Jasper

ADDISON-WESLEY

QUEST 2000

EXPLORING MATHEMATICS

AUTHORS

Ricki Wortzman Lalie Harcourt Brendan Kelly Peggy Morrow
Randall I. Charles David C. Brummett Carne S. Barnett

CONTRIBUTING AUTHORS

Linda Beatty Anne Boyd Fred Crouse Susan Gordon
Elisabeth Javor Alma Ramirez Freddie Lee Renfro Mary M. Soniat-Thompson

REVISED EDITION

Addison-Wesley Publishers Limited

Don Mills, Ontario • Reading, Massachusetts • Menlo Park, California • New York • Wokingham, England • Amsterdam • Bonn Sydney • Singapore • Tokyo • Madrid • San Juan • Paris Seoul • Milan • Mexico City • Taipei

Reviewers/Consultants
Marie Beckberger, Springfield Public School, Mississauga, Ontario
Jan Carruthers, Somerset and District Elementary School, King's County, Nova Scotia
Garry Garbolinsky, Tanner's Crossing School, Minnedosa, Manitoba
Darlene Hayes, King Edward Community School, Winnipeg, Manitoba
Barbara Hunt, Bayview Hill Elementary School, Richmond Hill, Ontario
Rita Janes, Roman Catholic School Board, St. John's, Newfoundland
Karen McClelland, Oak Ridges Public School, Richmond Hill, Ontario
Betty Morris, Edmonton Catholic School District #7, Edmonton, Alberta
Jeanette Mumford, Early Childhood Multicultural Services, Vancouver, B.C.
Evelyn Sawicki, Calgary Roman Catholic Separate School District #1, Calgary, Alberta
Darlene Shandola, Thomas Kidd Elementary School, Richmond, B.C.
Elizabeth Sloane, Dewson Public School, Toronto, Ontario
Denise White, Morrish Public School, Scarborough, Ontario
Elizabeth Wylie, Clark Boulevard Public School, Brampton, Ontario

Technology Advisors
Fred Crouse, Centreville, Nova Scotia; Flick Douglas, North York, Ontario; Cynthia Dunham, Framingham, MA; Susan Seidman, Toronto, Ontario; Evelyn J. Woldman, Framingham, MA; Diana Nunnaley, Maynard, MA

Editorial Coordination: McClanahan & Company
Editorial Development: Susan Petersiel Berg, Margaret Cameron, Mei Lin Cheung, Fran Cohen/First Folio Resource Group, Inc., Lynne Gulliver, Louise MacKenzie, Helen Nolan, Mary Reeve

Design: McClanahan & Company
Wycliffe Smith Design Inc.

Cover Design: The Pushpin Group

Canadian Cataloguing in Publication Data

Wortzman, Ricki.–
Quest 2000 : exploring mathematics, grade 3:
revised edition: student book

First and third authors in reverse order
on previous ed.

ISBN 0-201-55266-3

I. Mathematics – Juvenile literature. I. Harcourt,
Lalie, 1951– . II. Kelly, B. (Brendan),
1943– . III. Title.

QA107.K43 1996 510 C95–932763-0

This book contains recycled product and is acid free. Printed and bound in Canada.
D E F - MET - 01 00 99 98 97

Table of Contents

UNIT

1

Collecting and Analyzing Data

What patterns can we see in data?

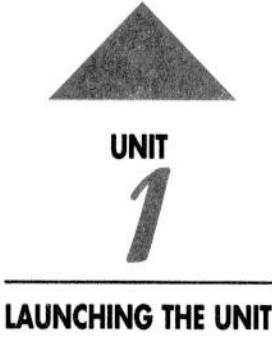

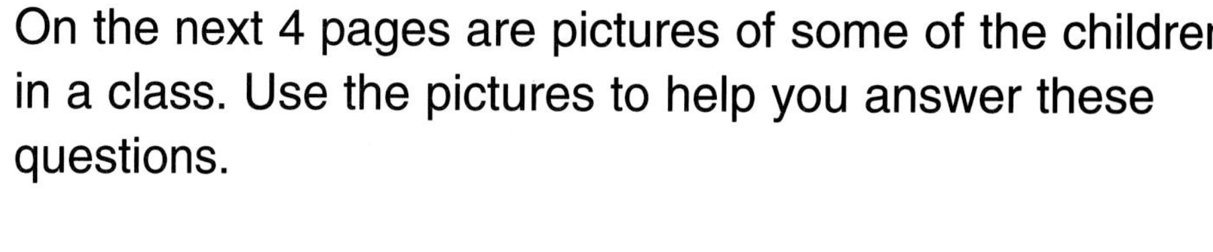

On the next 4 pages are pictures of some of the children in a class. Use the pictures to help you answer these questions.

1 • Are these graphs correct? Explain your thinking.
- If they are not correct, how would you change them?
- Look at the children in the pictures and the graphs that were made. What other data can you collect using these pictures?
- What kind of graph would you use to show the data?

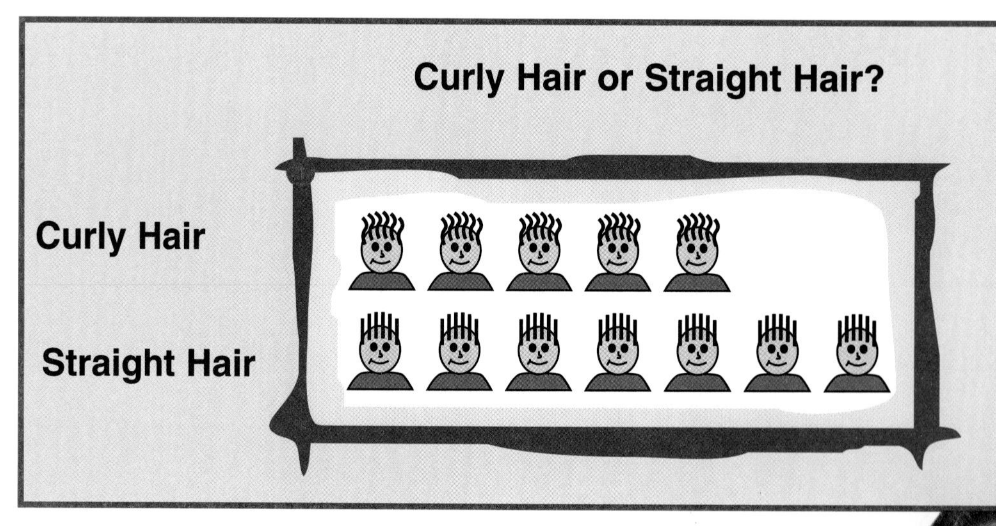

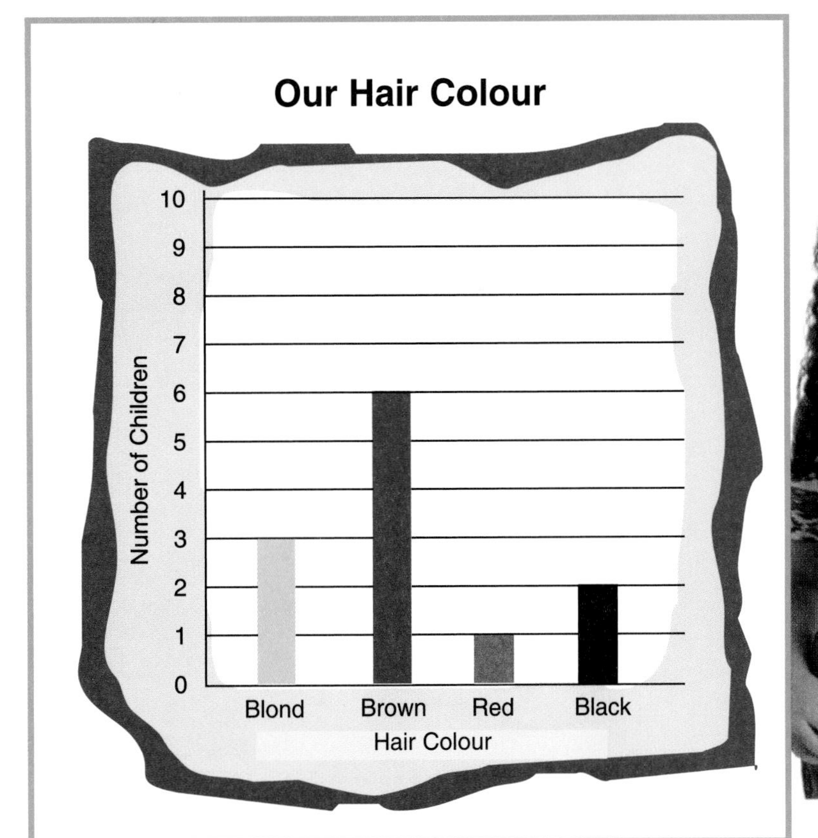

My Journal: Why do you use graphs?

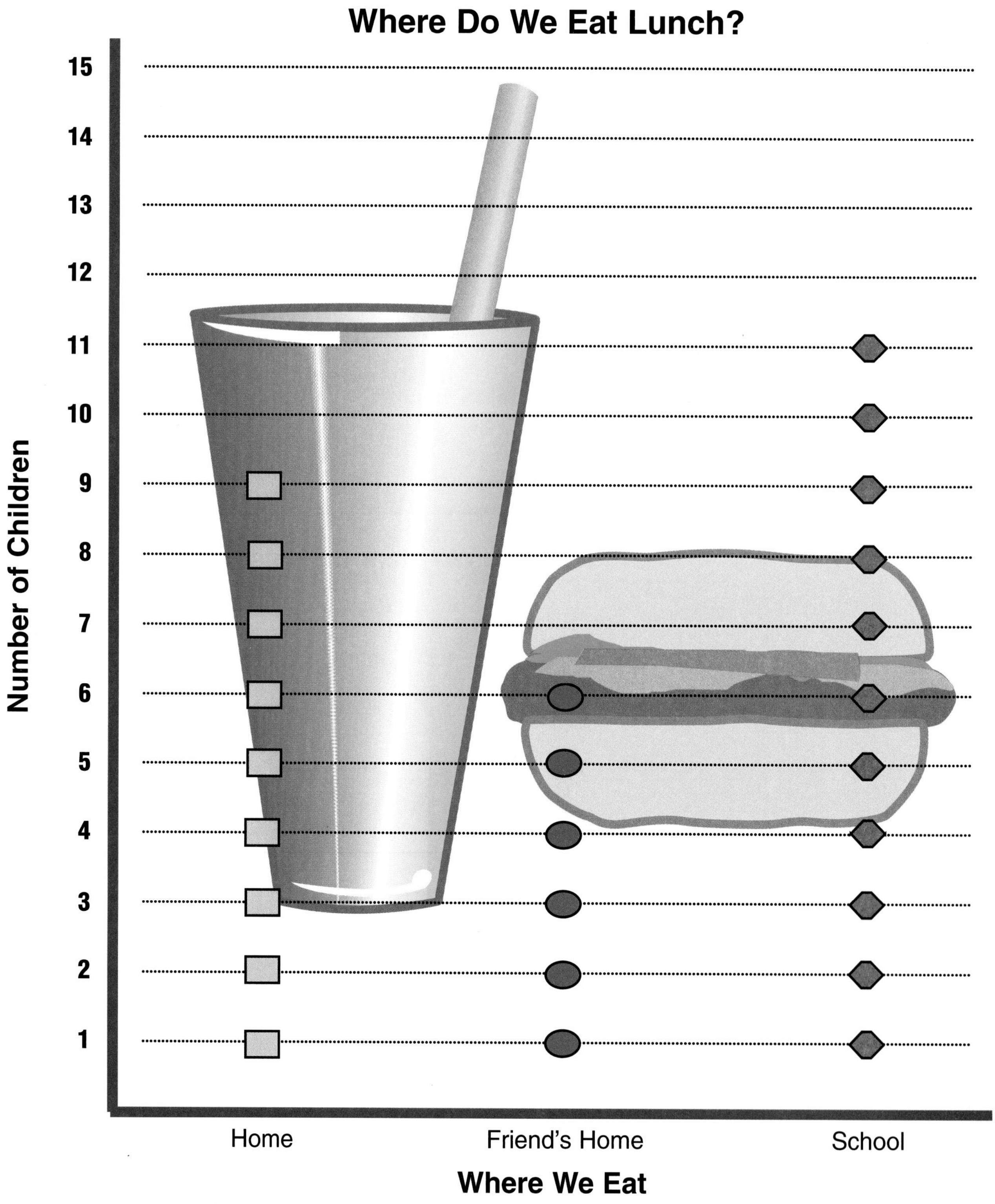

Where Do We Eat Lunch?

Number of Children

15
14
13
12
11
10
9
8
7
6
5
4
3
2
1

Home | Friend's Home | School

Where We Eat

2 • What information can you tell from looking at the sticker graph on page 10?

- If 4 people were away when the graph was made, how might it change when their data are added?
- Do more children eat lunch in school or outside of school? How can you tell?
- Look at the tally and decide whether the graph and the tally show the same data. How can you tell?

Where Do We Eat Lunch?		
Home	Friend's Home	School
𝍸	𝍸	𝍸
||||	|	𝍸

My Journal: What questions do you have about graphs?

Collecting Data

Think about these questions:

What's your favourite video?

What's your shoe size?

How many hours do you sleep at night?

How long does it take you to get to school?

What is your favourite snack?

What is your favourite sport?

How many people are in your family?

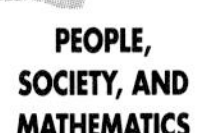

HAND-Y REPRESENTATION

Have you ever wondered how people at different times or in different places kept track of numbers?

In places around the world the hands and fingers were frequently used to represent data. In some languages the word for five and the word for hand were the same. Hands and fingers are a visual way of showing numbers and can be understood no matter what the language.

In First Nations picture writing, a hand drawn beside a tree could mean five trees.

Buyers and sellers in Indian, Arabian, and East African markets used a finger counting system for prices. Both buyers and sellers understood and, since no words were spoken, the deal was private.

1. Using First Nations notation, draw a picture that represents five boats.
2. If you count on your fingers, how do you represent six?
3. If you count on your fingers, how do you represent eleven?
4. Make up your own number system using your hands and fingers.

UNIT 1
ACTIVITY 2

Making Graphs

These graphs show data for some of the questions you have asked.

What do these graphs tell you?

1.

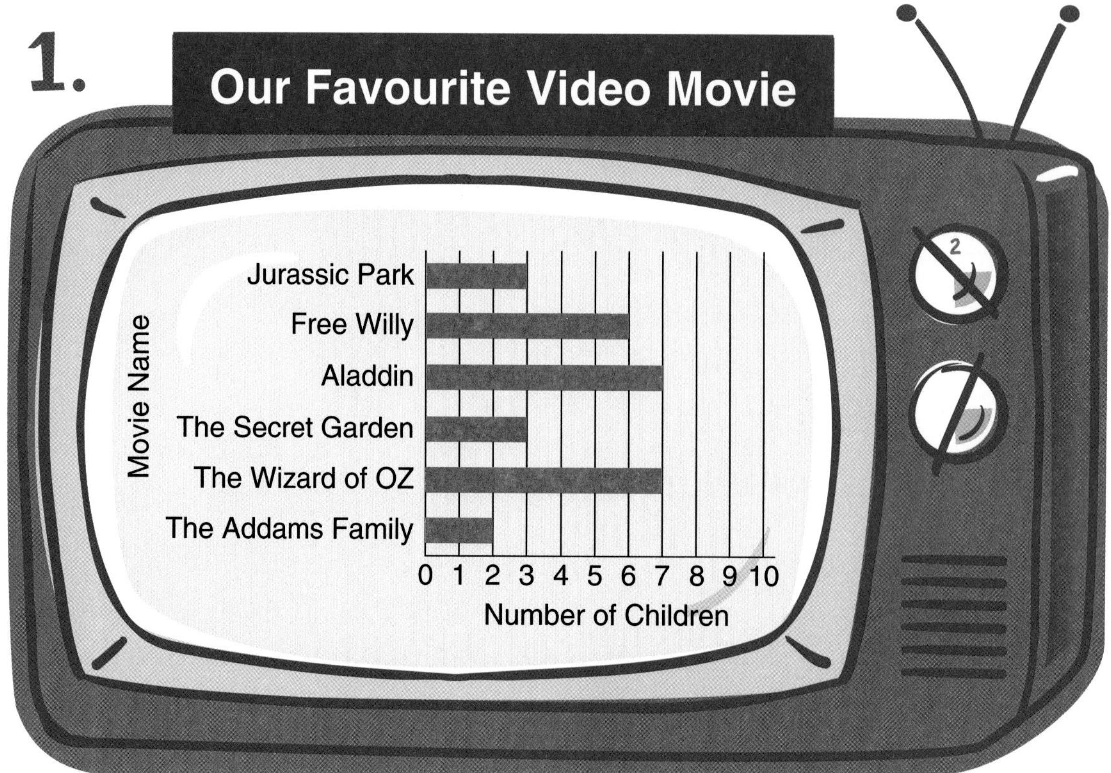

2.

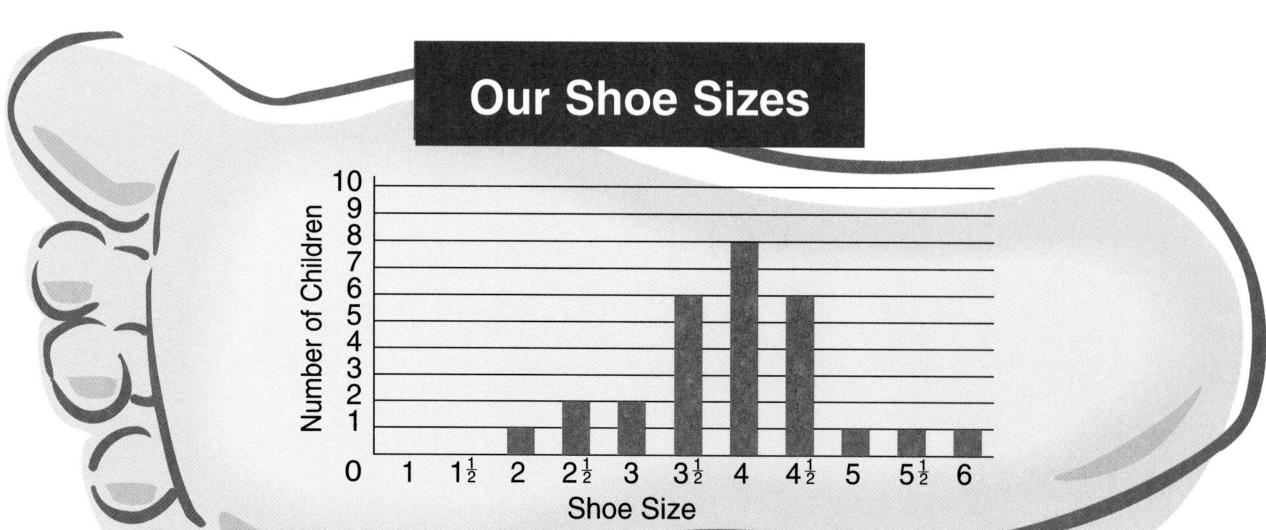

3.

How Many Hours We Sleep at Night

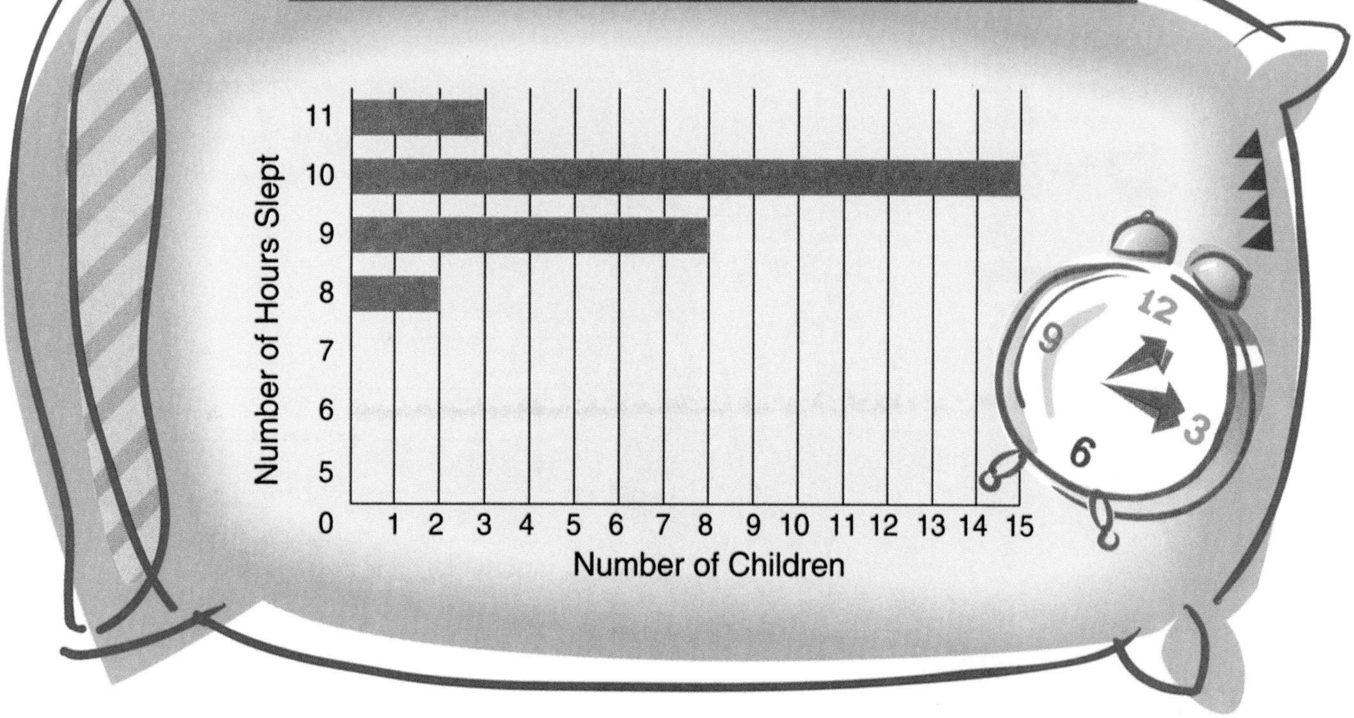

12
9
3
6
Number of Hours Slept
11
10
9
8
7
6
5
0
1 2 3 4 5 6 7 8 9 10 11 12 13 14 15
Number of Children

4.

How Long It Takes to Get to School

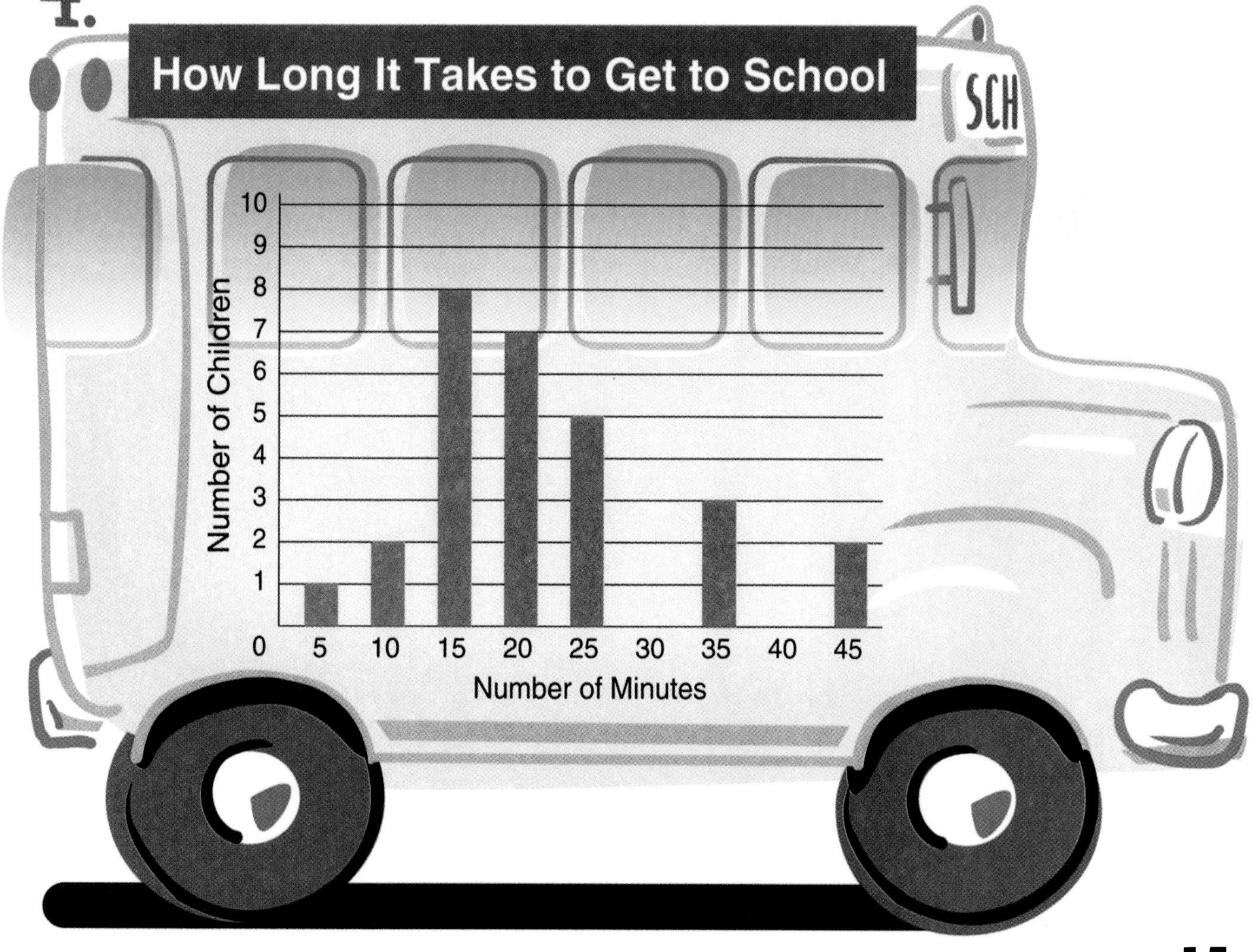

SCH
Number of Children
10
9
8
7
6
5
4
3
2
1
0
5 10 15 20 25 30 35 40 45
Number of Minutes

Look at this table. Then make a bar graph that shows the runners in an order. Answer the questions.

Runner	Seconds to complete 50 m dash
Ben	10
Jake	12
Owen	13
Paul	10
Fran	14
Fred	12
Gordon	13
Janelle	15
Elise	13
Kim	11
Onika	12
Zoë	10
Mei	13
Yolanda	14

1. Did Ben run faster or slower than Jake? Explain.
2. Is this statement true or false? Explain.
   All children finished in 15 seconds or less.
3. Was there a winner? Explain.
4. Write three statements about your graph.
5. *My Journal:* Which graph in this activity was the most interesting to you? Explain.

Data, Tallies, Graphs

The inspector of buckets at the Power Polygons factory needs your help. She needs to do a quality check and has asked if your class set of Power Polygons is complete and has the correct number of each shape. How could you find out?

▶ Two Ways to Record Your Data

Here is what a class found out about its favourite sports.

Our Favourite Sports	
Baseball	𝍸 ||||
Soccer	𝍸
Hockey	|||
Swimming	𝍸 𝍸 ||

1. Make a bar graph that shows these data. Make sure it shows the data from the most popular to the least popular sports.

2. What information does the graph tell you?

3. *My Journal:* What do you think makes a graph clear and easy to read?

Practise *Your Skills*

Here is a survey of the types of movies grade 3 students at one school like to watch.

Type of Movie	Tally	Total
Adventure	𝍸 𝍸 ||	
Comedy	𝍸 𝍸 𝍸 𝍸 |	
Cartoon	𝍸 ||||	
Scary	𝍸 𝍸 𝍸	
Mystery	𝍸 𝍸 |||	

1. Find the total for each type of movie.
2. How many students were in the survey?
3. Which type of movie is the most popular? The least popular?
4. Write three statements you know to be true based on this survey.

Saturday morning is peak time for cartoons.

How many minutes long is the longest cartoon program?

How many minutes long is the shortest cartoon program?

What length of program is most common during Saturday morning cartoon prime time?

Organize your data any way you choose. Write to tell what you discovered.

Would you expect to find the same lengths and types of programs on Saturday night from 7 p.m. to 11 p.m.? Explain.

SATURDAY NOV. 20 — MORNING

	7:00	7:30	8:00	8:30	9:00	9:30	10:00	10:30
2	Scratch	Nick News	Marsupllam (cc)	The Little Mermaid	Garfield & Friends		All New Dennis	Teenage Turtles (cc)
5	World in 80 Dreams	Hurricanes	Dog City	Droopy Detective	Bobby's World	Eekl & Thunderlizard	Tiny Toon Adventures	Taz Mania (cc)
7	The Mad Scientist Toon Club		Cro (cc)	Wild West O.O.W. Boys	Sonic the Hedgehog	The Addams Family	From the Cryptkeeper	The Bugs Bunny Show
11	Paid Programming				News Closeup	Best Talk	Bill Nye Science Guy	Energy Express
25	Les Fruittis	Mon Amie Maya	Tao Tao	L'ile aux Ours	Chat Boume!		Amis Ratons	

SATURDAY NOV. 20 — PRIME TIME

	7:00	7:30	8:00	8:30	9:00	9:30	10:00	10:30
2	News	Hard Copy (cc)	Dr Quinn, Medicine Woman				Walker, Texas Ranger (cc)	
5	Roseanne: Crystal is obsessed with her late husband.	Inside Edition Weekend (cc)	Cops: New York Transit Authority Police patrol subways	Cops: Briefing on drug warrants	Front Page (cc)		News	
7	News	Views	George: Tenant offers George a challenge.	Where I Live: The kids are growing up too fast.	The Paula Poundstone Show (cc)		The Commish: A would-be suitor is obsessed with Cyd; Tony learns a startling fact in the case of an elderly female banker.	
11	Star Trek: The Next Generation: Force of Nature. (cc)		MOVIE : THE RED STONE (G, '83) ★★ A documentary on Ayers Rock				News (cc)	
25	Spectacle de samedi soir							

UNIT 1

ACTIVITY 5

Exploring Time

- All tours meet at the Ranger Centre at Timberlake Park.
- Wear suitable clothing. Bring sunscreen.
- Arrive 10 minutes BEFORE the tour begins, to sign up.

TOUR	Leaves at—	Returns by—
Bike Hike Around the Lake (trail bikes available)	8:30 a.m. 4:00 p.m.	11:00 a.m. 6:15 p.m.
Bird Watch	7:30 a.m.	8:30 a.m.
Canoe Trip and Island Picnic	10:30 a.m.	3:45 p.m.
Cave Adventure	1:00 p.m.	3:20 p.m.
Cliff Trail Hike (must be 13 or older)	9:00 a.m. 2:30 p.m.	11:30 a.m. 5:00 p.m.
Exploring Ruins	11:00 a.m. 2:30 p.m.	12:30 p.m. 4:30 p.m.
Kids' Crafts (for ages 5–7) (for ages 8–10)	10:15 a.m. 1:30 p.m.	11:15 a.m. 2:45 p.m.
Nature's Picnic	12:15 p.m.	1:30 p.m.
Riverbank Horseback Ride	8:15 a.m. 2:15 p.m.	10:00 a.m. 4:00 p.m.
Wetlands Walk	8:15 a.m. 3:00 p.m.	9:00 a.m. 4:25 p.m.
Wild Berry Picking	1:40 p.m.	2:45 p.m.
Wildflower Walk	10:45 a.m. 12:40 p.m.	11:25 a.m. 1:20 p.m.

Solve these problems with your partner.

1. Which is the longest tour at Timberlake Park? How long does it last? Which is the shortest tour? How long does it last? Compare the lengths of these tours.
2. If you take the afternoon Wetlands Walk, how long will you be gone?
3. You have time for a tour that lasts $1\frac{1}{2}$ to 2 hours. What choices do you have?
4. You arrive at the park at 10:50 a.m. What is the earliest tour you can sign up for? Explain.
5. You want to take a tour that ends in time for you to meet a friend at 12:30 p.m. Which tour will you pick? How long is it from the end of the tour to 12:30 p.m.?

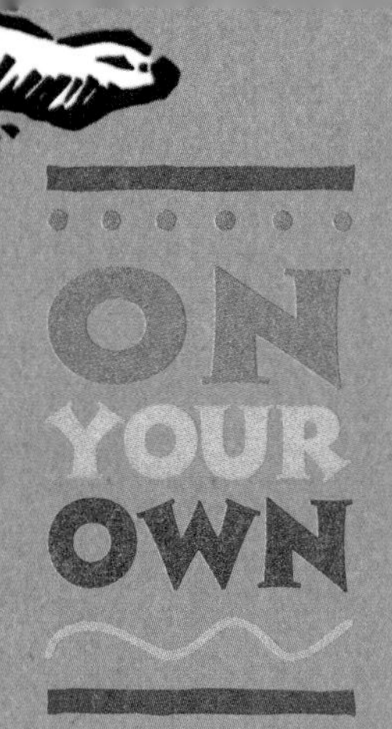

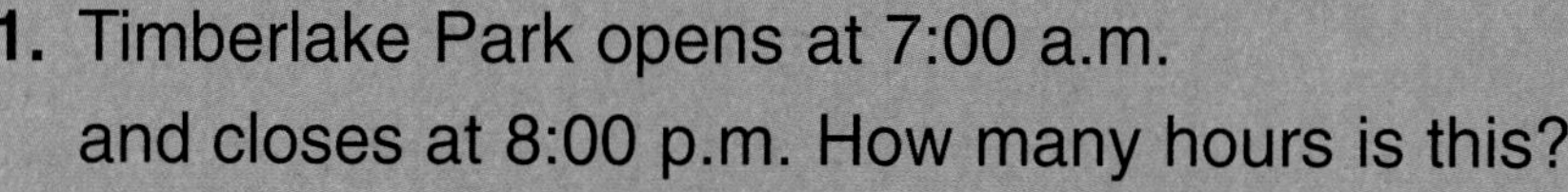

1. Timberlake Park opens at 7:00 a.m. and closes at 8:00 p.m. How many hours is this?

2. Talk to your family members about a day at Timberlake Park. Write a schedule that your family would enjoy. Tell when you must get there and when you would leave. How long will you be at the park altogether?

3. *My Journal:* Why is learning to read schedules important?

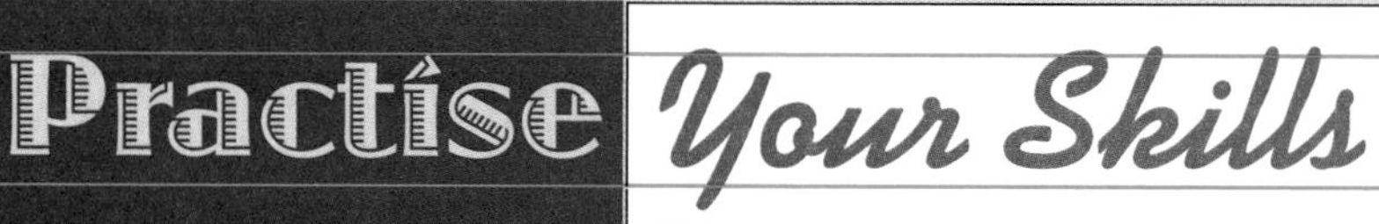

Practise Your Skills

Would you use seconds, minutes, hours, days, weeks, months, or years to measure:

1. tying your shoes
2. painting a picture
3. your age
4. playing a baseball game
5. a summer vacation
6. building a home
7. reading a story book

Making a Time Line

Things to think about when you make a time line:

- How many hours are in a day?
- When does your time line begin? When does it end?
- Which hours are a.m.? Which are p.m.?
- Which activities will you include?
- How long will each activity last? In what order will the activities go?
- How will you show the times and the activities?
- What will you do if times don't come out even?

Plan an ideal day. Don't forget about—

- eating
- sleeping
- relaxing

You might make a chart like this to help you get started.

Activity for My Ideal Day	How Long It Lasts	Possible Start Time

UNIT 1
ACTIVITY 7

Data and Shapes

▶ There are many ways you can make snowflakes. Here is one way:

1. Fold your paper in half.

2. Then fold your paper in half again.

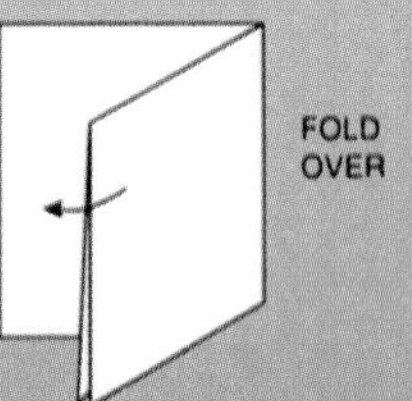

3. Cut holes along the folds. You can cut any shape holes you like.

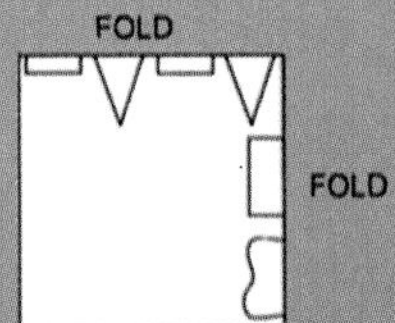

4. Cut the other edges any way you choose.

5. Open the paper and look at your snowflake.

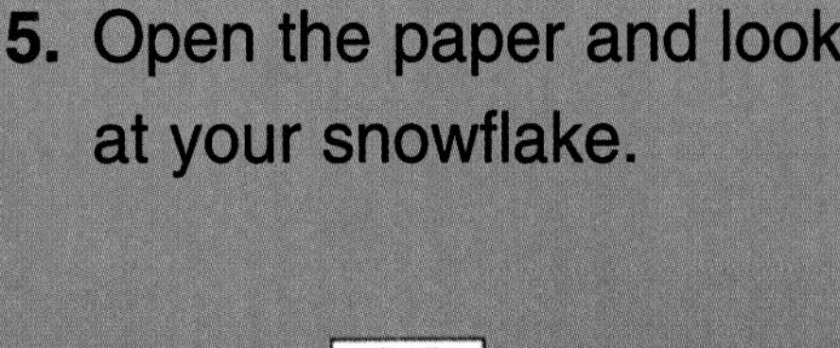

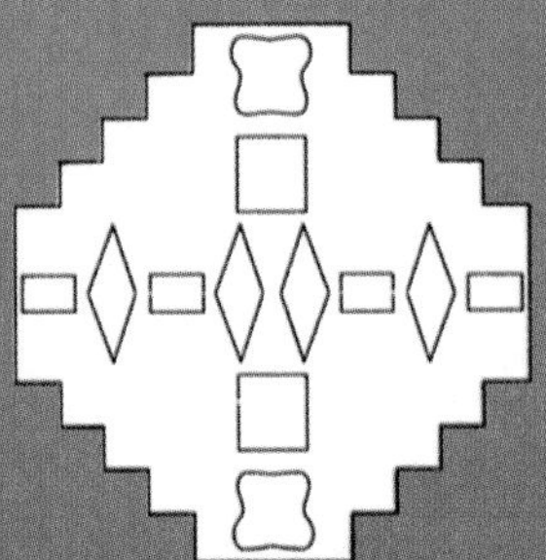

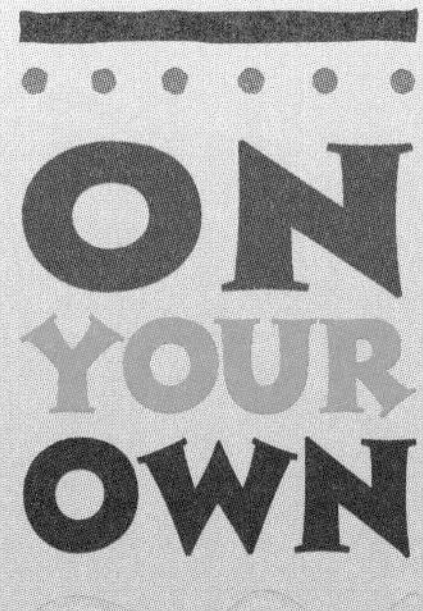

1. What shape will each hole be when you open up the paper?

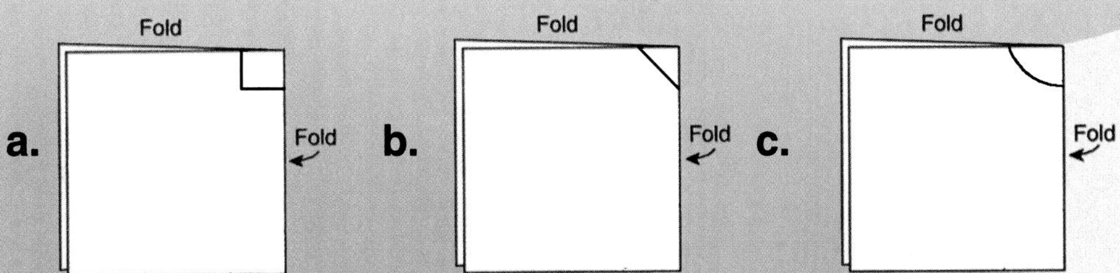

2. Find objects in your home that are box shapes, can shapes, ball shapes, and cone shapes. Make a bar graph to show how many of each shape you found.

3. *My Journal:* What do you now know about cutting paper to make snowflakes? Was this fun? Explain.

Practise *Your Skills*

Here is a picture graph made by a grade 3 class.

Favourite Types of Recess Games	
Skipping	☺☺☺☺☺☺☺
Tag	☺☺☺☺☺
Hopscotch	☺☺
Soccer	☺☺☺☺☺☺☺☺
Hide and Seek	☺☺☺☺☺

1. Make a list to show the choices in order.
2. Show a tally for these data.
3. How many children were asked?
4. What other statements can you make based on this graph?
5. Predict what your classmates would choose. Do a survey to find out.

Gathering Data for a Pen Pal Class

Do you have a friend or relative who lives in another city? Maybe you can help set up a pen pal exchange! Talk with your teacher about what you could do.

Look for some sources for pen pal classes. Besides asking friends and relatives, how else could you find a pen pal class? Your class can write a letter that asks for information. Talk about the most important data you'd give in your very first letter.

Tips for writing to pen pals

- Describe yourself, including your age. If possible, send a photograph.
- Share information about things people everywhere will understand, recognize, and enjoy, such as:

  sports, music, games, pets, foods, festivals, special school events, family events, riddles or puzzles, vacations and trips, special features of your community

- Include drawings, maps, charts, graphs, pictures, sketches, puzzles, or anything visual.
- When you get an answer, be sure to write back soon. Pen pals never like to wait too long!

Your data collection is complete and organized. You analyzed it and drew appropriate conclusions. You communicated these conclusions clearly in writing, and told how the data would help in a pen pal project.

1. This table shows how many marbles some of the children at Alley School had at the end of one day.

Student	Number of marbles
Alison	10
Bethany	8
Cristo	13
Raji	5
Elena	8
Frank	12
Antonio	15
Tiffany	11
Roger	9
Steven	10

   a. Draw a bar graph to show this information.
   b. How does your bar graph help you see who had the most marbles?
   c. What else can you tell from the graph?

2. **a.** Look at the shapes in this quilt. Tally the different shapes to find out how many shapes of each kind the quilter used.
   b. Show the data in a way a quilter could use it before starting to make a quilt. Why would your data be useful?

3. This is the schedule of events for your school picnic:

Time	11:30	12:00	12:30	1:00	1:30	2:00	2:30	3:00
Sand area	Sand castles							
Pond	Sketching		Fishing		Swimming			
Field	Warm-Up exercises	Simon Says	Nature hike		Sketching	Relay races		Cool down
Picnic area	Lunch			Rest Time	Board games			Snack

a. Which event takes the most time?

b. Which events take the least amount of time?

c. What time does swimming start?

d. What time does the nature hike end?

e. Decide how you would spend your day.
Write a schedule to show your choices.

1. Some children were surveyed. Each child named her or his favourite fruit.

a. Make a tally to show the children's choices.
b. Make a graph to show the choices.
c. How many chose each fruit? Write the choices from most popular to least popular.

2. Favourite Subjects

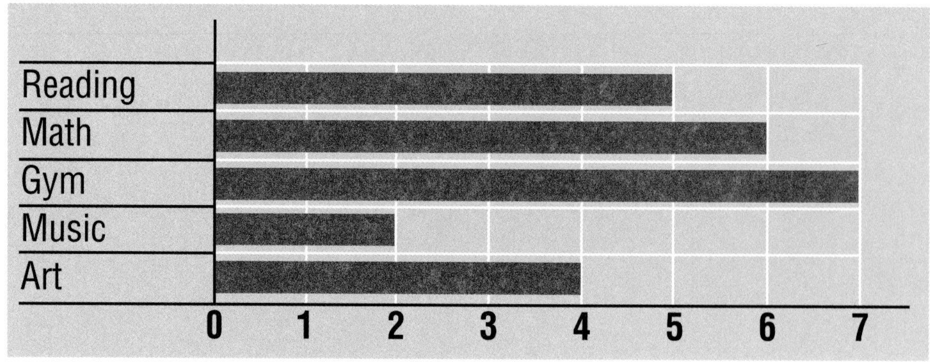

a. How many more children would need to choose art to have the same number as gym?
b. How would the graph change if you added your favourite?
c. Show what you think the children in your class would answer.

3. a. Make a time line like this. Show where the times on the clocks shown above might go.

b. Write what you might be doing at each time.

4.

Clock A

Clock B

a. How much time has passed from Clock A to Clock B?

b. What could you do in that amount of time?

Sports Stadium
Game Saturday
1:00 p.m.
$5.00
Seat #105
Sports Stadium
Game Saturday
1:00 p.m.
$5.00
Seat #104

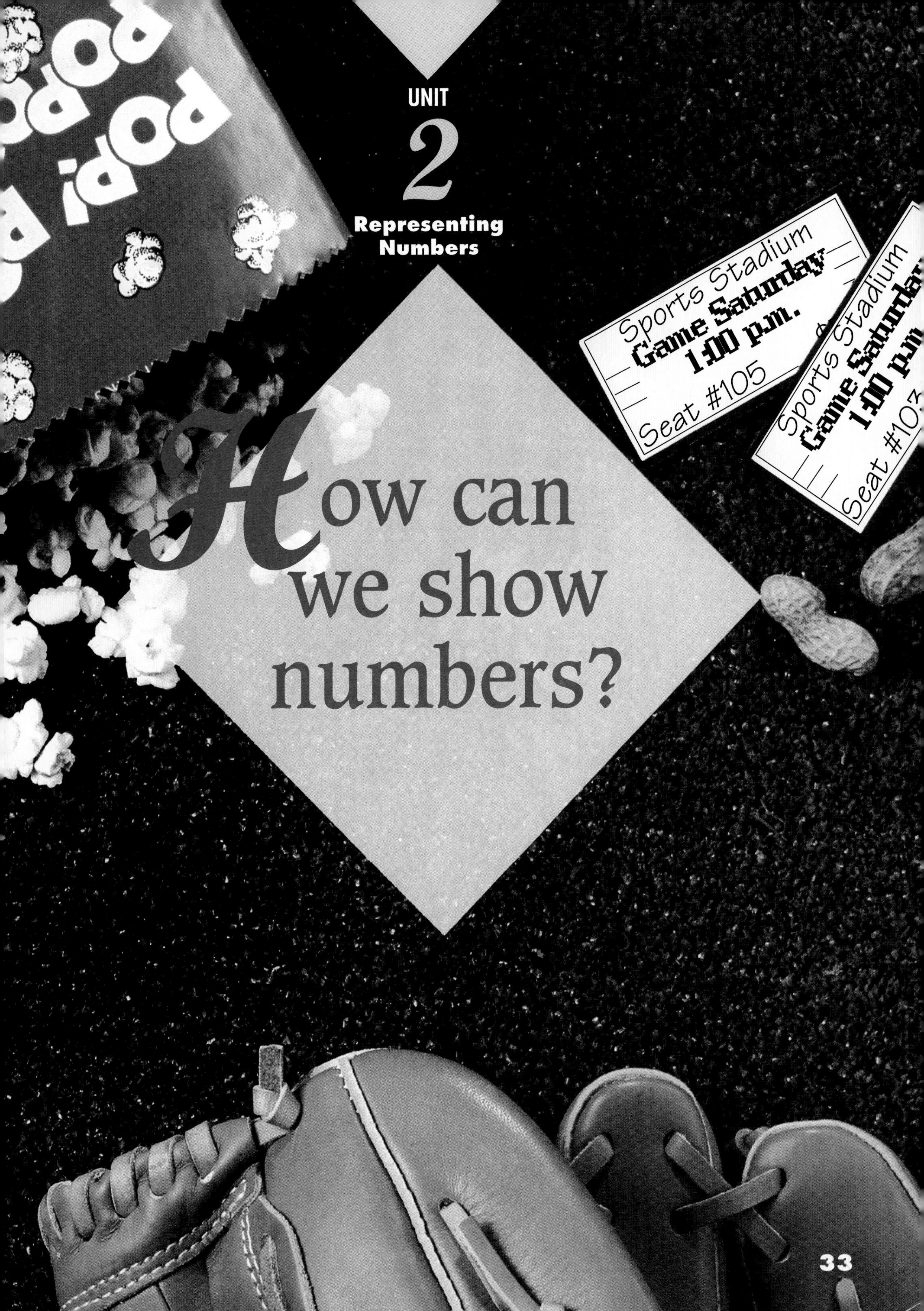

UNIT
2
Representing Numbers
How can we show numbers?
POP! POP!
Sports Stadium
Game Saturday
1:00 p.m.
Seat #105
Sports Stadium
Game Saturday
1:00 p.m.

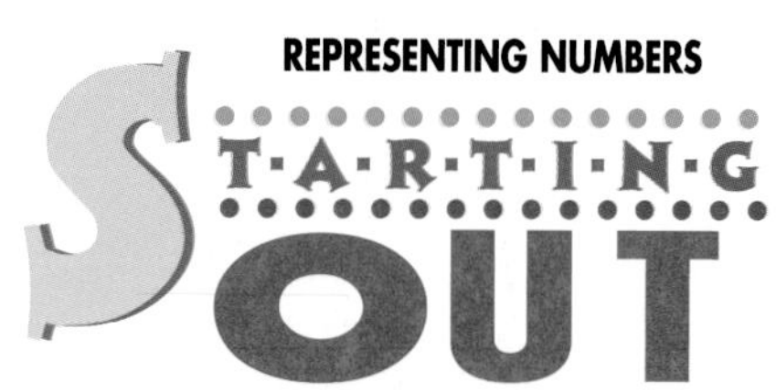
REPRESENTING NUMBERS
STARTING OUT

372 KIDS
RIDE FOR THOSE
WHO CAN'T

The Morning Standard
5948 SIGN PETITION
FOR NEW PARK

SALAD
HEAVEN
HUNDREDS
SERVED
EVERY
DAY!

1 • Which of these numbers are estimates?
- Which are not estimates?
- When are estimates useful?
- How can you tell which is the greatest number?
- Which is the least number? How do you know?

My Journal: When do you use large numbers? How do you know which numbers are the greatest?

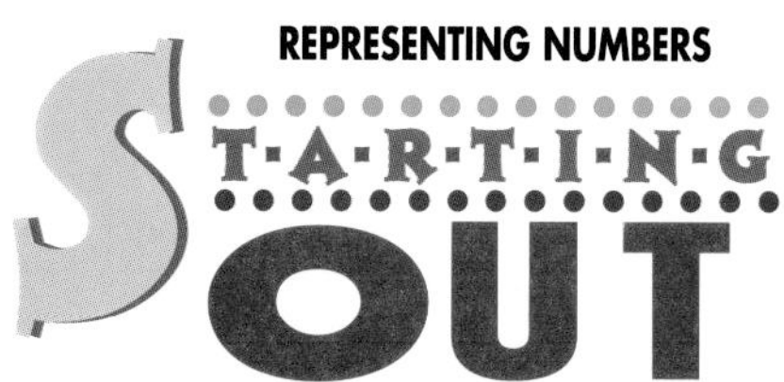

- 10 by 10 base ten block

- Bundle of 5 ten rods

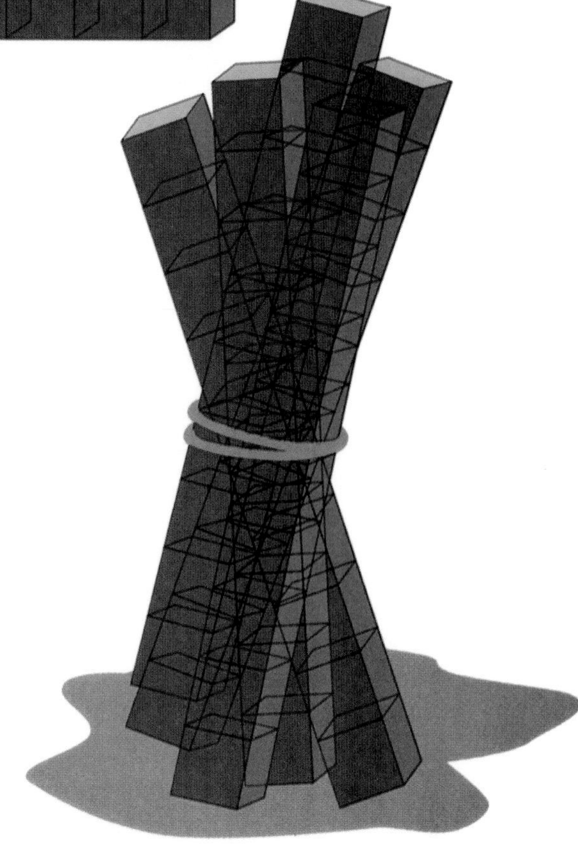

- Hundred chart

1	2	3	4	5	6	7	8	9	10
11	12	13	14	15	16	17	18	19	20
21	22	23	24	25	26	27	28	29	30
31	32	33	34	35	36	37	38	39	40
41	42	43	44	45	46	47	48	49	50
51	52	53	54	55	56	57	58	59	60
61	62	63	64	65	66	67	68	69	70
71	72	73	74	75	76	77	78	79	80
81	82	83	84	85	86	87	88	89	90
91	92	93	94	95	96	97	98	99	100

- Place value chart

thousands	hundreds	tens	ones
1	0	0	0

2
- What number does each picture show?
- Why is it important to know how to read large numbers?
- What is the greatest number on this page?
  Explain how you know.
- What is the least number? Explain how you know.
- Where have you seen large numbers?

My Journal: What do you know about writing and reading large numbers?

Estimating and Counting

1 unit

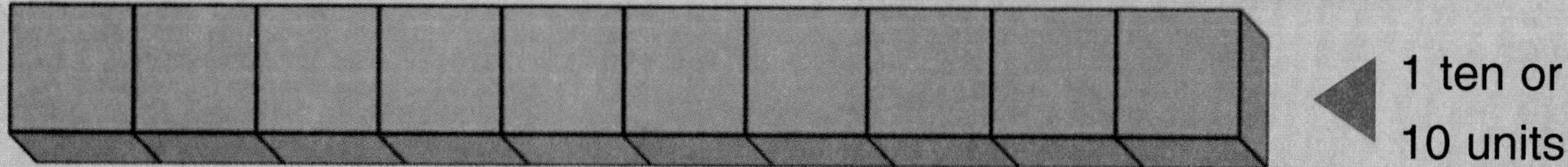

1 ten or
10 units

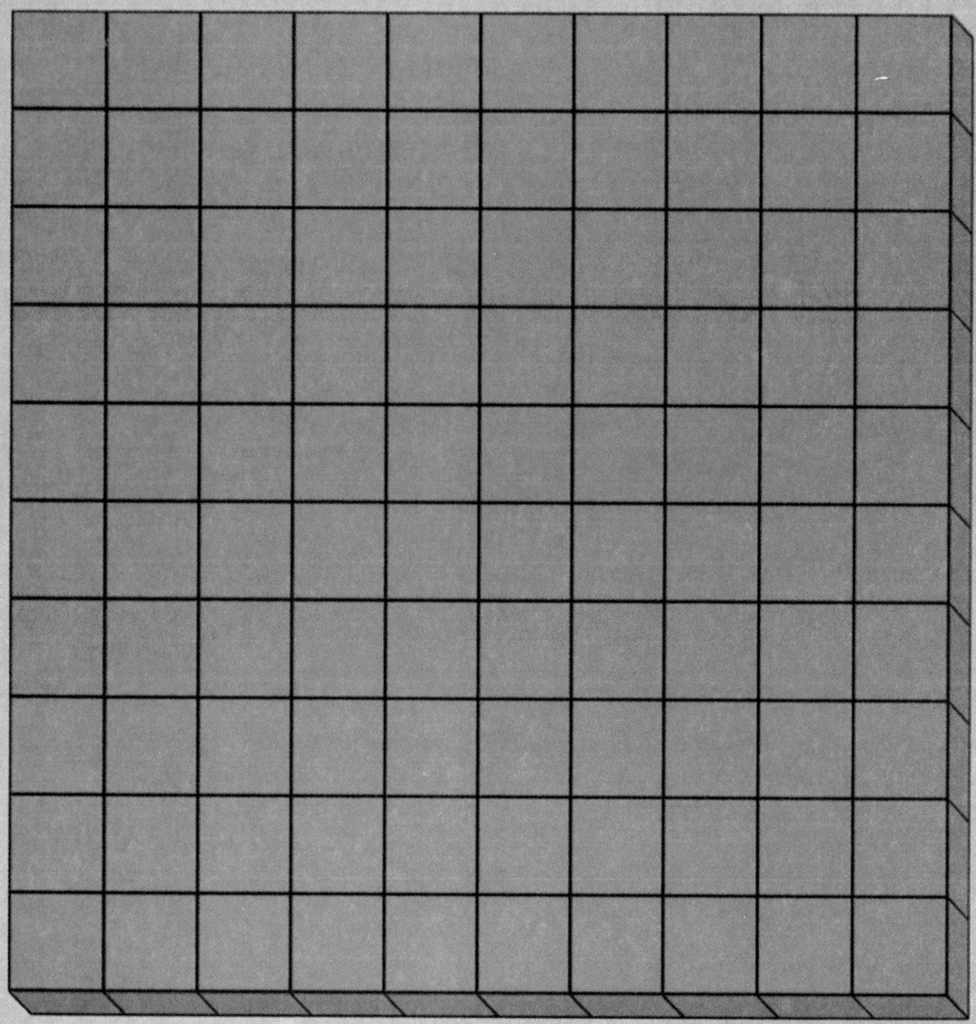

1 hundred or
100 units or
10 tens

ON YOUR OWN

▶ Write each number using symbols and words.

Draw blocks to show how many.

7. 496

8. two hundred thirty-four

9. 581

10. three hundred seventy-six

11. 405

12. five hundred sixty

13. *My Journal:* Write about the greatest number you know. Where did you see it? What was it used for? Do you think it is an estimate or an exact number?

Making Large Numbers

▶ Use any of these blocks to make models of numbers. How many different numbers can you make?

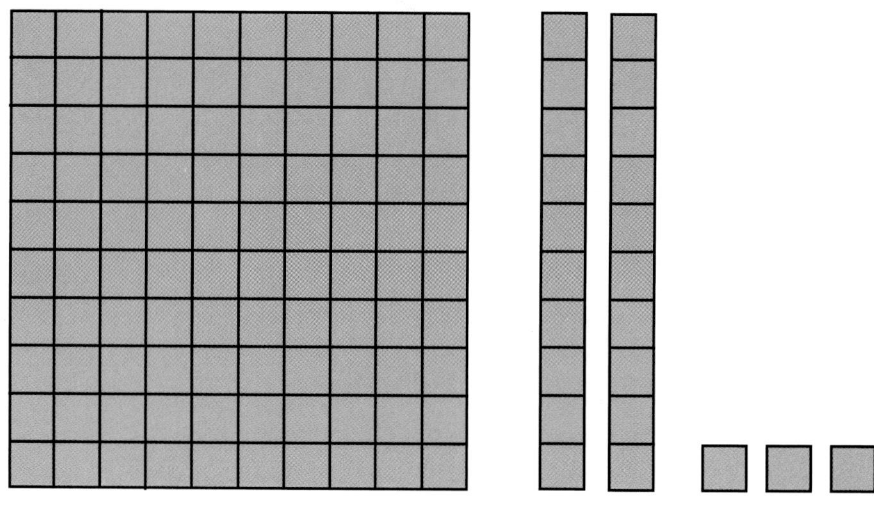

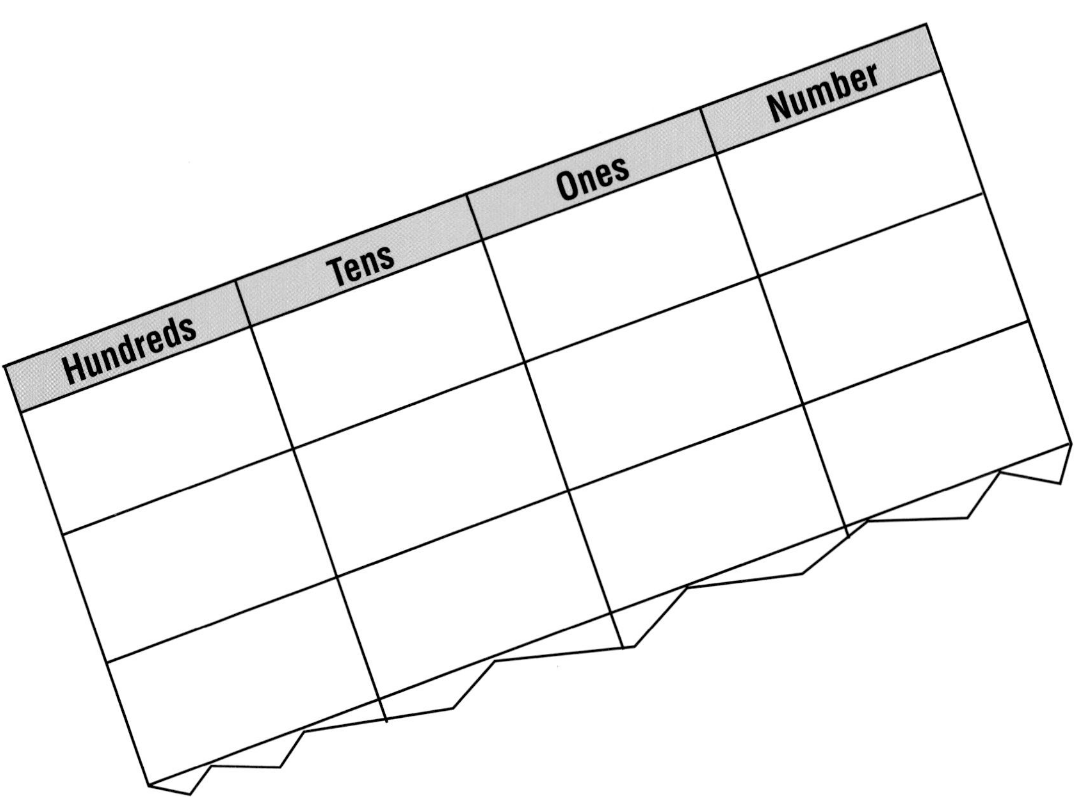

1. Sanda is building numbers. She is using four blocks. Here are the numbers she has made so far.

What other numbers can she make using four blocks?

Hundreds	Tens	Ones	Number
			400
			130
			121

2. Here is one way to build 235 with base ten blocks.

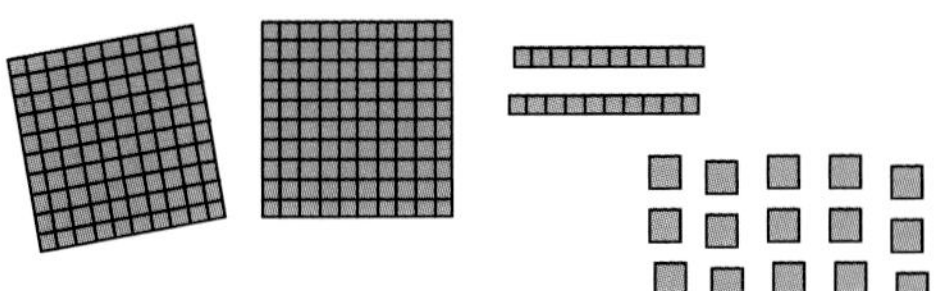

200 + 20 + 15 = 235

What other ways can you find? Record each way you find with pictures and a number sentence.

3. ***My Journal:*** What did you learn about making models of numbers?

Look for patterns. For each list, write the next 4 numbers and describe each counting pattern.

1. 265, 275, 285, 295,

2. 150, 250, 350, 450,

3. 325, 350, 375, 400,

4. 982, 882, 782, 682,

5. 450, 440, 430, 420,

6. 540, 560, 580, 600,

7. Think of a number pattern. Write 6 numbers that show it. Ask someone to guess your pattern.

UNIT 2

ACTIVITY 3

Looking for Number Patterns

▶ How many packages of balloons does the shopper need to buy for the party? Explain how you know.

1. How many packages of balloons do you need to buy to get 1000 balloons? Explain how you know.

2. Find something that comes with more than one in a package. How many packages would you need to have 100? 200? 300?

3. Look in the newspaper for numbers that are close to 1000. Record them.

4. How much would each member of your family receive if you were to share $100 equally? Explain your thinking.

5. ***My Journal:*** What do you think is a large number?

Practise *Your Skills*

What is the value of the 5 in each of these numbers? Write your answer as 5, 50, or 500.

1. 257	**2.** 591	**3.** 905
4. 501	**5.** 350	**6.** 795

7. These blocks show a number.

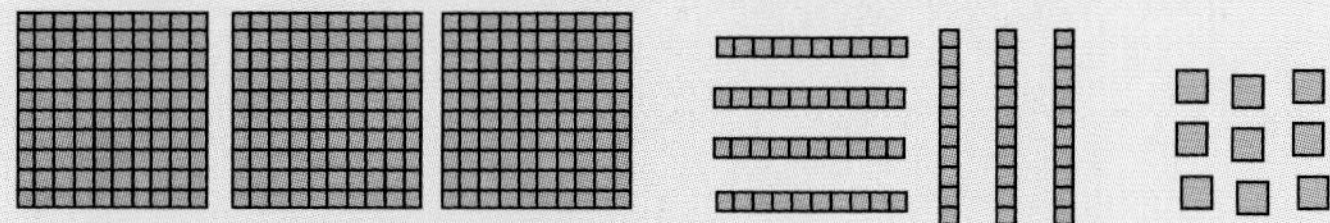

a. Write an estimate of the number.
b. Write the exact number.
c. Tell how the numbers compare.

UNIT 2

ACTIVITY 4

Making 1000 Dollars

1. Suppose you were to be paid in 2 equal payments. How much would each payment be? How much would you get if there were 4 equal payments? 5 equal payments? 8 equal payments? 10 equal payments?

2. Suppose you were given 3 unequal payments. Show some ways you could be paid. Show some ways you could be paid in 4 unequal payments.

1. Time how long it takes you to write your name 10 times. Use this information to estimate how long it would take to write your name 1000 times. Explain your estimate.

2. Imagine a stack of dinner plates. How high do you think 1000 would reach? How did you estimate?

3. Imagine 1000 pennies. How high do you think they would reach when stacked in a pile? How far do you think they would reach placed side by side? Tell how you estimated.

4. *My Journal:* What do you know about 1000 that you didn't know before?

Practise *Your Skills*

10	20	50	100	250	500

Use these numbers to build the numbers below. Build each number 4 different ways. You may use each number above as many times as you like.

1. 100

2. 200

3. 500

4. 1000

PEOPLE, SOCIETY, AND MATHEMATICS

Counting with WOLVES

Have you ever wondered how people in different times or places represented large numbers?

A bone from a young wolf that died thirty thousand years ago was found in Czechoslovakia. The bone has 55 notches arranged in two groups, 25 in the first group and 30 in the second. What do you think this represents? Is it 55? Within each group the notches are arranged in groups of five.

Africans from the area that is now Zaire used marks on a bone to record numbers also.

The Ishango bone is an example. Researchers are not sure whether the marks show a number system or a type of calendar. What do you think?

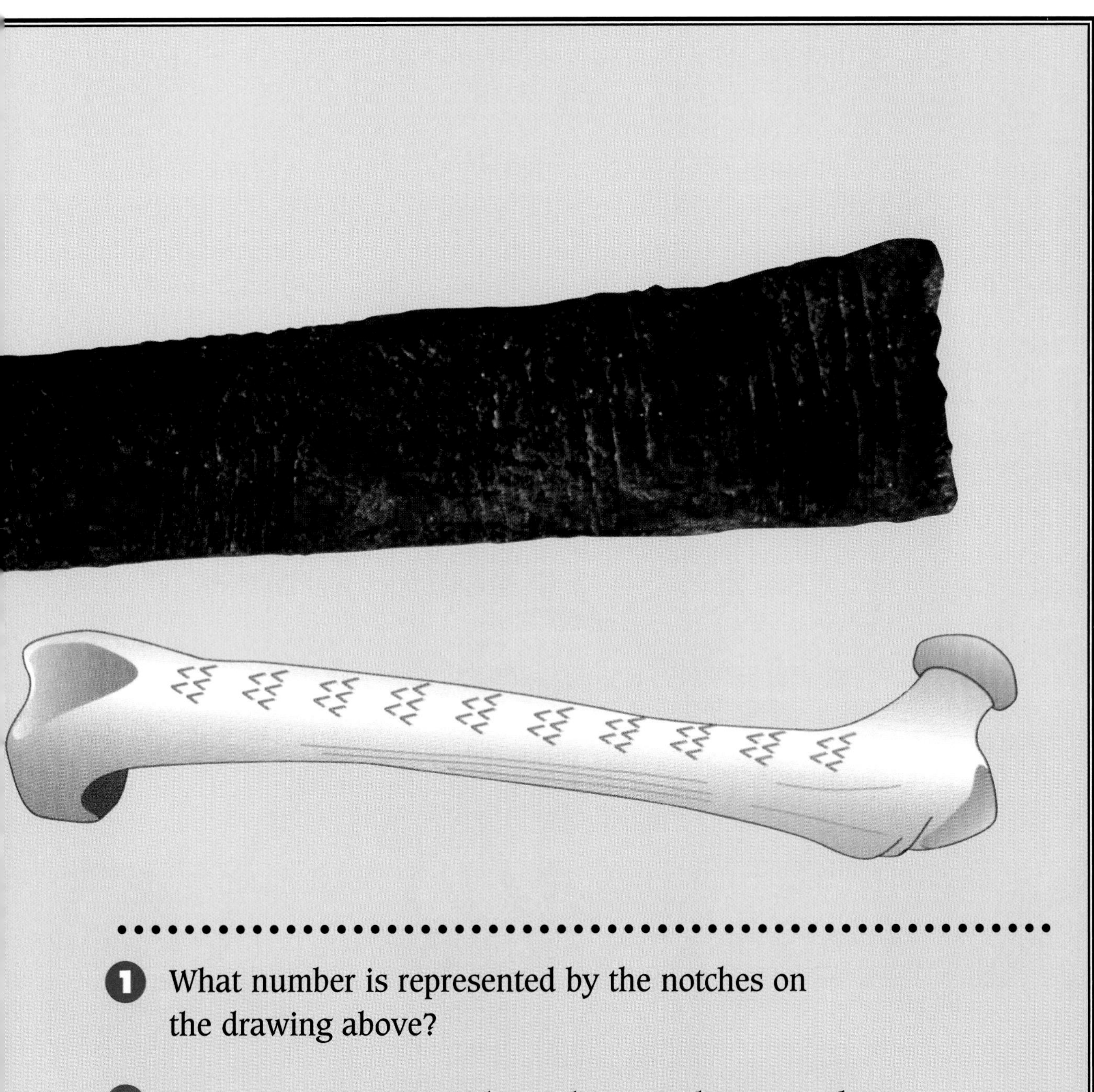

1. What number is represented by the notches on the drawing above?

2. Represent your age with notches on a bone you draw.

3. Represent the total number of students in your class with "bone" notation.

Numbers to 9999

[3] [5] [2] [1] can be used to make a 4-digit number.

What are the possible numbers?

1. Tell which number is greater, 1042 or 1420. Write to tell how you decided.

2. Here are some data about recycling.

Recycling Centre Report for April

Material	Amount
Glass:	
Clear	1503 kg
Brown	740 kg
Green	295 kg
Newspaper	9550 kg
Cardboard	4020 kg
Cans	425 kg
Plastic	1248 kg

a. Is more glass or more newspaper recycled? Tell how you decided.
b. Which is the greatest amount of material recycled? Tell how you decided.
c. Show the recycled materials in order from least to greatest.

3. *My Journal:* How do you compare large numbers?

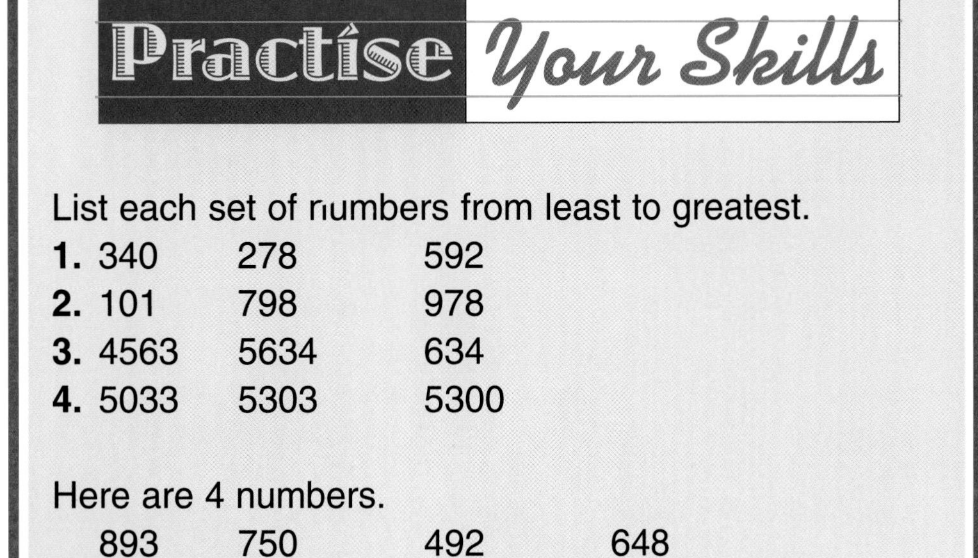

Practise Your Skills

List each set of numbers from least to greatest.

1. 340 278 592
2. 101 798 978
3. 4563 5634 634
4. 5033 5303 5300

Here are 4 numbers.

893 750 492 648

5. Which are greater than 599?
6. Which are less than 705?

EXPLORING PLACE VALUE: BUILD THE GREATER NUMBER Game

Game Rules

1. Play with a partner. Arrange your place value cards in order in front of you.
2. Mix both players' sets of number cards together. Place them face down in the centre.
3. Toss a number cube to see who goes first. The first player picks a number card and places it beneath one of the place value cards. Then the second player does the same.
4. Play until both you and your partner have chosen 4 number cards, and placed one number card beneath each place value card.
5. Say your numbers aloud. Compare numbers. Who built the greater number? That player is the winner of that round. Play again.

THOUSANDS

HUNDREDS

Tip

You can also play a Build the Smaller Number Game with the same rules. In this game, the player with the smaller number is the winner.

ONES

TENS

Making Larger Numbers

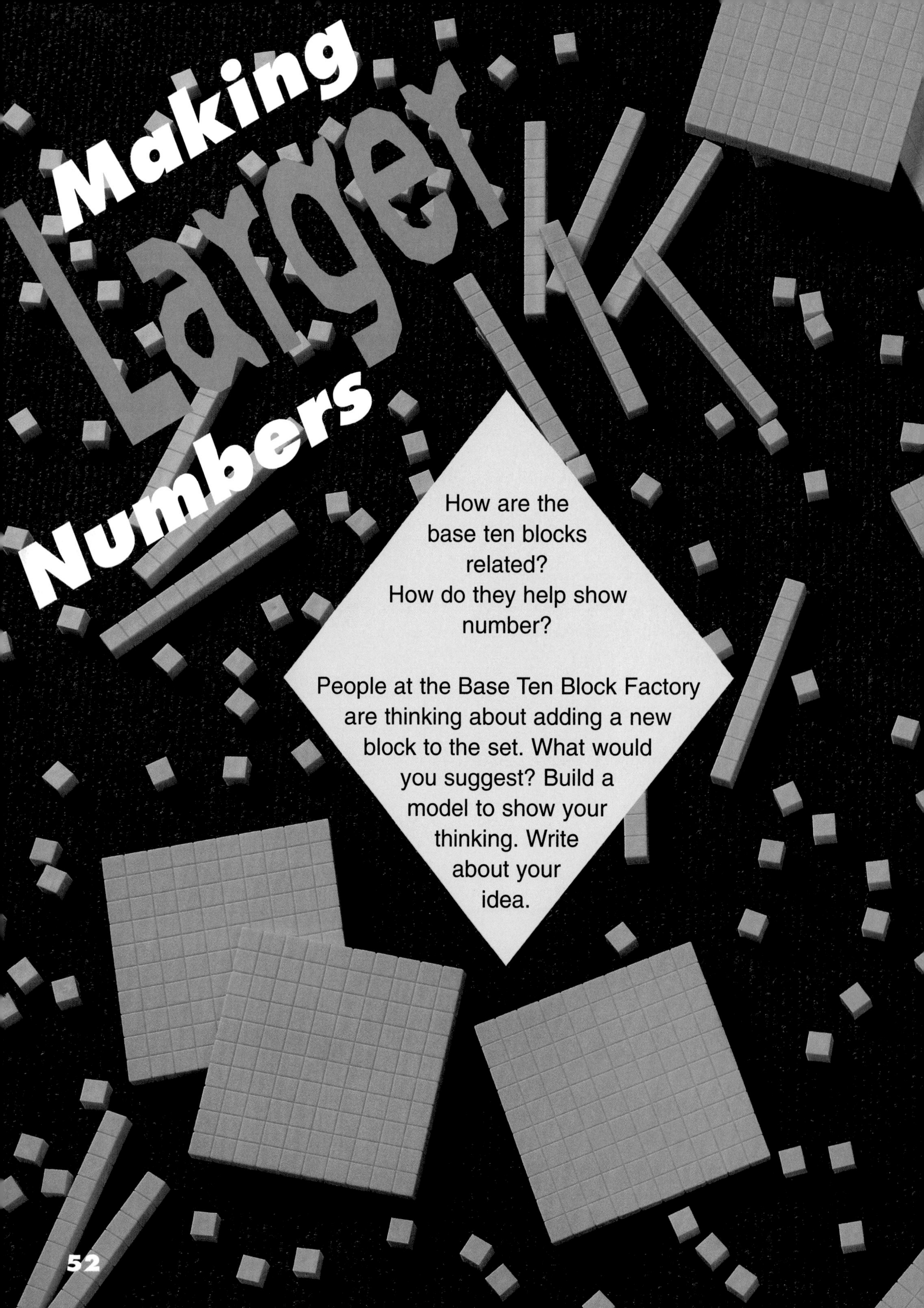

How are the base ten blocks related? How do they help show number?

People at the Base Ten Block Factory are thinking about adding a new block to the set. What would you suggest? Build a model to show your thinking. Write about your idea.

Check YOURSELF

Your description is complete. You have explained how the blocks are related. You made a model to show your new block and you have written a report to show how it is related to the other blocks. Your ideas about why the new block is useful are clear.

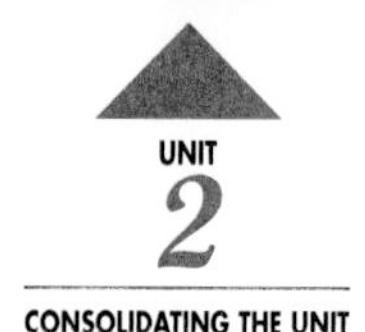

PROBLEM BANK

1. Use base ten blocks to build a structure.

a. Write to tell which blocks you used.

b. How many units are in your structure?

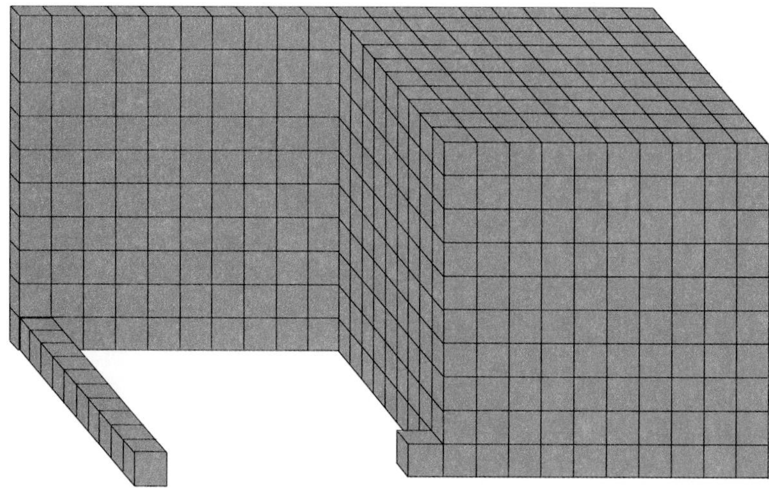

2. Build structures that have the following numbers of units. Tell which blocks you used to build each one.

a. 367

b. 428

c. four hundred sixty-three

d. five hundred twenty-nine

3. Use base ten blocks to show these numbers in different ways. Record the ways for each number on a chart.

a. 374 **b.** 710 **c.** 2953

Thousands	Hundreds	Tens	Ones

4. Here is how these marbles are sold. What different ways could you buy packages to have a total of 1000 marbles? Record each combination.

5. Sometimes a lottery is won by more than one person. How much will each person get if 1000 dollars is won by 4 people? By 5 people? By 10 people?

6. Here are the scores of a video game.

Player	Score
Harinder	1856
Sue	2016
Dani	1995
Barry	2234

a. Arrange the scores in order from greatest to least.
b. If Sue scored another 200 points, would she win? Explain.
c. About how many more points does Dani need to win? Explain.

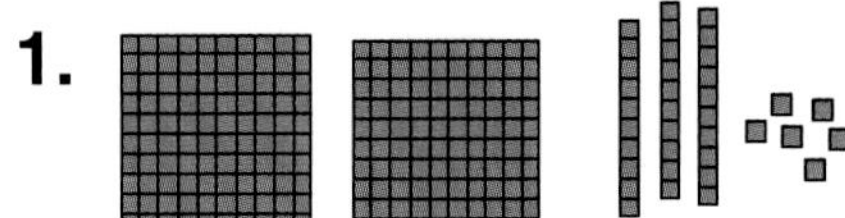

1.

Write this number in as many ways as you can.

2. What are the next 6 numbers in each pattern?
What is the pattern?
   a. 225, 250, 275, 300
   b. 685, 695, 705, 715
   c. 520, 620, 720, 820

3. Write each number.
   a. two hundred eighty
   b. nine hundred sixty-three
   c. 700 + 4 + 50
   d. four thousand two hundred six
   e. 300 + 70 + 1000 + 9

4. What is the value of 7 in each number?
Give your answer as 7, 70, 700, or 7000.
   a. 307 **b.** 754 **c.** 371
   d. 1072 **e.** 7593 **f.** 2740

5. Which number is greater, 794 or 947?
Write to tell how you decided.

6. At Maple School, there are 386 students. Pencils are sold in packages of 100.
   a. How many packages of pencils must be bought for each student to get 1 pencil?
   b. How many packages of pencils must be bought for each student to get 2 pencils?

1. Here is a tally chart showing books borrowed from the library.

Books Taken Out	
Mystery	𝍸 𝍸 𝍸 𝍸 𝍸 |
Sports	𝍸 𝍸 |
Fairy Tale	𝍸 𝍸 𝍸 𝍸 |
Adventure	𝍸 𝍸 𝍸 |||
Animal	𝍸 ||||

a. Write the book types in order, from those borrowed most to those borrowed least.

b. Make a graph to show these data.

c. Write 3 true statements about the data.

d. What advice would you give to a librarian about buying new books?

2. Look at the list of activities. Think about how long it takes to do each. Write each in one column of a chart like the one shown.

Activities

- paint the school
- blink
- draw a picture
- take a camping trip
- tie your shoes
- bake a cake
- have a bath
- sing a song
- paint a picture
- read a long book
- travel to the ocean
- play a game of hockey

1–10 seconds	1–10 minutes	1–10 hours	1–10 days

3. Write each time. Tell how much time passed between the times shown:

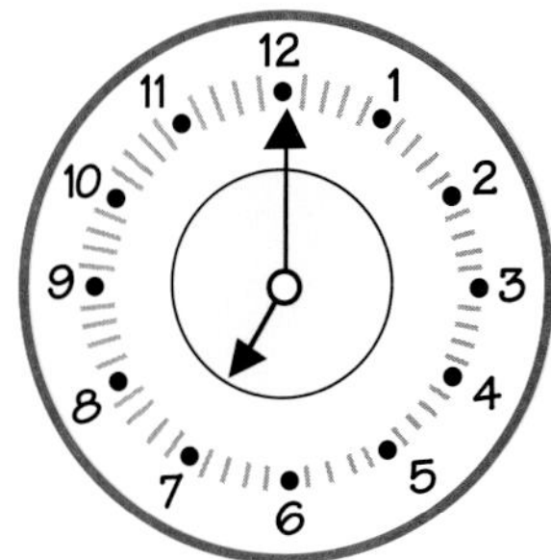

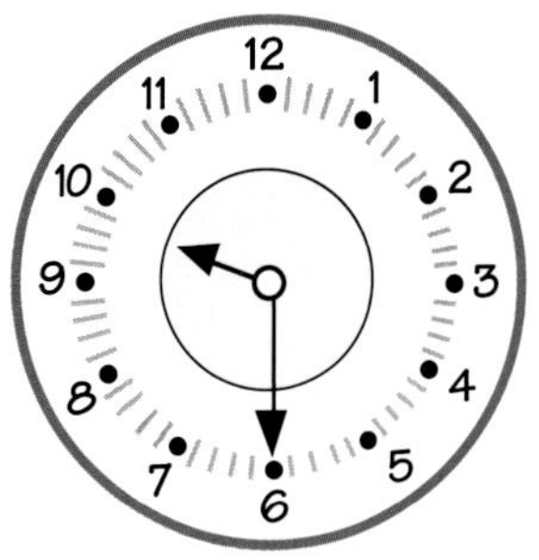

UNIT

3

Combining, Comparing, and Separating

What are addition and subtraction?

COMBINING, COMPARING, AND SEPARATING

STARTING OUT

1 • Where can you see addition on this farm?
- Where can you see subtraction on this farm?
- Make up a problem about this scene that someone could solve using addition.
- Make up a problem about this scene that someone could solve using subtraction.

My Journal: When do you add? When do you subtract?

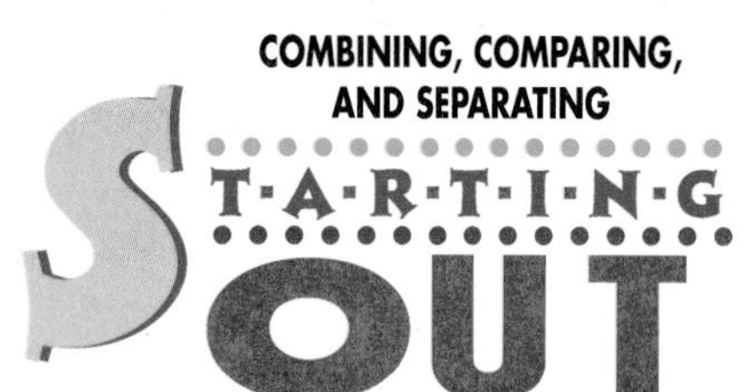
STARTING OUT

1

2 • Use numbers to tell about each frame in the story.
• What pictures and number sentences would you use to make this story longer?
• How do you decide when to add?
• How do you decide when to subtract?

My Journal: How do you think adding and subtracting are related?

Combining Groups

Don't look now, but there are 13 chickens and pigs playing in the barnyard. Altogether there is a total of 36 legs. How many chickens and how many pigs are playing in the barnyard?

▶ Solve the problems below about legs, wheels, tables, and stools. Explain your solutions.

1. Rashida has a total of 12 ducks and sheep. Altogether, these animals have 38 legs. How many ducks and how many sheep does Rashida have?

2. The Country Kitchen restaurant has 13 4-legged tables and 3-legged stools altogether. There is a total of 42 table and stool legs in the restaurant. How many tables and how many stools are there?

3. From his hiding place Dwayne saw 15 bicycles and tricycles pass by. He counted a total of 36 wheels. How many bicycles were there? How many tricycles?

4. ***My Journal:*** Which problem was most interesting to you? Explain.

Practise *Your Skills*

Find the sum.

1. 2 3 + 2	**2.** 4 7 + 4	**3.** 5 5 + 8	**4.** 6 6 + 6	**5.** 3 4 + 4
6. 9 1 + 1	**7.** 8 2 + 2	**8.** 7 3 + 7	**9.** 2 5 + 5	**10.** 1 8 + 1

11. 2 + 7 + 7 = ■ **12.** 6 + 4 + 6 = ■

13. 2 + 7 + 2 = ■

14. How are the questions above alike?

Combining More Groups

▶ Solve. Use reasoning and pattern blocks.

1. You have some triangles and squares. There are more squares than triangles. There are 18 sides altogether. How many triangles and how many squares do you have?

2. You have the same number of triangles and squares. There are 35 sides altogether. How many triangles and how many squares do you have?

3. You have squares and hexagons with a total of 22 sides. How many squares do you have? How many hexagons?

4. You have squares and triangles. Altogether, there are 20 sides. How many squares and how many triangles do you have?

5. You have triangles and hexagons with a total of 24 sides. How many triangles and how many hexagons do you have?

6. You have triangles, squares, and hexagons. There are the same number of hexagons as triangles. There are 30 sides altogether. How many squares, triangles, and hexagons do you have?

ON YOUR OWN

▶ Solve. Use reasoning and pattern blocks. Draw pictures of the shapes if it helps.

1. You have some squares and triangles. There are fewer squares. Altogether, there are 34 sides. How many squares and how many triangles do you have?
2. You have only triangles and hexagons. Altogether, there are 15 sides. How many triangles and hexagons do you have?
3. Make up two shape problems of your own. Try to write one that has more than one solution. Record your answers.
4. *My Journal:* Which of the problems you solved were easy? Which were difficult? Explain why.

Practise *Your Skills*

Find the difference.

1. 15 − 5	2. 9 − 6	3. 16 − 7	4. 12 − 8	5. 13 − 6
6. 17 − 8	7. 12 − 9	8. 9 − 2	9. 18 − 9	10. 12 − 5

Find the sum or difference.

11. 8 + 7 = ■	12. 8 + 3 = ■	13. 5 + 7 = ■	14. 8 + 8 = ■
15 − 7 = ■	11 − 3 = ■	12 − 7 = ■	16 − 8 = ■

15. What strategy can you use for questions 11 to 14?

Estimating Sums

▶ Try these estimations. Check each estimate you make with a calculator. If your sum does not fall within the range, try again with another number.

What number can I add to 277 to get a sum between 600 and 700?

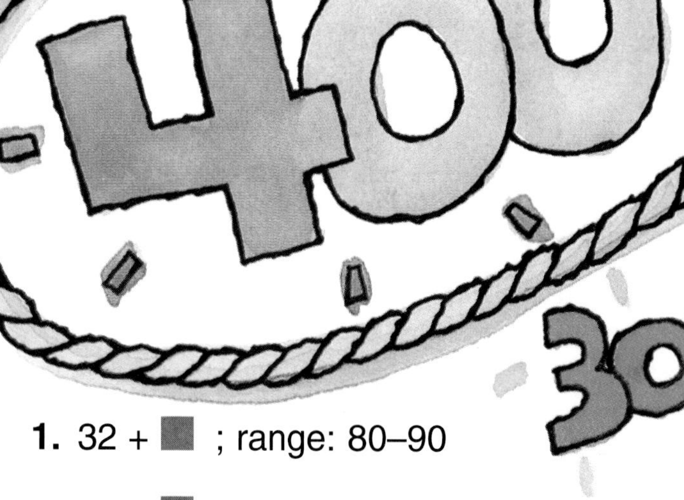

1. 32 + ■ ; range: 80–90
2. 87 + ■ ; range: 120–130
3. 274 + ■ ; range: 600–700
4. 316 + ■ ; range: 800–900
5. 438 + ■ ; range: 730–780
6. 73 + ■ ; range: 520–560
7. 198 + ■ ; range: 900–975
8. 582 + ■ ; range: 750–770

▶ Estimate the number of boxes, cartons, and cases needed for the horseshoe totals. Then find the exact number for each. Use your calculator. Compare your estimate with your exact answer.

Box

Carton

Case

1. Horseshoes = 144
   - ■ boxes
   - ■ cartons
   - ■ cases

2. Horseshoes = 648
   - ■ boxes
   - ■ cartons
   - ■ cases

3. Horseshoes = 1512
   - ■ boxes
   - ■ cartons
   - ■ cases

4. ***My Journal:*** What did you find out about making estimates?

Practise *Your Skills*

Estimate the sum. Show your thinking.

46 + 31 → 50 + 30 = 80

1.	2.	3.	4.	5.
37 + 22	49 + 48	78 + 35	92 + 27	24 + 39

6.	7.	8.	9.	10.
121 + 237	248 + 248	373 + 194	155 + 699	350 + 449

11. How does rounding numbers to the nearest 10 or 100 help you estimate sums?

UNIT 3 ACTIVITY 4

Adding Large Numbers

▶ Estimate each sum. Then find the exact answer.

1. There are about 180 school days a year. About how many days has a child spent in school by the end of grade 2? By the end of grade 4? Explain your answer.

2. These children play a game every day after school. Here are their scores for Monday and Tuesday.

Name	Monday	Tuesday
Jessica	285	360
Rahim	190	295
Chris	255	220

Who has the highest total score? Explain how you know.

3. Read how these children add 57 + 28. Then draw a picture of yourself. Write a thought bubble that tells how you add 47 and 38.

57 + 28
First I add the tens;
50 + 20 = 70.
Then I add the ones;
7 + 8 =15.
Then I add
those sums;
70 + 15 = 85.

57 + 28

$$\begin{array}{r} {}^{1}57 \\ +\ 28 \\ \hline 85 \end{array}$$

I add the ones.
I trade a ten if there is one.
Then I add the tens.

57 + 28
I think 57 is about 60.
28 is about 30.
60 and 30 is 90.
But I need to
subtract 5.
90 – 5 = 85.

4. Interview someone older than you to find out how someone else adds 57 and 28. Draw that person and the thought bubble that explains that person's thinking.

5. ***My Journal:*** What questions do you have about addition?

Group

This is a game for two players.

Materials

Each pair needs 4 sets of 0–9 number cards.

Game Rules

1. Shuffle all the cards. Place them face-down in a stack.
2. In turn, each player draws 1, 2, or 3 cards from the deck and records the number formed by the cards in the order they were drawn. For example, if you draw a 5, then a 7, and then a 3, your number is 573. Put all the used cards on the side.
3. Each player takes another turn. This time the player can draw 0, 1, 2, or 3 cards and adds the new number formed to the first number.
4. Players continue taking turns, adding each new number formed to the total.
5. The game continues until one player gets a sum over 1000. The player with the sum closest to 1000 wins.
6. If there is a tie, each player draws a card, and the player with the greater number wins.

ON YOUR OWN

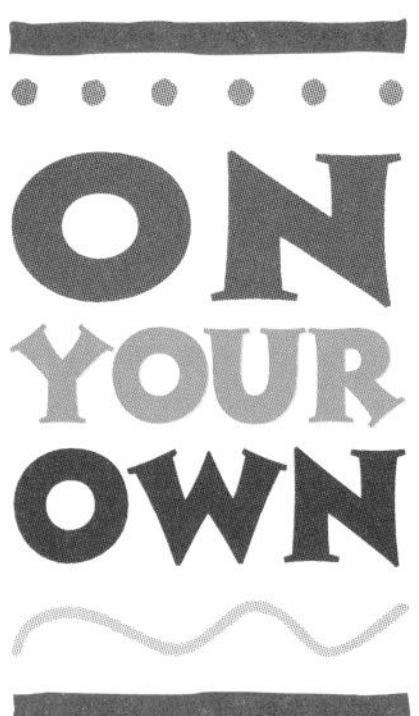

▶ Imagine that you are playing a game of Closing in on 1000 with a partner named Ed. You have each drawn three times. So far, these are the sums each of you has made:

My draws
273
+ 465
738
+ 156
894

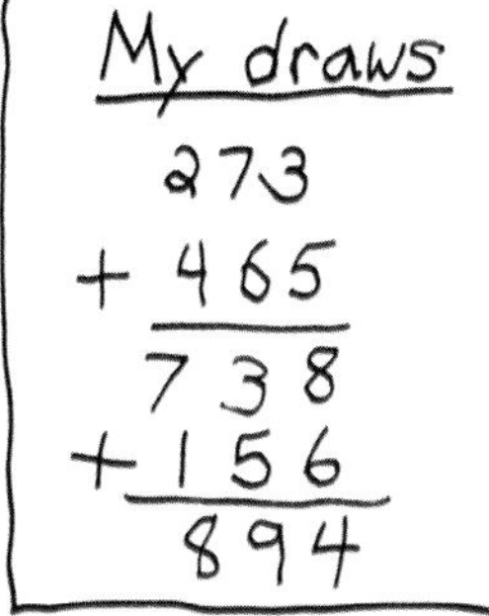

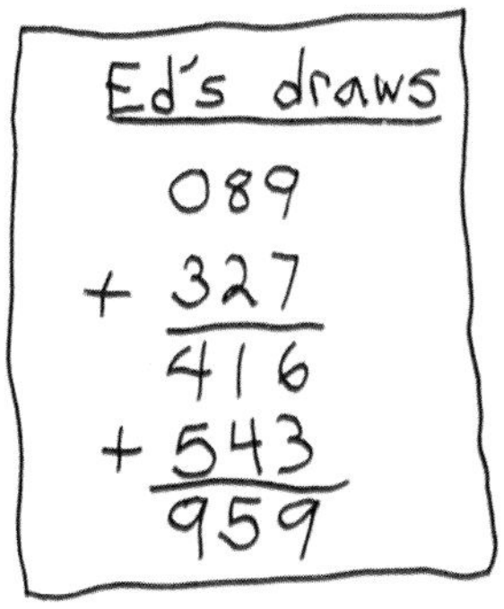

Ed's draws
089
+ 327
416
+ 543
959

Look at the two running totals.

1. Will you draw any cards? If so, how many? Explain.

2. What should Ed do? Why?

3. *My Journal:* What did you learn that was new in this activity?

3

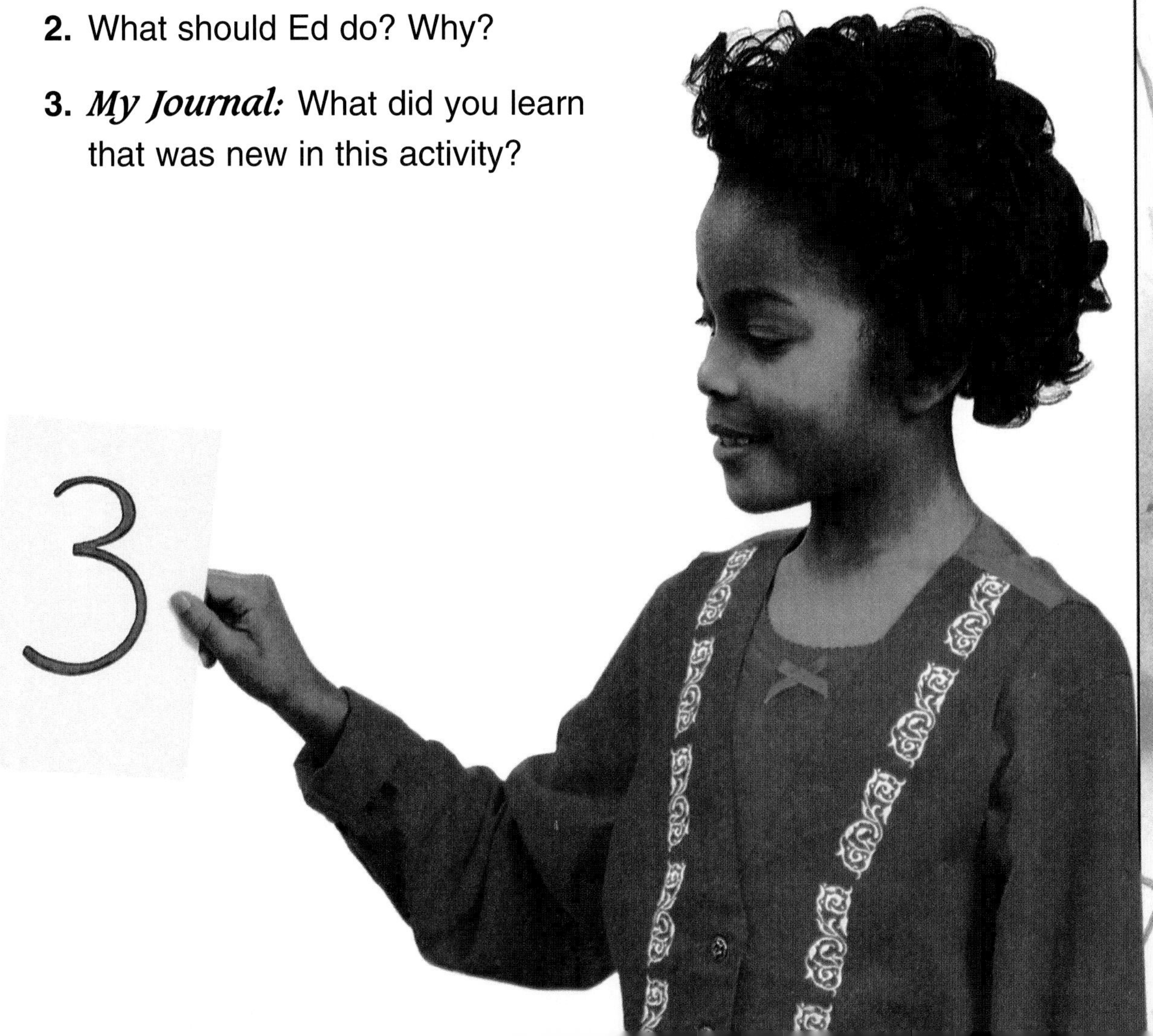

PEOPLE, SOCIETY, AND MATHEMATICS

The CASE OF THE Missing ARROW

Have you ever wondered how people in different times or different places counted and compared? This First Nations tale tells about one common way.

Little Eagle was 9 years old and his task was to guard a stack of arrows. He did not know the names of numbers, but he always knew if even one arrow was missing. He gathered rocks—one for each arrow—and placed them in a pile next to the arrows.

One day he saw that there were fewer arrows than rocks, so he knew some arrows were missing. He looked all around until he saw his little sister playing with the arrows. When he put the missing arrows back, he saw there were as many arrows as rocks.

Across the ocean a similar system was in use. Because some African people believed that it was bad luck to count animals, a herder would put one small stone in a bag for each animal and then match them to the animals one-to-one.

1. How are the First Nations and African methods similar?

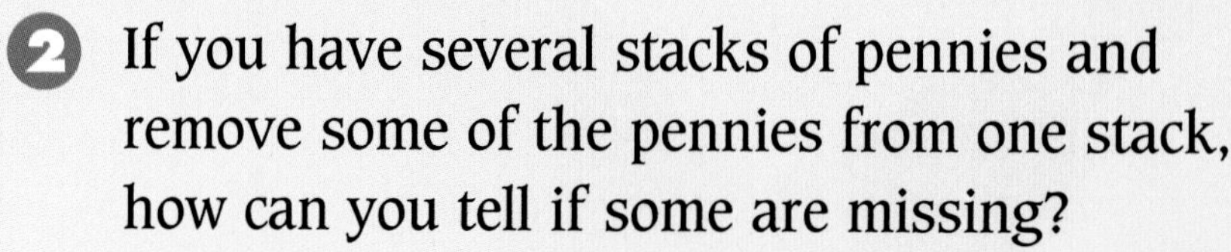

2. If you have several stacks of pennies and remove some of the pennies from one stack, how can you tell if some are missing?

Data Collection

UNIT 3
ACTIVITY 6

▶ You can do an experiment to find out who has the biggest hand. Here's how:

1. Get a jar large enough to put your hand in.
2. Use a centimetre ruler to mark and label a strip of paper from 0 to 25 cm in half centimetres. Tape this strip to the side of the jar.
3. Fill the jar with enough water to cover anyone's hand completely. Measure the water level to the nearest half centimetre. Record this measurement in a table.
4. Place your hand in the jar. Find the water level now. Record it in the table, too.
5. Find the difference between water levels. Record this in your table. What have you learned about hand sizes in your group?

Using Subtraction

▶ How will you measure?
How do the measures compare?

Choose 2 books. Use square grid paper or square tiles to find out how much space each book covers. Which book covers more space? How much more space does it cover?

Measure your height in centimetres. Measure your longest step in centimetres. Which is longer? What is the difference between the two lengths?

Take a handful of small cubes. How many did you get? Use both hands together to scoop up cubes. How many did you get? How many more did you get the second time?

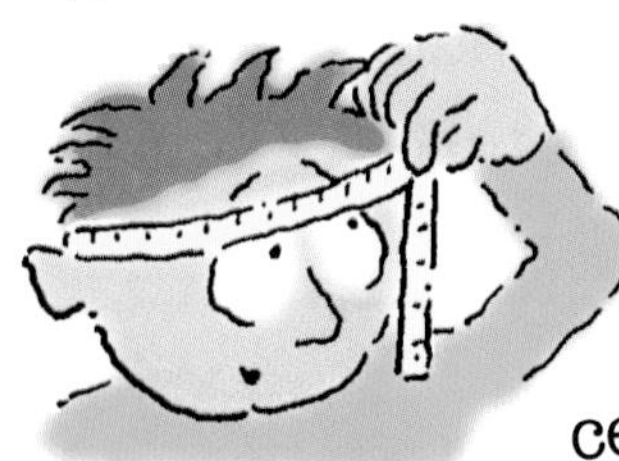

Measure around your head in centimetres.

Measure around your knee in centimetres. What are the measures? What is the difference between them?

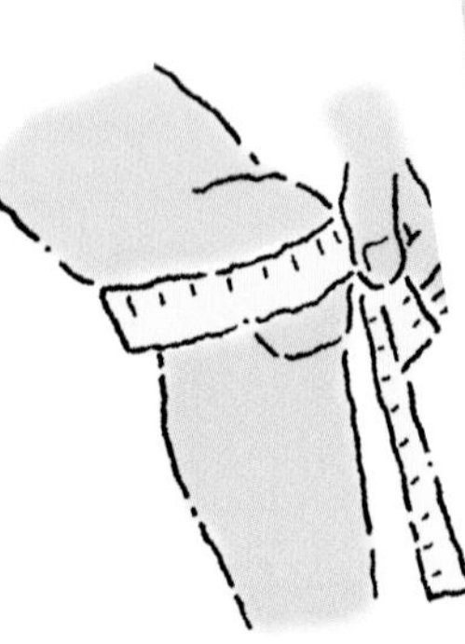

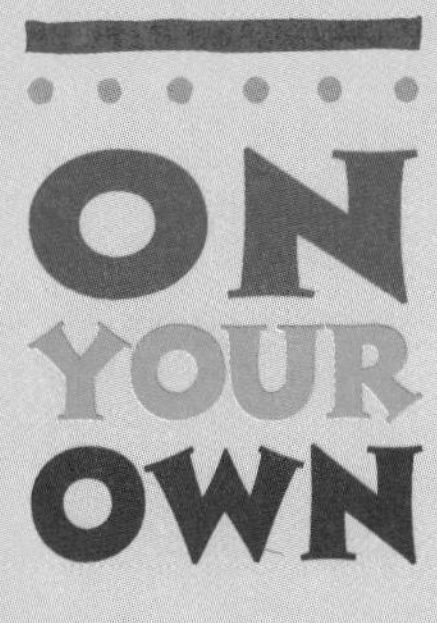

1. Measure your height. Measure the height of someone in your family. What are the measures? What is the difference between the two measures?

2. Trace your hand on grid paper. Trace an adult's hand. What is the area of each? What is the difference between the two measures?

3. Find a small drinking glass. Find out how many pieces of macaroni fit in it. Find out how many large beans fit in it. What is the difference between the two counts?

4. ***My Journal:*** What other things might you measure and compare?

Practise *Your Skills*

Add.

1. 53 + 37	**2.** 28 + 45	**3.** 29 + 47	**4.** 35 + 35	**5.** 49 + 54
6. 120 + 75	**7.** 295 + 37	**8.** 348 + 297	**9.** 204 + 340	**10.** 570 + 235

What can you add to give a sum in the range?

11. 57 + ■; range 100–110

12. 180 + ■; range 500–550

Subtracting Large Numbers

▶ Estimate each difference. Then find the exact answer.

Chalkboard Talk

1. 42 − 16 = ____
2. What is 56 − 33? ____
3. What is the difference between 73 and 37? ____
4. 329 − 114 = ____
5. Find 656 − 244 ____
6. What is the difference between 382 and 66? ____
7. $\begin{array}{r} 717 \\ -\underline{534} \end{array}$
8. $\begin{array}{r} 852 \\ -\underline{351} \end{array}$

1. There are 365 days in one year. You go to school about 180 days. How many days in a year do you not go to school? How did you find out?

2. These children play a game each day after school. Here are their scores for Monday and Tuesday.

Name	Monday	Tuesday
May	272	308
Selina	291	267

a. How much higher was May's second score than her first?
b. How much lower was Selina's second score than her first?

3. Read how these children solve 84 – 58. Then draw a picture of yourself. Write a thought bubble that tells how you find 93 – 46.

84 – 58
I add on to the smaller number: 58, 68, 78 makes 2 tens. I count up 2 to 80 then 4 to 84.
20 + 2 + 4 = 26,
84 – 58 = 26.

84 – 58
I think 58 is about 60;
84 – 60 = 24.
Then I add 2 more;
24 + 2 = 26.

84 – 58
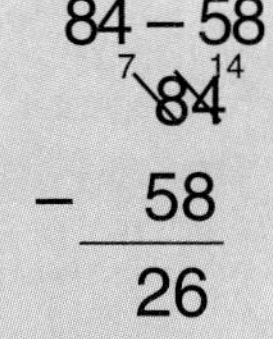

I subtract ones first. I trade a ten for 10 ones if I need to. Then I subtract the tens.

4. Interview someone older than you to find out how someone else solves 84 – 58. Draw that person with a thought bubble to show that person's thinking.

5. ***My Journal:*** What questions do you have about subtraction?

Using Addition and Subtraction

Yikes! It's Mickies!

The Main Stuff

Chicken taco	$0.89
Corn dog	$0.75
Veggie burger	$1.19
Giant salad	$1.25
Buffalo burger	$1.39
Stomper	$0.89
Double Stomper	$1.49

The Side Stuff

Coleslaw	$0.65
Curly fries	$0.75
Plantains	$0.45
Tomato salad	$0.59

The Wet Stuff

Soda	$0.59
Lemonade	$0.69
Iced tea	$0.39

The Sweet Stuff

Fruit cup	$0.59
Pudding	$0.49
Chocolate cake	$0.95
Giant cookie	$0.35

Munchy Meal #1
Corn dog
Tomato salad
Lemonade
Only $1.90

▶ Show the menu at Mickie's to two members of your family. Do this before dinner, so they'll be hungry.

Ask each of them to use the menu to plan his or her favourite meal. (If they don't like this menu, let them choose a menu they do like!)

Whichever menu they choose, tell your family members to write down their choices and give them to you.

1. Estimate and then find the total cost of each meal. Write down these amounts.
2. Create a special Munchy Meal price for each person's order. Figure out the savings. Ask each person to check your work.
3. *My Journal:* What did you learn from this activity?

Practise Your Skills

Find the difference. Use addition to check your answer.

1. 86 − 27   **2.** 50 − 48   **3.** 93 − 62   **4.** 127 − 35   **5.** 293 − 246

Estimate the difference. Show your thinking.

93 − 47 → 90 − 50 = 40

6. 57 − 39   **7.** 83 − 68   **8.** 70 − 32
9. 155 − 83   **10.** 247 − 193   **11.** 578 − 294

Pet Care Costs

How much does it cost to keep a dog or a cat for one year?

At an animal shelter, it can cost about $125 to buy a dog. A cat costs about $85.

The costs of some things your pet will need are given. Think about how long some of these supplies will last.

Foods

Can of dog or cat food: $0.79–$1.69

Dry food for dogs or cats: $25 – $29 for a 9-kg bag

Medical Care

Rx

Visit to vet: $30

Rabies or distemper shots: $40 for both

Leukemia shots: 3 for $4 each

Spaying or neutering: $120

Flea or tick powder: $3.59

Check YOURSELF

Your plan is complete in all ways. It shows that you understand how to use addition and subtraction. You added and subtracted successfully to find all costs. Your estimates of expenses are reasonable. Your written plan communicated your ideas clearly to others.

PROBLEM BANK

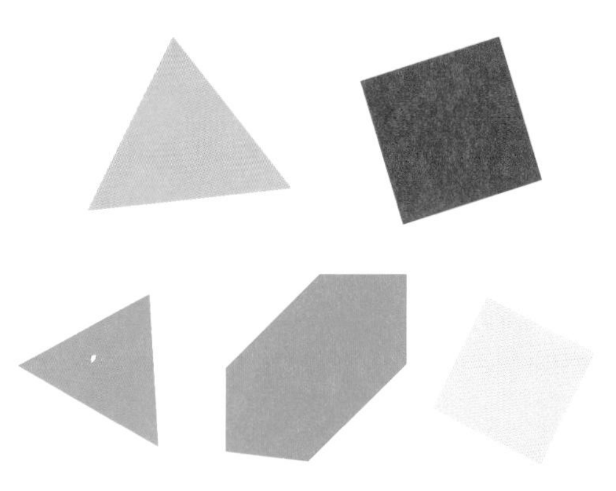

1. The Cycle Store sells bicycles and unicycles. Altogether there are 19 wheels. How many bicycles and unicycles are there for sale? Explain how you know. List at least two other possible answers.

2. You have some triangles and some squares. There are the same number of each. There are 21 sides. How many triangles and how many squares do you have altogether? (Use blocks if you wish)

3. You have hexagons and triangles. There are twice as many hexagons as triangles. There are 30 sides. How many hexagons and how many triangles do you have? (Use blocks if you wish)

4. Estimate the number of boxes, cartons, and cases needed for the marbles. Then find the exact number for each. Compare your estimate with your exact answer.

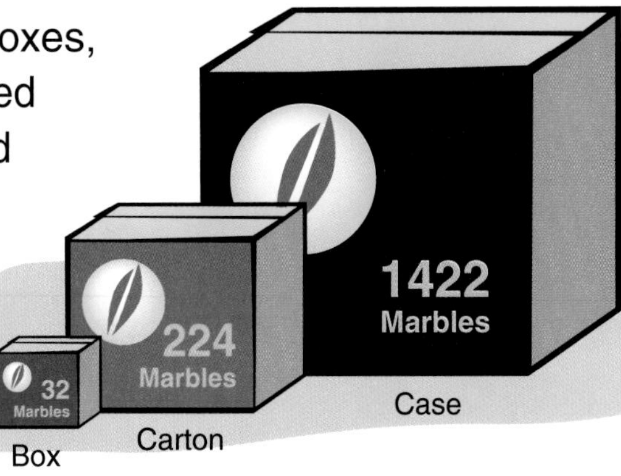

a. Marbles = 256
■ boxes
■ cartons
■ cases

b. Marbles = 320
■ boxes
■ cartons
■ cases

c. Marbles = 1646
■ boxes
■ cartons
■ cases

5. a. Use a calculator to play this game with a partner. Using the numbers 1, 2, 3, 4, and 5, your goal is to add numbers until you reach exactly 37. Each person gets a turn entering a number on the calculator. The player who adds the number that gets to the total of 37 wins.

b. Is there a strategy you can use so you will always win?

6. 245 children are travelling to a cross-country track meet. One type of bus has seats for 50. Another bus has seats for 80. What different ways could the school arrange to order buses? Record each way. For each way, tell how many empty seats there will be.

7. Your team needs new baseball gloves and hats. Gloves cost $15 and hats cost $12. From fundraising, you have $112. What can you get for the money you have raised? List all the possibilities.

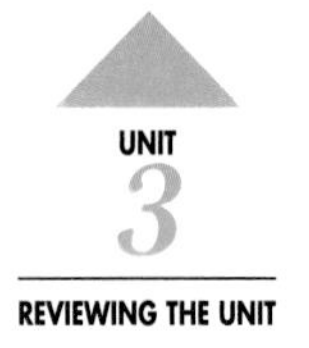

What can you add to each number to get a sum within the range?

1. 47 + ■; range 80–90
2. 55 + ■; range 100–110
3. 254 + ■; range 500–530
4. 415 + ■; range 800–900
5. 525 + ■; range 700–750
6. 678 + ■; range 900–950

Estimate each sum.

7. 29 + 32
8. 52 + 39
9. 127 + 48
10. 353 + 460
11. 592 + 175

Estimate each difference.

12. 83 − 59
13. 27 − 19
14. 158 − 62
15. 395 − 283
16. 625 − 458

Add or subtract.

17. 95 − 68 = ■
18. 158 + 227 = ■
19. 350 + 86 = ■
20. 245 − 113 = ■

21. Here are the scores four children got in their favourite video game this week.
Anna: 326 Kimi: 455 Tenisha: 390 Brady: 422
a. How many more points does Anna need to tie Kimi?
b. Last week Brady scored 100 more points than this week. What is his total score?
c. If Tenisha were to score another 125 points, what would her total score be?

1. This tally shows children's answers to two surveys.
   a. Was the same number of children asked each question?
   b. Write 3 statements about each tally. Use numbers in your statement.
   c. Make a graph to show each set of data.

Do you like vegetables?	
Yes	𝍸 𝍸 ||
No	𝍸 𝍸 𝍸 |||

How do you like to eat potatoes?	
Mashed	𝍸 ||||
French Fries	𝍸 𝍸 𝍸 ||
Baked	||||

2.

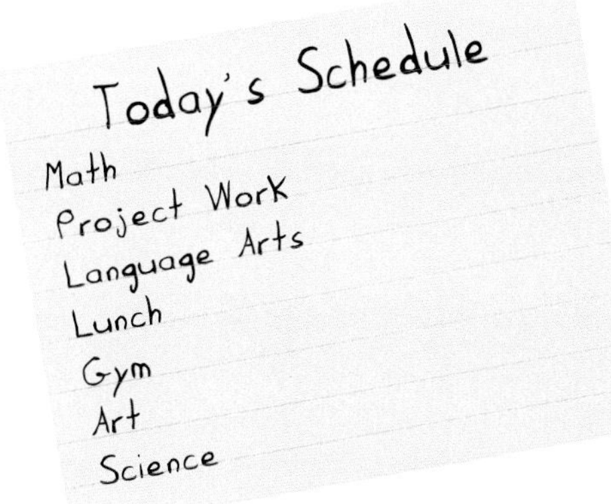

a. What do children do first?
b. What is the fifth activity?
c. Add starting and ending times for the activities.

3. Write the time shown on each clock. Then answer the question.

a.

What time was it 5 minutes earlier?

b.

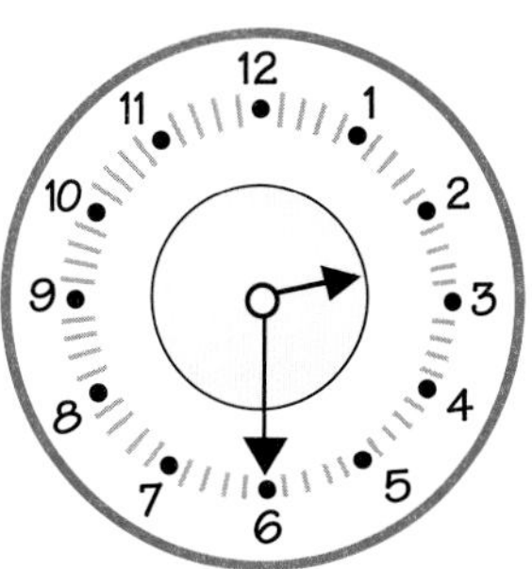

What time will it be in 15 minutes?

c.

What time will it be in half an hour?

4. Complete these number sentences.
   a. 1649 = 1000 + ■ + 40 + ■ **b.** 5060 = 5000 + ■

5. Write the numeral.
   a. 2 thousands, 6 hundreds, 4 tens **b.** six hundred forty-seven

6. Write the next 5 numbers in each pattern.
   a. 3155, 3055, 2955,... **b.** 625, 650, 675, ... **c.** 470, 460, 450, ...

QUEEN
MON. SEP. 26
Time Line
A telephone number is posted on every bus and streetcar stop. When you call that number, the talking computer tells you when the next two vehicles are scheduled to come.
17108
Proof of Payment
Paid to
DOWN
MON. SEP. 26
00999
UP
DOWN
Zone 3
Zone 1
SPC
Steeles
Shepp.
Y. Mills
Davis.
Welles.
Front
Rosedale
Bloor Yonge
Sherbourne
Castle Frank
Wellesley
College
Dundas
Queen
St. Patrick
Osgoode
St. Andrew
Dupont
Bay
Bathurst
Campbellton
Rimouski
GASPÉ
PENINSULA
Chatham
Newcastle

UNIT
4
Locating and Mapping
How can we make and use maps?

LOCATING
AND MAPPING
STARTING
OUT

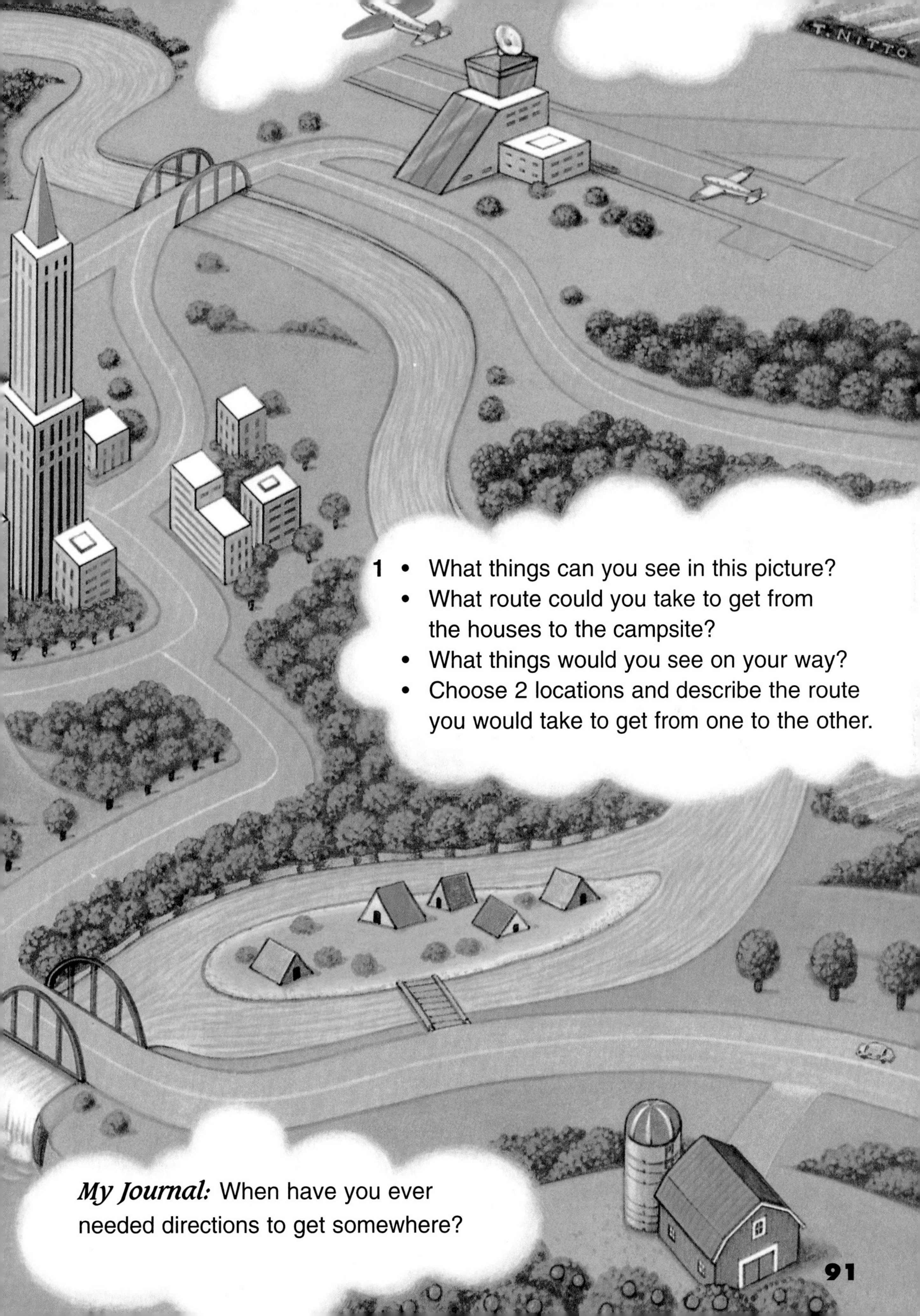

1 • What things can you see in this picture?
- What route could you take to get from the houses to the campsite?
- What things would you see on your way?
- Choose 2 locations and describe the route you would take to get from one to the other.

My Journal: When have you ever needed directions to get somewhere?

LOCATING AND MAPPING

STARTING OUT

Four different people on four different airplanes looked out their windows onto the scene from pages 90–91.

2 • Describe where the plane would be for each picture. Which way do you think it is heading? Explain how you know.

• If the airplane was above the large hill heading toward the airport, what would you be able to see out the window? How do you know?

My Journal: When have you seen maps being used? Why do you think they are useful?

UNIT 4

ACTIVITY 1

Exploring Maps

▶ Match each map to a place on the drawing.

UNIT 4
ACTIVITY 2

Mapping the Classroom

▶ Match the photographs to the maps.

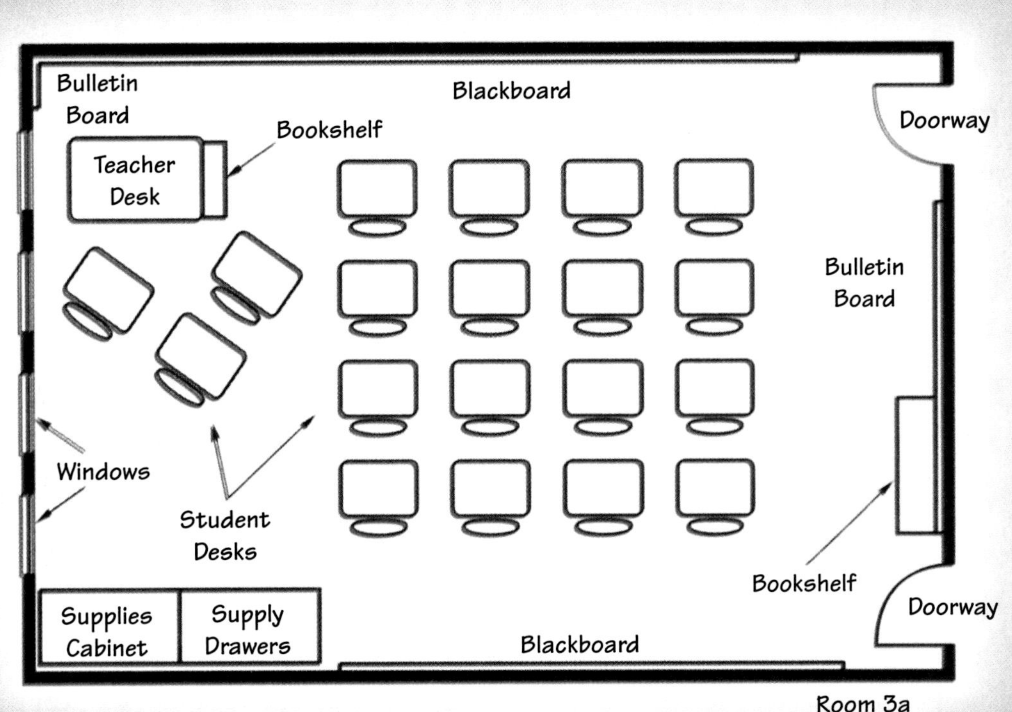
Bulletin Board
Blackboard
Bookshelf
Doorway
Teacher Desk
Bulletin Board
Windows
Student Desks
Bookshelf
Doorway
Supplies Cabinet
Supply Drawers
Blackboard
Room 3a Classroom

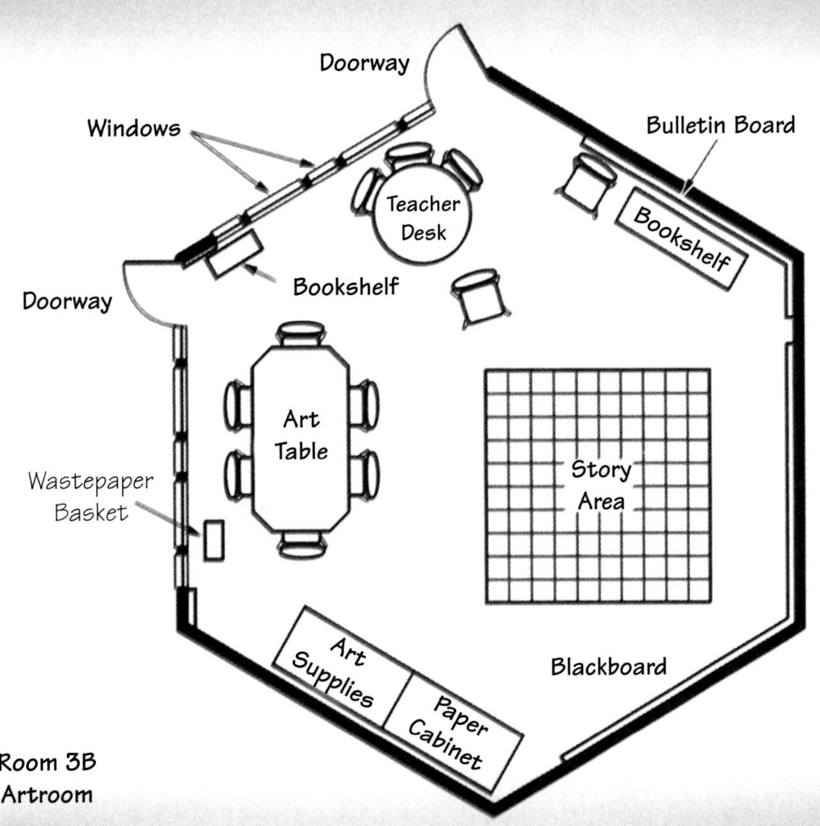
Doorway
Windows
Bulletin Board
Teacher Desk
Bookshelf
Bookshelf
Doorway
Art Table
Story Area
Wastepaper Basket
Art Supplies
Paper Cabinet
Blackboard
Room 3B Artroom

SEA SHELL MAPS

Have you ever wondered if there were different ways to make maps?

Maps were frequently made from handy materials. Some of the earliest maps were made by the Babylonians on tablets of damp clay that were baked in the sun. Chinese people used their beautiful silk fabrics for map making.

Some of the most interesting maps were made by Polynesian Islanders in the South Pacific. They made maps from reeds, sea shells, and palm leaves. The reeds made a grid, the shells represented islands, and the curved leaves represented the ocean's waves and currents.

1. Using some handy materials, make a map of your neighbourhood.
2. Pretend you are burying treasure somewhere nearby. Draw a map to show where it is buried.
3. When someone sends you a birthday card, how does the postal worker find your home to deliver it?

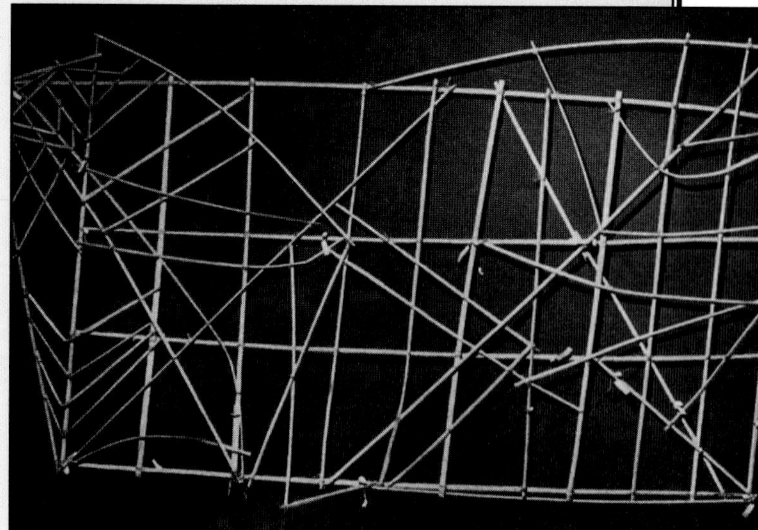

Reed Map

Giving Directions

▶ Describe how to get from X to Y.

1. Write directions for going from your home to school.
2. Write directions for going from school to your home. How do they differ from the directions in problem 1?

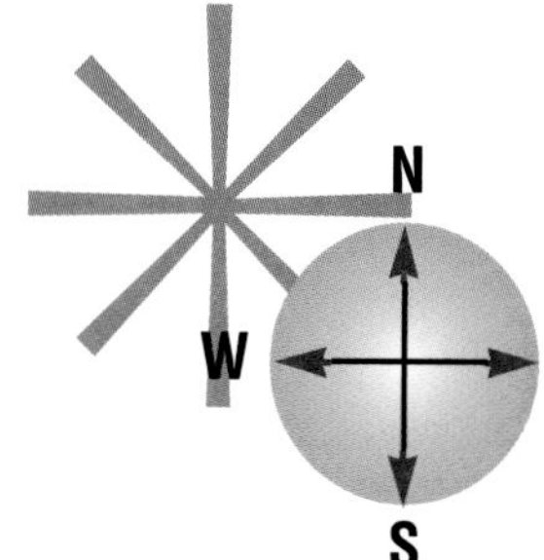

3. Write directions for going from your bedroom to the kitchen.
4. *My Journal:* What did you learn about directions from this activity? Explain.

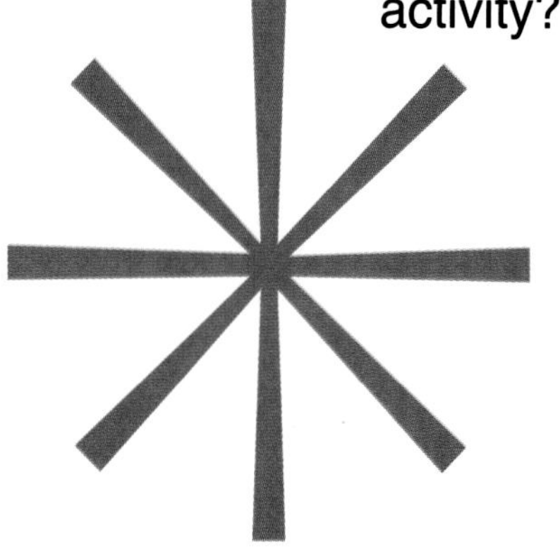

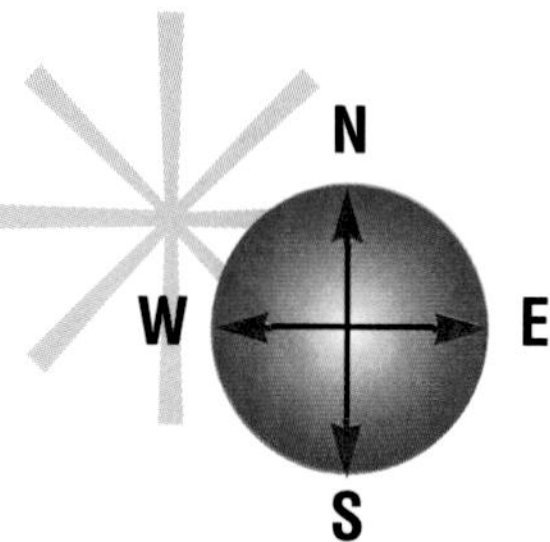

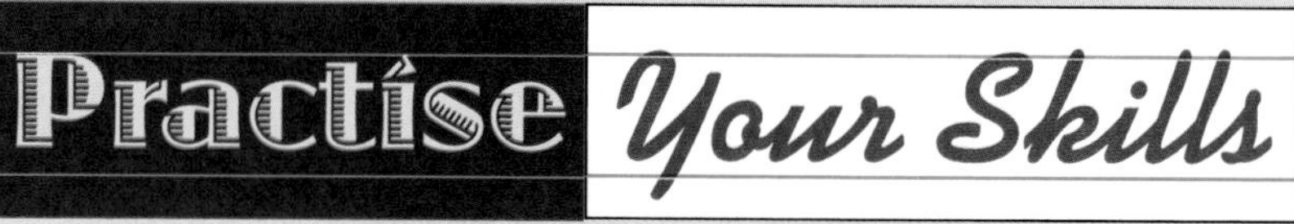

1. a. Trace or draw this grid.
   b. Draw a path from A to B. Write directions that tell about the path.
   c. Draw another path. Write directions that tell about it.

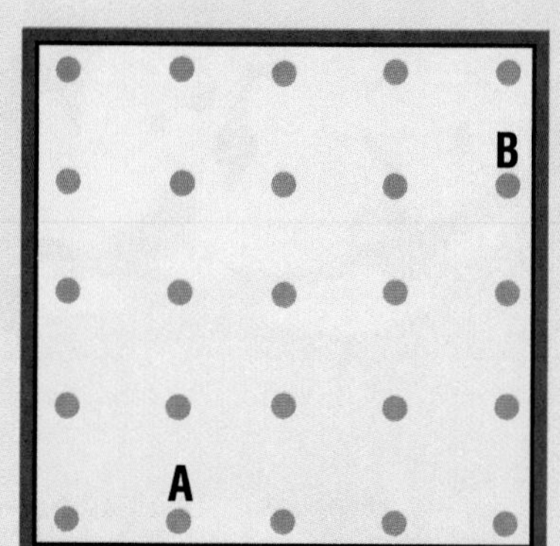

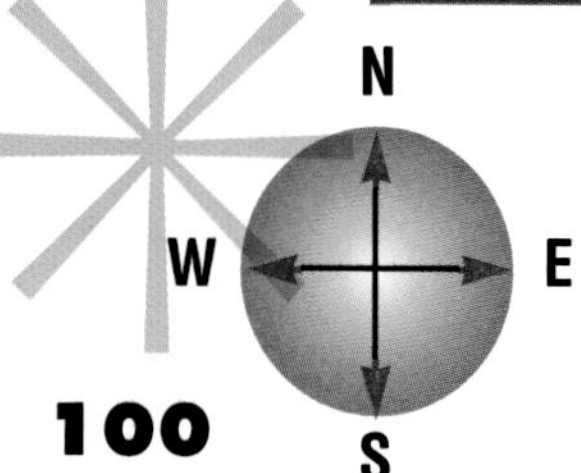

Reading a Map

1. Name a city in the E, 5 section of the map.
2. What sections would you pass through going from Surrey to Victoria?
3. What lettered section is directly east of C? What numbered section is directly south of 4?
4. *My Journal:* What did you learn about making maps from this activity?

Practise Your Skills

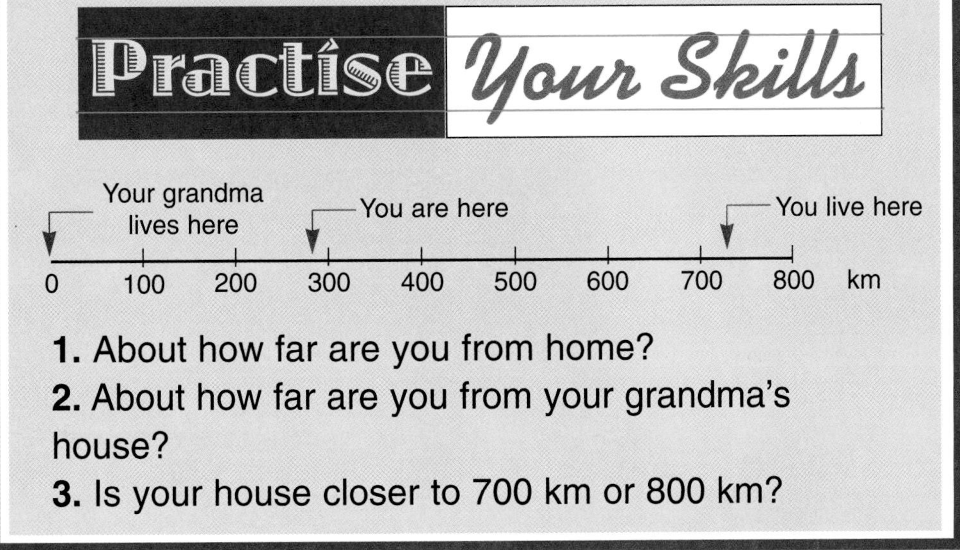

1. About how far are you from home?
2. About how far are you from your grandma's house?
3. Is your house closer to 700 km or 800 km?

UNIT 4
ACTIVITY 5

DINOSAUR DISCOVERY

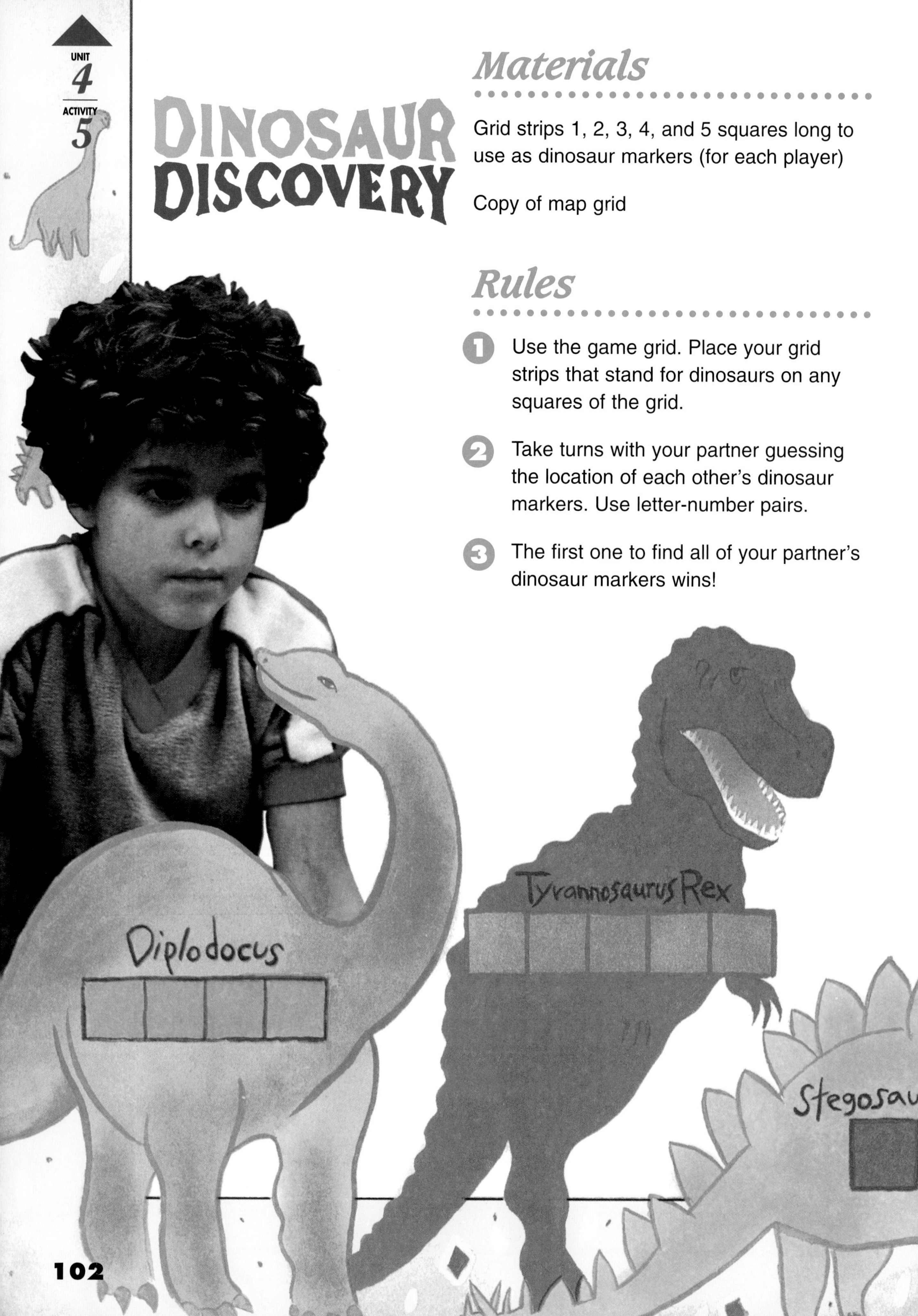

Materials

Grid strips 1, 2, 3, 4, and 5 squares long to use as dinosaur markers (for each player)

Copy of map grid

Rules

1. Use the game grid. Place your grid strips that stand for dinosaurs on any squares of the grid.
2. Take turns with your partner guessing the location of each other's dinosaur markers. Use letter-number pairs.
3. The first one to find all of your partner's dinosaur markers wins!

10
9
8
7
6
5
4
3
2
1
A B C D E F G H I J
Triceratops
Corythosaurus

MAKING MAPS

Have you ever made a map? What was the map for? What are some things that should be on a good map?

Work with your group to make a map of your school so that family and friends can find their way around. Some things to think about:

- What things should go on the map? What doesn't need to be on the map?
- How can pairs of numbers and letters help someone use your map?
- Where would be the best places in the school to have the map?

Check YOURSELF

The map you made is complete and easy to use. It includes all the important places in your school. You explained clearly, in writing, how pairs of numbers and letters were used on your map.

PROBLEM BANK

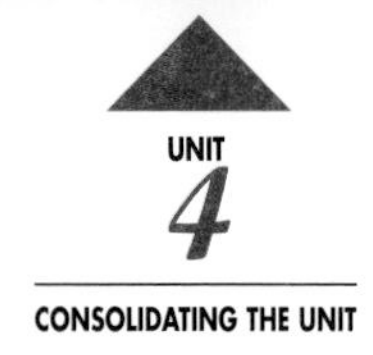

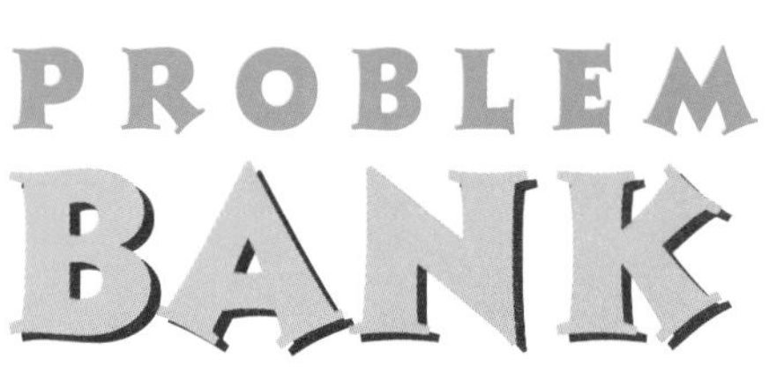

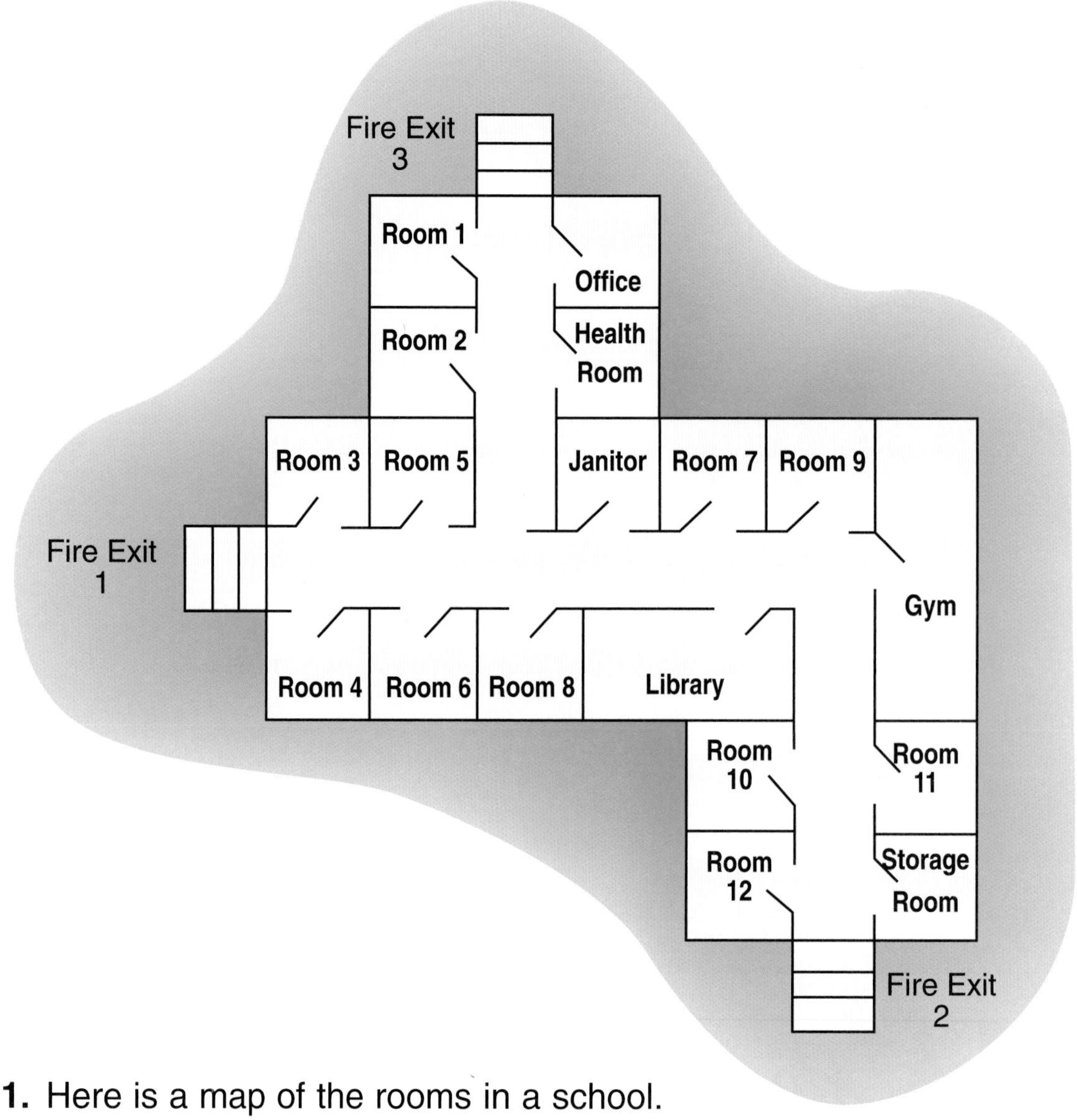

1. Here is a map of the rooms in a school.
   a. Describe the route you would take to get from the library to the office. What rooms would you pass?
   b. If you were to leave Room 12 and head toward the gym, what rooms would you pass?
   c. Draw a fire route for Room 8. What exit should the students use?
   d. Use this map to write another problem about routes and mapping for a friend to solve.

2. **a.** The library is getting two more computers and two more computer desks. Draw a new floor plan for the library to show where they could go.
b. The library is getting two large couches, a rocking chair, and another bookshelf. Draw a new floor plan for the library to show where they could go.
c. Write another problem, using this floor plan, for a friend to solve.

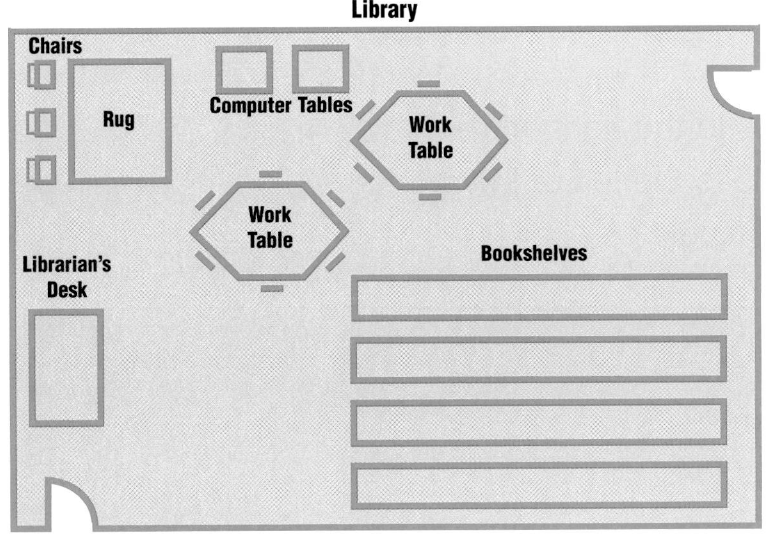

3. Square City is made up of perfectly square city blocks. The path marked on the map shows how to get from A to B by walking 3 blocks.
a. Trace two other, different ways to get from A to B walking only 3 blocks.
b. Find a path from A to B that is 5 blocks long. How did you arrive at your answer?
c. Which letters can be reached from other letters following paths that are 2 blocks long? 4 blocks long?
d. Trace a path that is 15 blocks long. Write a set of directions to explain your path.

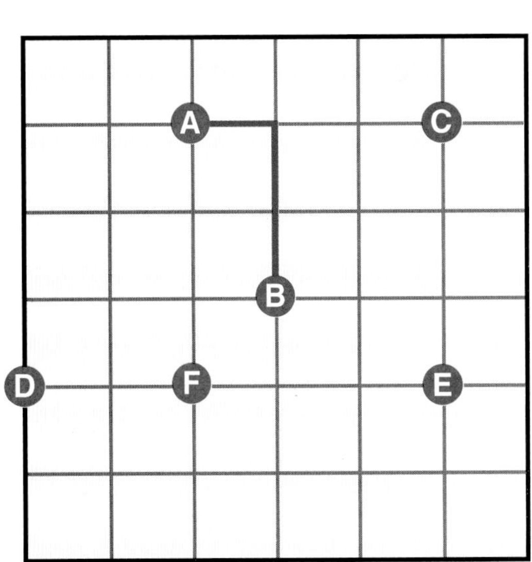

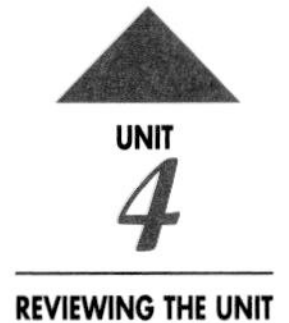

1.

a. Which shape is to the right of the circle?
b. Which shape is to the left of the star?
c. Where is the triangle?

2. a. Which room is across from the office?
b. Where is Room 4?
c. Write directions for going from Room 3 to Room 6.

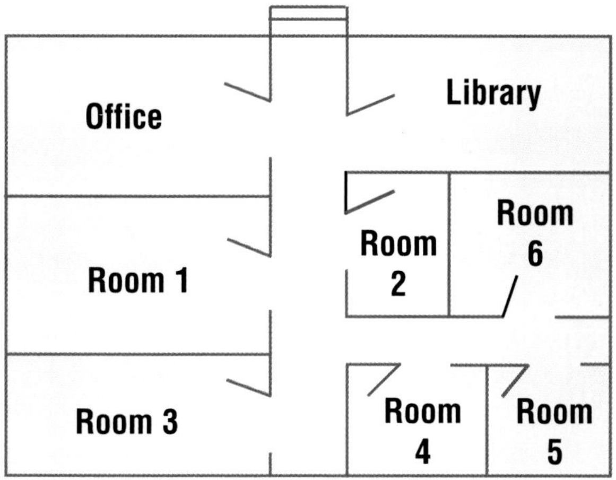

3.

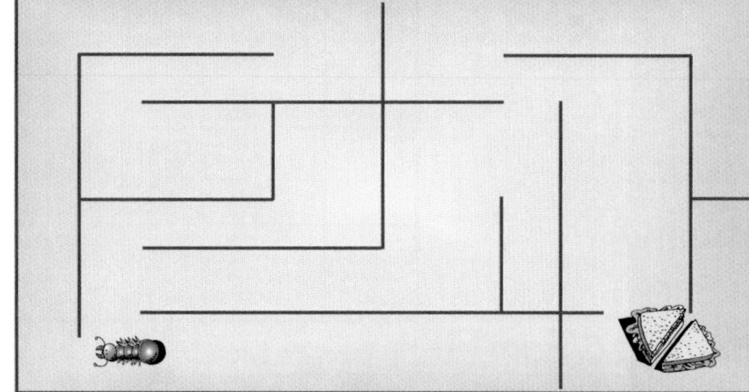

a. Trace this maze. Find a path from the ant to the food.
b. Write directions for the path you drew.

4. What direction does each letter stand for?

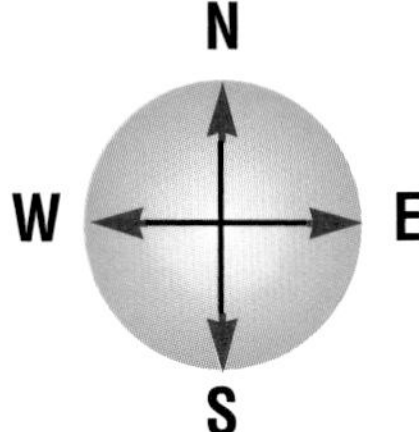

1. Write the number that is:
   a. 10 greater than 189
   b. 100 greater than 463
   c. 10 less than 2365
   d. 100 less than 1846

2. Write the following as numbers:
   a. 500 + 40 + 20 + 7
   b. 4000 + 300 + 5
   c. five hundred seventy-five
   d. four thousand two hundred six

3. a. Estimate the number of hearts in the whole picture.
   b. How did you decide on your estimate?

4. a. What number is shown below?
   b. Write 2 numbers greater than this one.
   c. Write 2 numbers smaller than this one.

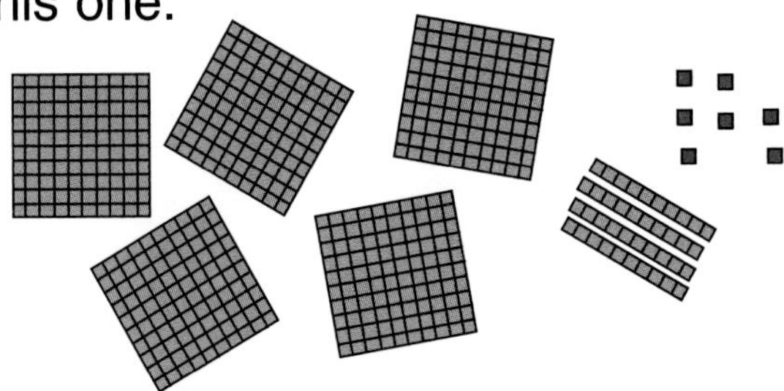

5. a. How can you buy about 200 crayons?
   b. How can you buy about 500 crayons?

6. Complete the exercises that have answers between 300 and 400.

a.	b.	c.	d.	e.
600	163	227	863	527
− 295	−129	+ 55	−692	−138

CANADA

UNIT
5
Grouping
and
Sharing
How can we use equal groups?
Canada
CANADA 43
COLLECTION

GROUPING AND SHARING

STARTING OUT

1 • What equal groups do you see in this kitchen?
- What equal groups could you add to your list?
- How would you find out how many chair legs there are?
- How would you find out how many buns there are in 2 bags?
- Did you use equal groups to help you find out how many? Explain.

My Journal: What do you know about multiplication?

UNIT 5 ACTIVITY 1

Exploring Equal Groups

For about every 89 births there is one set of twins born. Identical twins occur once in about 1000 births.

The constellation Gemini is called the twin constellation. Can you see why?

Practise Your Skills

1. Draw a picture for each number statement.
   a. 4 + 4 + 4
   b. 2 + 2 + 2 + 2 + 2
   c. 3 groups of 2

2. Write a number sentence to tell how many.
   a. 
   b. 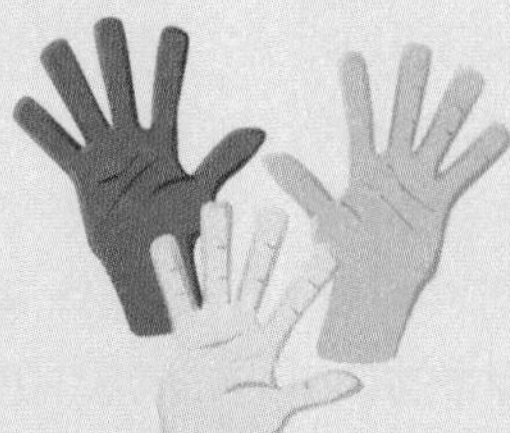

Multiplication Patterns

▶ Describe the pattern. What numbers come next?

1	2	3	4	5	6	7	8	9	10
11	12	13	14	15	16	17	18	19	20
21	22	23	24	25	26	27	28	29	30
31	32	33	34	35	36	37	38	39	40
41	42	43	44	45	46	47	48	49	50
51	52	53	54	55	56	57	58	59	60
61	62	63	64	65	66	67	68	69	70
71	72	73	74	75	76	77	78	79	80
81	82	83	84	85	86	87	88	89	90
91	92	93	94	95	96	97	98	99	100

UNIT 5 ACTIVITY 2

1. Use a hundred chart to record the numbers you land on when you count by 3. Use the same hundred chart to record the numbers you land on when you count by 6. Write about patterns you see.

2. Try shading in a hundred chart with another pair of numbers between 2 and 10. Write about what you observe. Compare with problem 1.

3. Predict and write what will happen if you try another pair of numbers between 2 and 10. Use another hundred chart and count by the two numbers you selected. Write about what actually happened.

4. *My Journal:* Which counting patterns do you find easiest to remember? Why?

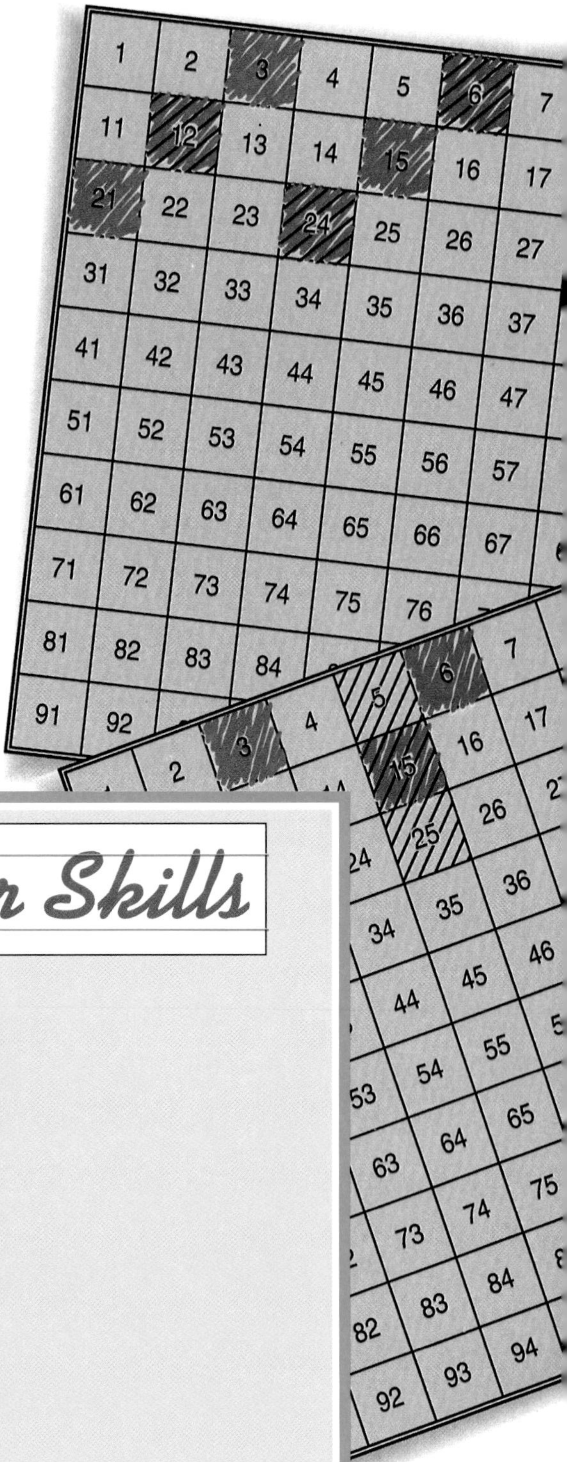

Practise *Your Skills*

Complete these counting patterns.

1. 4, 8, 12, ■, ■, ■, ■, ■, 36
2. 2, 4, 6, ■, ■, ■, ■, ■, 18
3. 5, 10, 15, ■, ■, ■, ■, ■, 45
4. 3, 6, 9, ■, ■, ■, ■, ■, 27
5. 6, 12, 18, ■, ■, ■, ■, ■, 54

Counting with Equal Groups

How many stamps are on a sheet?

How many stamps are there in 2 sheets?

What is the total cost for all of the stamps on 1 sheet?

1. How many stamps are on each sheet? What does each sheet cost?

   a. 

   b. 3 rows of 4 stamps each, 3 sheets in the book
   Each stamp costs 15¢.

2. Ramona has 80¢. Can she buy 2 sheets of the stamps shown in problem 1a?

3. You can buy aerograms from Canada Post. They are stamped and cost only the price of the stamp. This one is for 45¢. Write a multiplication sentence for the cost of 10 of these aerograms.

4. *My Journal:* What did you learn that was new?

Practise *Your Skills*

1. Write a multiplication sentence for each picture. How many wheels are there?

   a. 

   b. 

2. Write two multiplication sentences for each array.

   a.

   b.

Patterns in Arrays

What patterns do you see in the quilts?

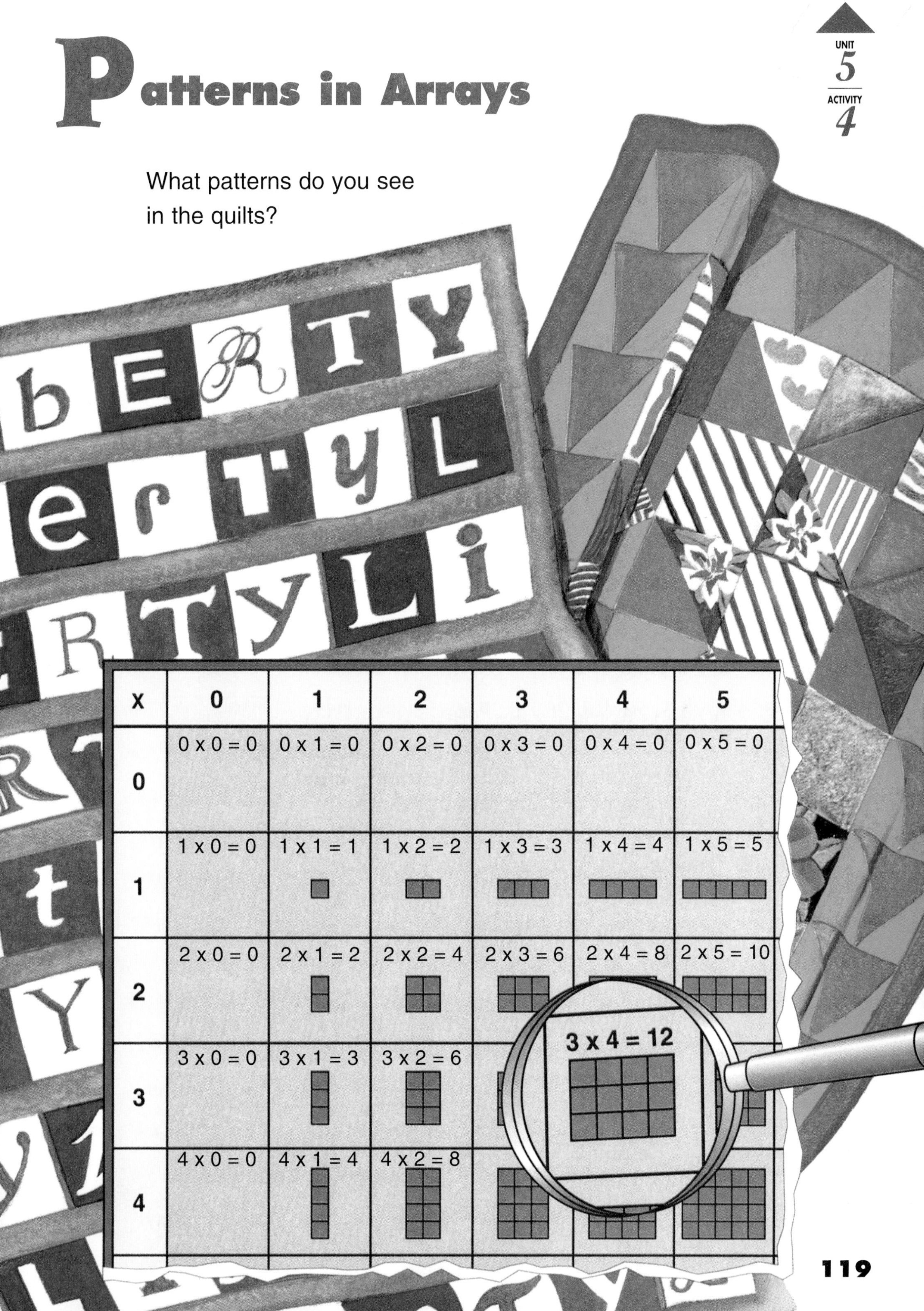

x	0	1	2	3	4	5
0	0 x 0 = 0	0 x 1 = 0	0 x 2 = 0	0 x 3 = 0	0 x 4 = 0	0 x 5 = 0
1	1 x 0 = 0	1 x 1 = 1	1 x 2 = 2	1 x 3 = 3	1 x 4 = 4	1 x 5 = 5
2	2 x 0 = 0	2 x 1 = 2	2 x 2 = 4	2 x 3 = 6	2 x 4 = 8	2 x 5 = 10
3	3 x 0 = 0	3 x 1 = 3	3 x 2 = 6			
4	4 x 0 = 0	4 x 1 = 4	4 x 2 = 8			

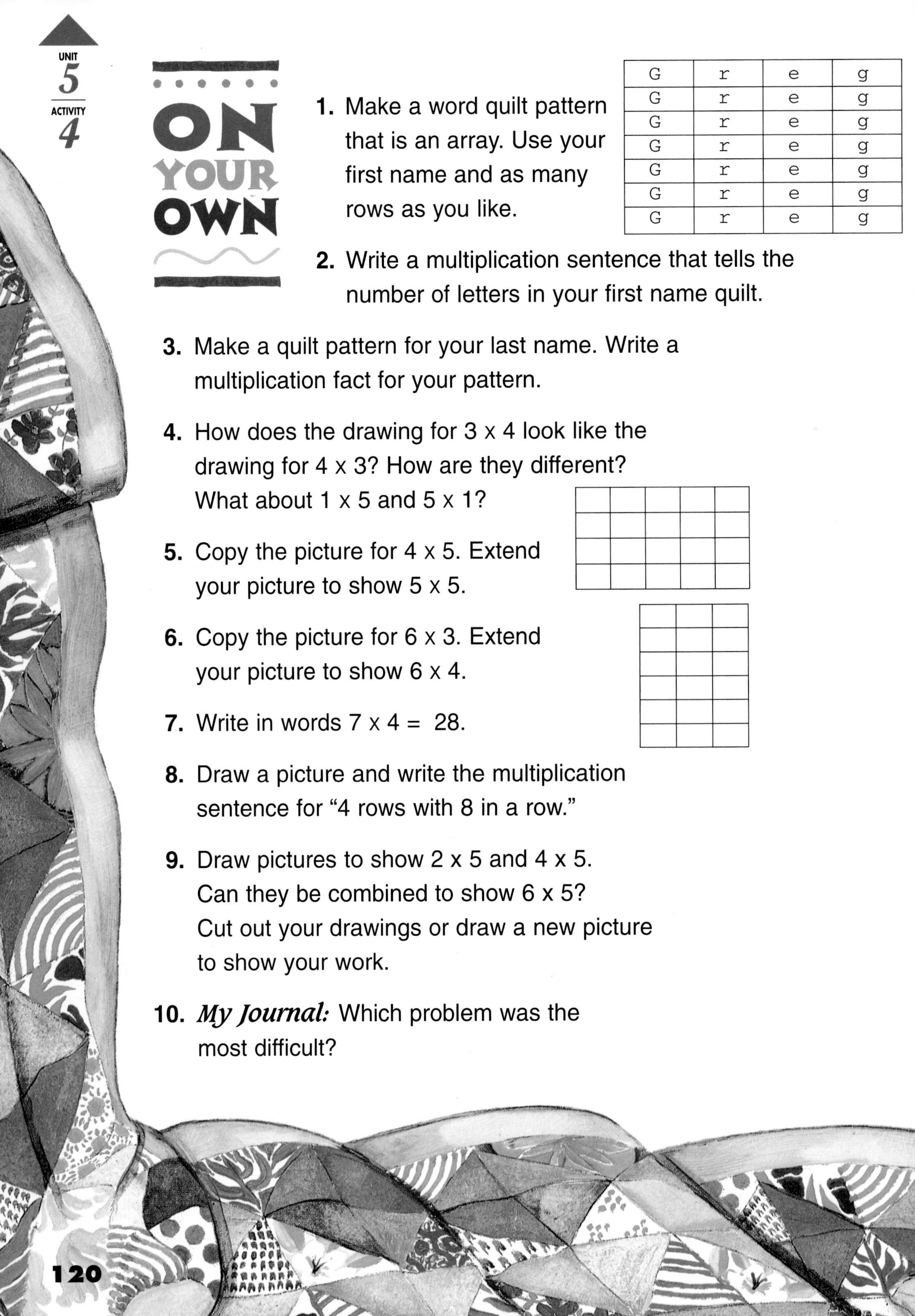

UNIT 5 ACTIVITY 4

ON YOUR OWN

1. Make a word quilt pattern that is an array. Use your first name and as many rows as you like.

G	r	e	g
G	r	e	g
G	r	e	g
G	r	e	g
G	r	e	g
G	r	e	g
G	r	e	g

2. Write a multiplication sentence that tells the number of letters in your first name quilt.
3. Make a quilt pattern for your last name. Write a multiplication fact for your pattern.
4. How does the drawing for 3 x 4 look like the drawing for 4 x 3? How are they different? What about 1 x 5 and 5 x 1?
5. Copy the picture for 4 x 5. Extend your picture to show 5 x 5.
6. Copy the picture for 6 x 3. Extend your picture to show 6 x 4.
7. Write in words 7 x 4 = 28.
8. Draw a picture and write the multiplication sentence for "4 rows with 8 in a row."
9. Draw pictures to show 2 x 5 and 4 x 5. Can they be combined to show 6 x 5? Cut out your drawings or draw a new picture to show your work.
10. *My Journal:* Which problem was the most difficult?

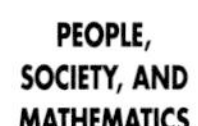

ARE YOU GAME?

Have you ever wondered about the kinds of games people played before there were video games?

The Haida, who live in the Pacific Northwest, played a stick game that made use of both their reasoning and wood-carving skills. The Haida played the game with 18 beautifully carved sticks with different designs.

You and a partner can play a version of the game by using 18 counters. Mark one of the counters on the bottom with a piece of tape. You divide the counters into equal groups and your partner gets a certain number of chances to guess which group the marked counter is in.

1. How many different equal groups can you divide the counters into?

2. Why do you think 18 was chosen as the number of sticks? What other number might be a good choice? What number would be a bad choice?

3. If you divide your counters into 6 groups, should your partner have more or fewer chances to guess than if you divide the counters into 2 groups?

UNIT 5
ACTIVITY 5

THE ARRAY game

Group

3 players, 1 banker

Materials

Each group needs:
Eight sets of array cards cut from Activity Master 16

A pair of number cubes showing 1, 2, 3, 4, 5, and W

Each player needs:
A 100-square centimetre game board or centimetre grid paper

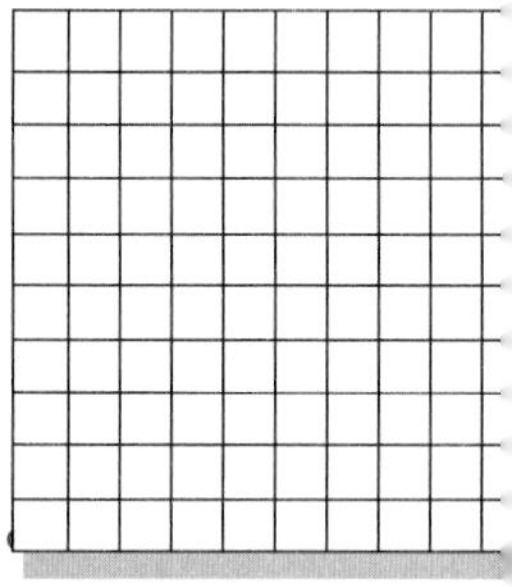

Game Rules

1. The banker keeps all the array cards.
2. The player to the right of the banker rolls the number cubes and names the product of the 2 numbers that are face up on the cubes. Note: If "W" comes up, choose a "Wild Number" – any number from 1 to 5.
3. The banker gives the player an array card for the product.
4. The player places the array card anywhere on his/her game board. Once the array card is placed, it cannot be moved. Array cards cannot overlap on the game board.
5. The other two players take turns. The game continues until one player completely fills her or his game board and wins.
6. Play again with a different banker.

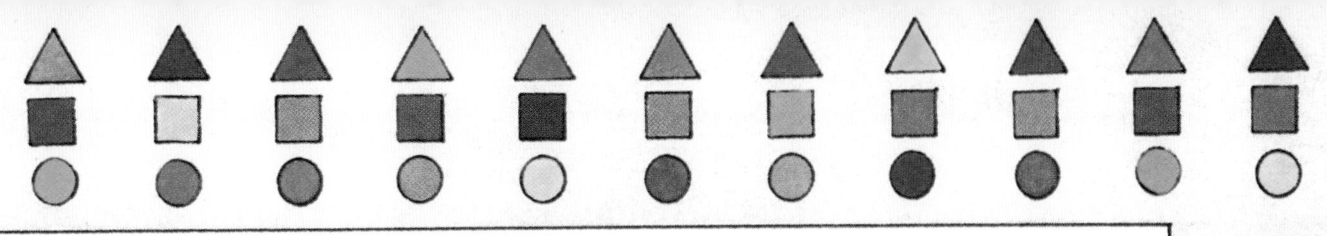

Sometimes the array for a set of rolled numbers will not fit on the game board. You can break the product apart and ask for smaller array cards.

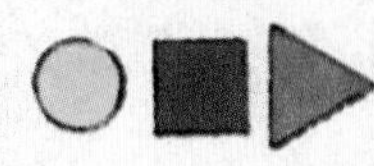

Example

Two 5s were rolled.
25 is the product.

The 5 by 5 array card looks like this: Suppose it doesn't fit in the space left on the board.

5 X 5 = 25

But a 5 by 1 and a 5 by 4 might fit.

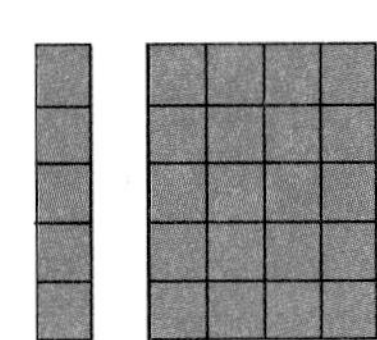

5 X 1 = 5
5 X 4 = 20
5 X 5 = 25

Or a 5 by 2 and a 5 by 3 might fit.

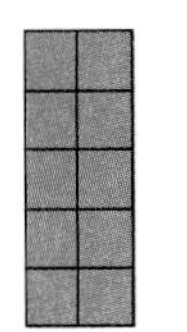

5 X 2 = 10
5 X 3 = 15
5 X 5 = 25

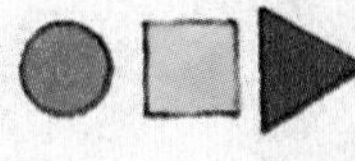

If none of the pairs of smaller arrays works, the next player takes a turn.

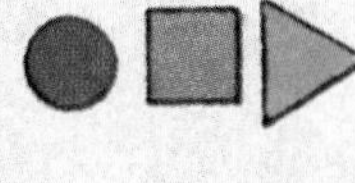

Would any of the smaller arrays fit on this part of the gameboard?

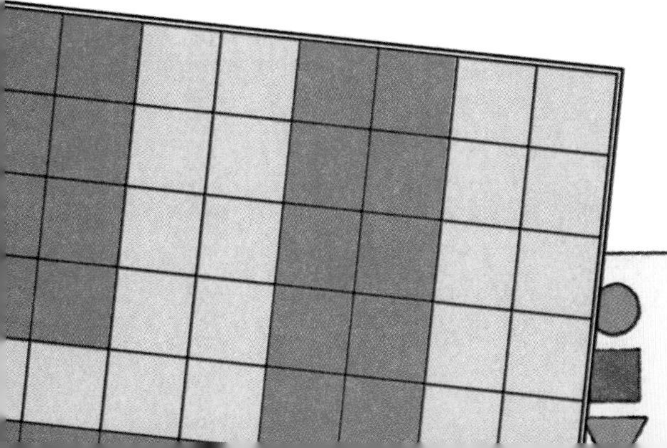

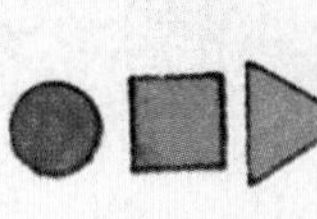

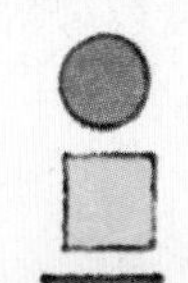

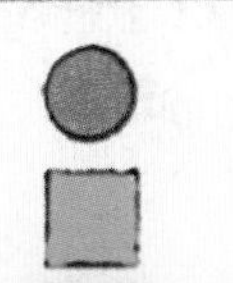

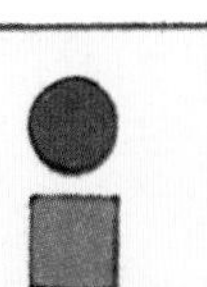

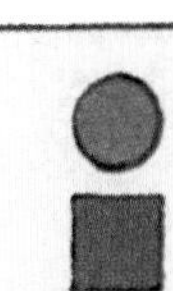

Division Using Arrays

Coin albums usually have equal rows.

How many rows are there?

How many are in each row?

How many coins are there altogether?

▶ Solve. Use any method you like. Tell how you solved the problem.

How many lire in each row?

How many rows of rupees are neede

▶ Solve. Use any method you like.
Tell how you solved the problem.

Carrie was given 50 collector coins and a new coin album for her birthday.

There are 6 rows on a page, and one row in the coin album holds 5 coins.

How many pages does Carrie need for her coins? How many rows does she need?

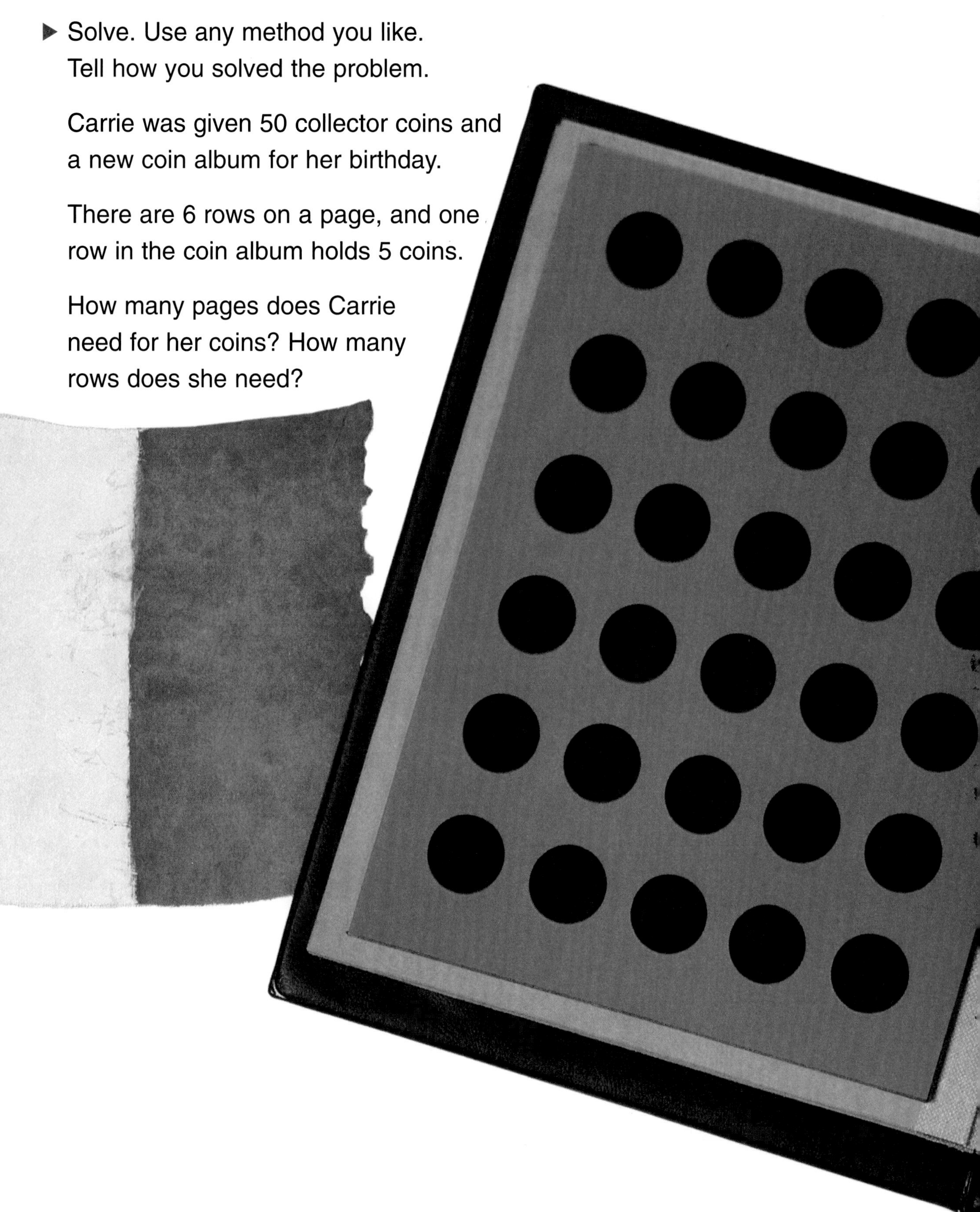

UNIT 5
ACTIVITY 7

Division Using Equal Groups

There are 35 party favours.
How many are there for each bag?

There are 8 monster stickers on a sheet. How many sheets are in the package?

24 MONSTER STICKERS

▶ Solve. Use any method you like. Tell how you solved the problem.

6 sheets of stickers
How many on each sheet?

Six girls bought a booklet of stickers to share. They want to share them equally. How many stickers should each one get?

Showing Division

▶ Solve these problems.
Show your work and record your answer.

3 stacks of comic books

27 comic books

How many comic books are in each stack?

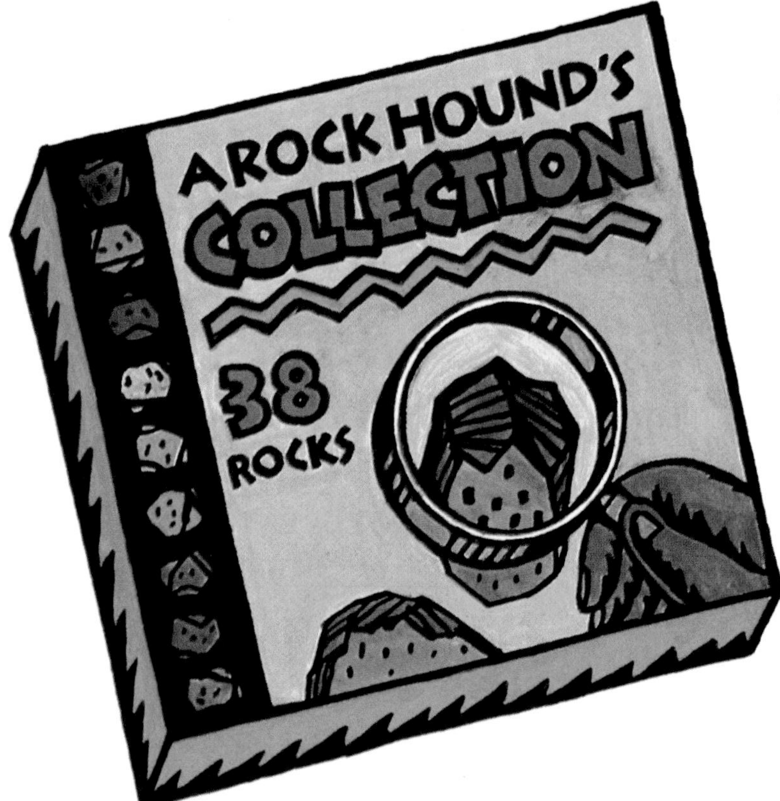

9 rows
How many rocks are in each row?

How many battery packs are in the box?

▶ Solve these problems. Record your work using division symbols.

1. 15 videos
   How many showcases are needed?

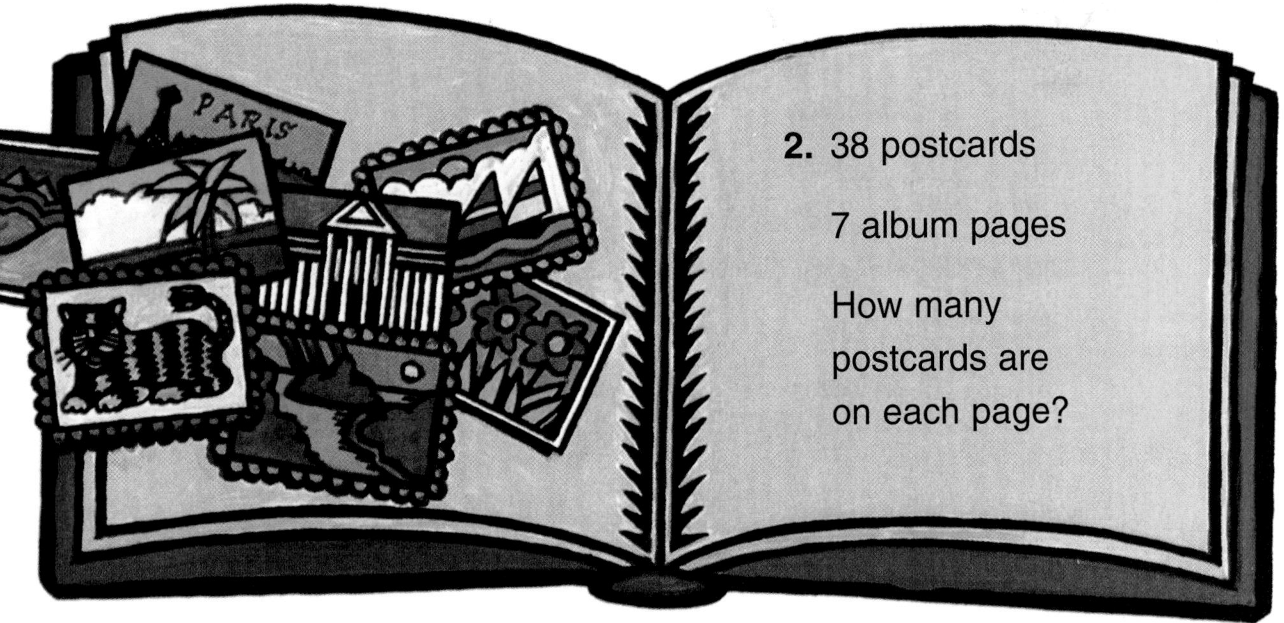

2. 38 postcards

   7 album pages

   How many postcards are on each page?

3. *My Journal:* When will division help solve the problem?

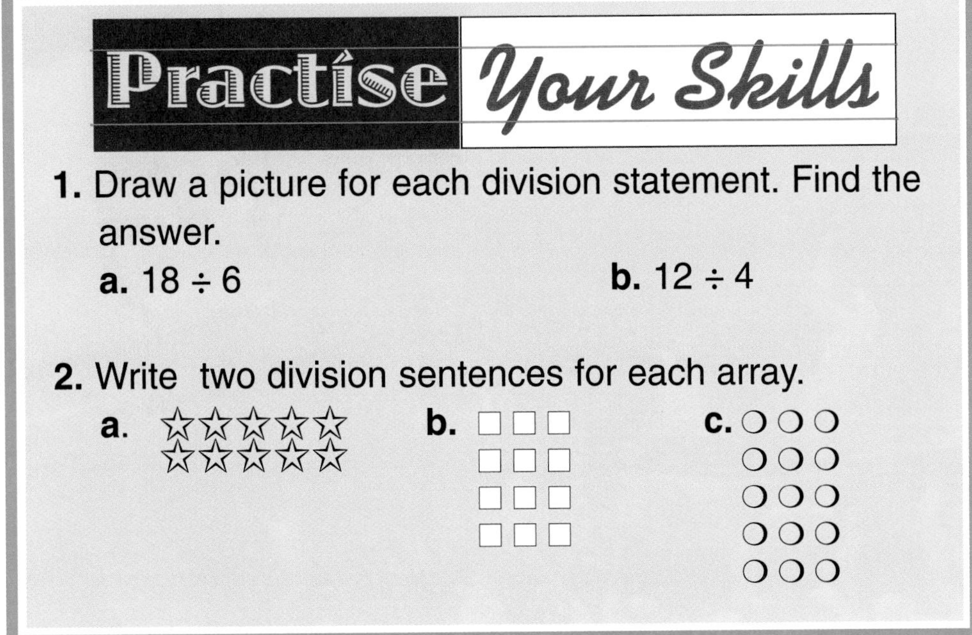

Practise *Your Skills*

1. Draw a picture for each division statement. Find the answer.

   a. 18 ÷ 6 **b.** 12 ÷ 4

2. Write two division sentences for each array.

   a.
   ☆☆☆☆☆
   ☆☆☆☆☆

   b.
   □□□
   □□□
   □□□
   □□□

   c.
   ○○○
   ○○○
   ○○○
   ○○○
   ○○○

UNIT 5
ACTIVITY 9

Connecting Multiplication and Division

▶ Write a question for each situation. Then solve the problem any way you choose.

15 days
7 days
in a week

23 potholders
8 campers

▶ Use the pictures. Write a problem and solve it.

5 tents
8 campers
in each

Bag of 56 marshmallows
6 sticks

▶ Write a question. Then solve your problem any way you choose.

1. 45 campers
8 fit in each van

2. 9 players
on a team
5 teams

3. 34 floating buoys
8 lines

4.

5. ***My Journal:*** Is there anything about division you do not understand? Explain your difficulties.

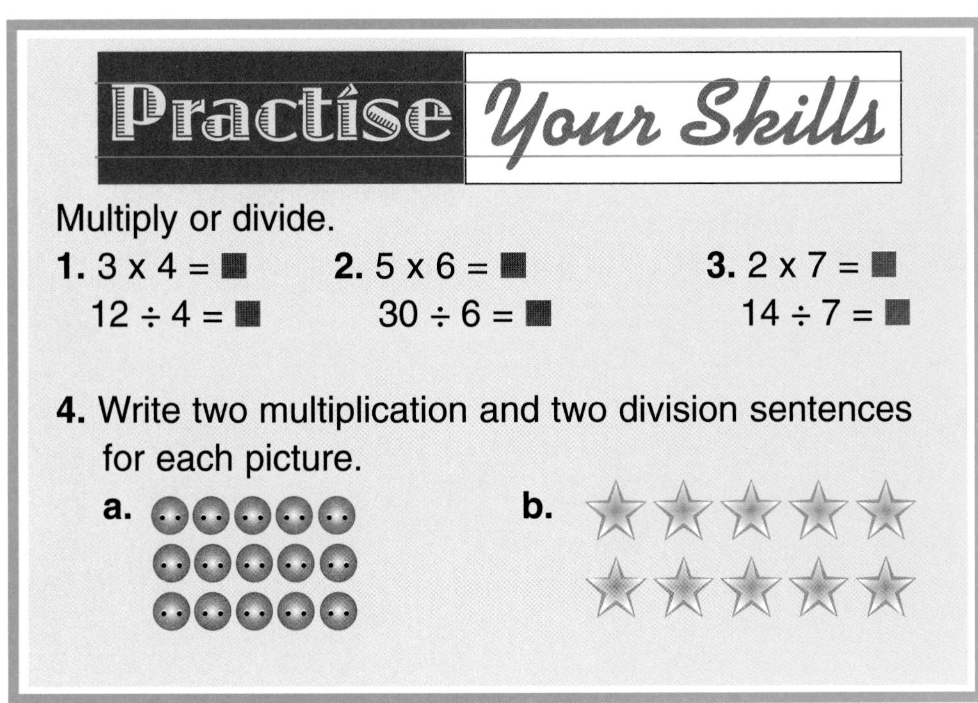

Practise *Your Skills*

Multiply or divide.

1. 3 x 4 = ■
12 ÷ 4 = ■

2. 5 x 6 = ■
30 ÷ 6 = ■

3. 2 x 7 = ■
14 ÷ 7 = ■

4. Write two multiplication and two division sentences for each picture.

a.

b.

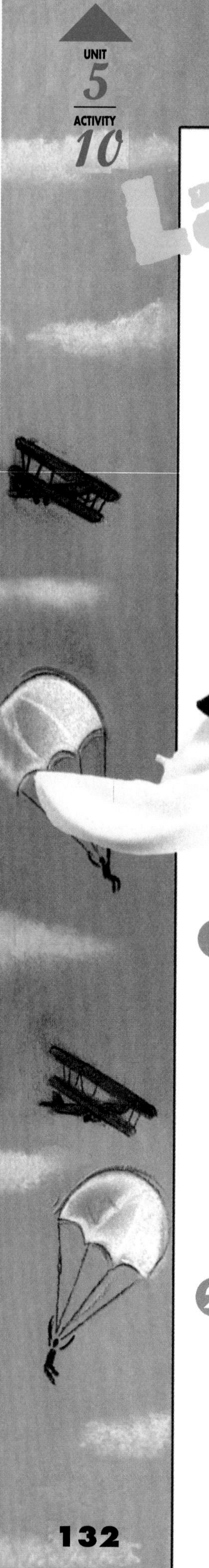

Land On "O" Game

Group

Pairs

Materials

Each pair needs:
2 differently coloured markers

2 hundred charts (with 0 added on)

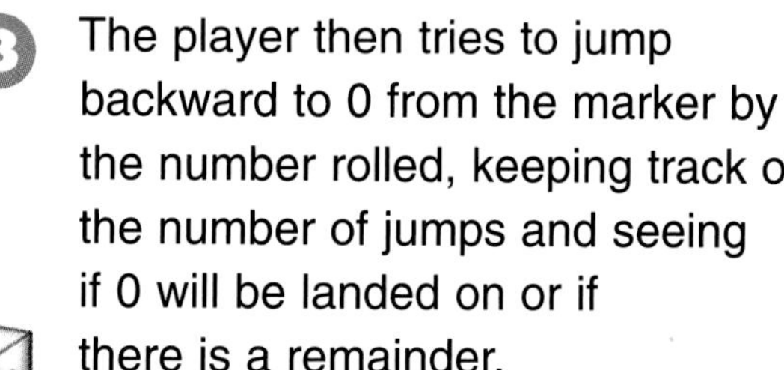

2 number cubes
one numbered 1 to 6
one numbered 0, 7, 8, 9, W_1, W_2

2 score sheets

calculator

Game Rules

1. Each person adds 0 to her or his hundred chart and rolls the 2 cubes. The person who can make the greater 2-digit number is the first player. (W_1 can be any number from 0 to 4; W_2 can be any number from 5 to 9.)

2. The first player puts a marker on any number of his or her choice on the hundred chart and then rolls the number cube numbered from 1 to 6.

3. The player then tries to jump backward to 0 from the marker by the number rolled, keeping track of the number of jumps and seeing if 0 will be landed on or if there is a remainder.

Marked Number	Number Rolled	Jumps	Remainder
27	5	5	2

4. The player writes the division statement and records only the remainder on the score sheet.

Score
2

5. The second player checks the work on the calculator using repeated subtraction.

6. The second player takes a turn.

7. At the end of 5 turns, each player totals his or her score sheet. The player with the lower score wins.

Score
2
3
0
1
1
7

winner!

Score
1
4
0
3
1
9

8. Repeat the game using the number cube labelled 0, 7, 8, 9, W_1, W_2 in step 2. If you roll a 0, you roll again.

Do you want all your stamps to look alike?

How many layers will you put in your booklet?

How much will each of your stamps cost?

How much will your booklet cost?

What will you put on the cover?

Have fun!

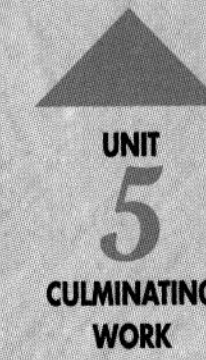

CheckYOURSELF

Great Job! Your stamp booklet shows an understanding of the concepts of multiplication and division. You used multiplication sentences to show the number of stamps and to price your booklet. You used arrays as a model. You wrote clearly about your work.

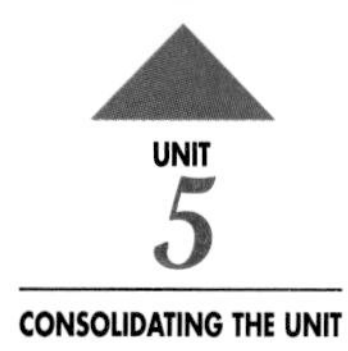

PROBLEM BANK

1. **a.** If everyone in your class were a twin, how many would there be if all of you and all your twins got together? How did you figure out how many?
   b. If everyone in your class were a triplet, how many would there be if all of you and all your triplets got together? How did you figure out how many?

2. There are many equal groups in nature.

   a. What other equal groups can you think of in nature?
   b. Make up some nature problems that use equal groups. Write the problems and the solutions. Share the problems with a friend.

3. Get a calculator and enter a number from 2 to 10. Press the [+] key. Then press the [=] key. Keep pressing [=] and shade on a hundred chart the numbers you see on the calculator display. Write about the patterns that you see on the chart.

4. Jamal is sure that 6 x 5 is double 3 x 5. Do you agree? Use arrays to help show your thinking.

5. Martina has set up the chairs for a puppet play. They are arranged in 7 rows with 4 in a row. Draw a picture to show the set-up. Write a multiplication sentence for your picture. Can you think of more than one way to set up the chairs?

6. There are 24 seats in a section at a stadium. There are 6 rows in a section. How many seats are in each row? Draw a picture to show your thinking.

7. There are 48 children ready for play day. You get to make teams. Each team should have the same number of players. What size teams could you have? Draw pictures to show your ideas. Write a division sentence for each.

8. The prizes for play day are tennis balls. The balls come in cans of 3. How many cans are needed so that there are enough for 28 prizes? Explain how you know.

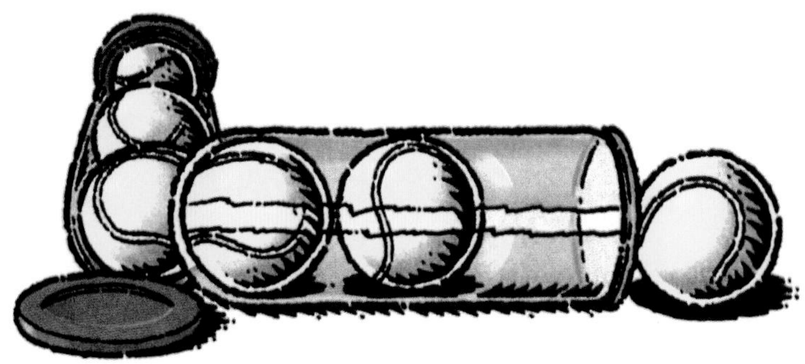

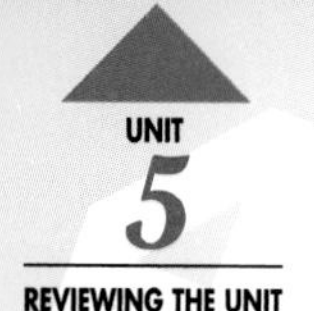

1. Complete these statements.
   a. 3 x 7 is 2 x 7 plus ...
   b. 5 x 5 is 5 x 3 plus ...
   c. 7 x 8 is 7 x 4 plus ...

2. a. Draw a picture that shows 3 rows with 6 in each row.
   b. Write two multiplication and two division sentences for your picture.

3. Write a problem for each of these statements. Solve your problems.
   a. 6 x 2 b. 7 x 6 c. 18 ÷ 3 d. 20 ÷ 4

4. Multiply and then write and solve a related division sentence.
   a. 4 x 3 b. 7 x 6 c. 8 x 4 d. 5 x 2 e. 6 x 4

5. Multiply and then write a related division sentence.
   a. 6 x 7 b. 5 x 9 c. 3 x 8 d. 2 x 3 e. 1 x 7

6. Divide.
   a. 21 ÷ 3 b. 15 ÷ 6 c. 20 ÷ 6 d. 14 ÷ 2

1. What number can you add or subtract to get an answer in the range?
   - **a.** 48 + ■; range 80–90
   - **b.** 125 + ■; range 200–250
   - **c.** 586 + ■; range 850–900
   - **d.** 94 – ■; range 50–60
   - **e.** 270 – ■; range 120–140
   - **f.** 463 – ■; range 225–250

2. Find the answer.

a. 87 + 23	**b.** 125 + 395	**c.** 275 – 132
d. 686 – 299	**e.** 700 – 430	**f.** 484 + 367

3. **a.** You need 500 marbles. What different ways can you buy them?
   b. Juni bought 2 boxes and 1 carton. She needs 225 marbles. Does she have enough?

144 Marbles
Carton
48 Marbles
Box

4. Look at the scores these children got playing a video game.

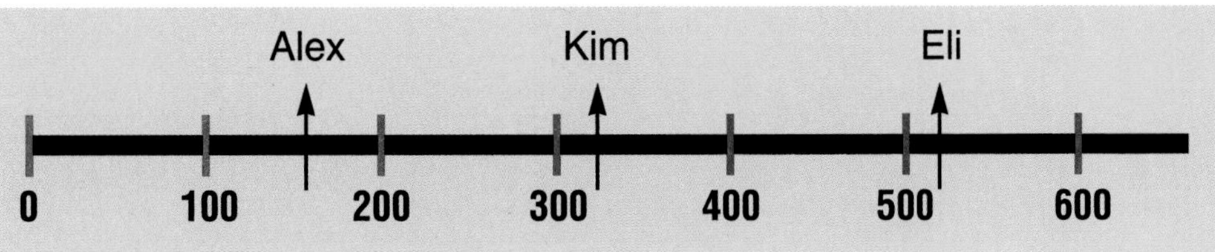

   - **a.** Who got close to 500?
   - **b.** Did Kim score closer to 300 or 400?
   - **c.** About how many more points does Alex need to get 600?
   - **d.** About how many more points does Eli have than Kim?

The Hongkong and Shanghai Banking Corporation
20
10
500

UNIT
6
Counting and
Exchanging
Money
How can we
use money?

COUNTING AND EXCHANGING MONEY

1 • If you had 1 dollar, what items might you buy?
• What items could you buy for about 2 dollars?
• What would you buy to send a friend? What combination of coins and paper money could you use to pay for it?
• Write a problem that someone could solve using the information in this picture.

My Journal: What do you think is a fair weekly allowance? Explain your thinking.

Souvenirs
$15.00
CHOCOLATE LOONIES.
MAPLE SUGAR LOLLIPOPS
0.89
$1.99
99¢
$1.75
25¢
$1.50
CANADA
COOKIES
MOUNTIE COOKIES
MOUNTIE
$2.50
$6.00
$10.00

Counting and Writing Money Amounts

▶ How are the vending machines alike? How are they different? What would you choose to buy?

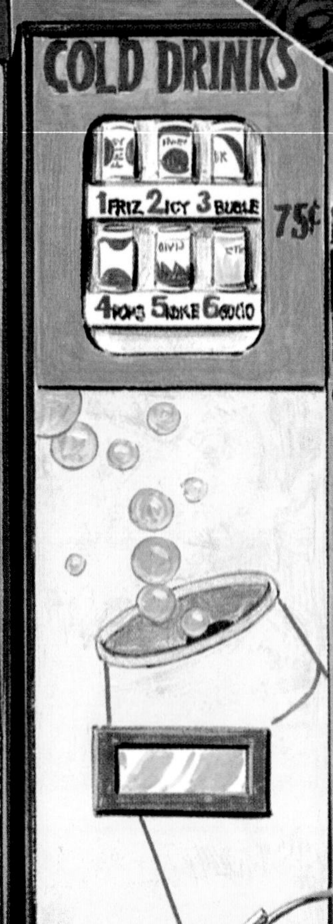

Here is one way to keep track of your work.

Item	Price	How many?	Total cost?	Coins needed?
Chips	$0.45	2	$0.90	9 dimes or 18 nickels or 2 dimes, 14 nickels 3 dimes, 12 nickels
Banana				

1. List all the different ways you can find to make $0.40.
2. How many ways can you make $1.50 without using pennies, nickels, or dimes?
3. Look at each pile of coins. What trades would you make to get as many bills as possible? As few coins as possible? Explain.

4. Figure out the value of each full roll of coins. Copy and complete the table.

Coin	Full roll has	Value of roll
penny	50	
nickel	40	
dime	50	
quarter	40	
dollar	25	

5. *My Journal:* What have you learned about money?

Practise *Your Skills*

1. Show another way to write each amount.
   a. 37¢ **b.** $0.75 **c.** 46¢ **d.** $0.99
2. Michael has 2 quarters, 3 dimes, 1 nickel, and 4 pennies. Can he buy a sticker that costs $0.85?
3. What is the total value of these coins?

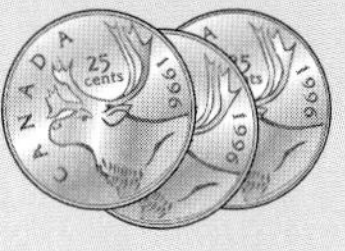

UNIT 6 ACTIVITY 2

Exploring Money Problems

You have $10.00. What could you order for a meal?

GRANDE MEXICANA

BLACK BEAN SOUP	$ 1.95
TACO	2.50
BURRITO	3.75
CARNE ASADA	6.95
QUESADILLA	4.75
CHEESE ENCHILADA	3.50
CHICKEN ENCHILADA	3.75

SIDE ORDERS

TORTILLA CHIPS	$ 1.50
REFRIED BEANS	1.95
MEXICAN RICE	1.75
SALSA RANCHERA	1.95

DRINKS AND DESSERTS

MILK	$ 0.75
FLAN	1.75

PASTA PASTA

SALADS

Mixed Green	$ 3.25
Caesar Salad	4.75
Tomato & Cheese	4.25

PASTA

Spaghetti with Meat Balls	$ 8.75
Linguine with Clam Sauce	10.95
Fettuccine Alfredo	8.95
Ravioli	8.95
Lasagna	7.25
Chicken Parmesan	9.50
Pasta and Burger	8.25
	6.95

DRINKS

Milk	$ 1.25
Fresh Juice orange, apple, tomato	1.50

Egg Roll	$ 1.25
Fried Wontons	1.95
Beef with Bean Cake	6.25
Beef with Broccoli	5.85
Chicken with Black Bean Sauce	6.95
Chicken with Pineapple	7.85
Egg Foo Yung	4.25
Shrimp Lo Mein	6.70
Shrimp Fried Rice	4.25

SOUP

Egg Drop	$ 1.55
Chicken Noodle	1.75
Wonton	2.00

DRINKS

Milk	$ 1.55
Juice	1.10

DELI

Salads

GRILLED CHICKEN	$ 7.90
SPINACH	4.50

Sandwiches

HAMBURGER	$ 4.95
CHICKEN	7.50
TURKEY CLUB	7.50
BRISKET	7.95
BARBECUE	7.50

Dessert

KEY LIME PIE	$ 4.75
MUD PIE	3.50

Drinks

Milk	$ 1.20
Juice	1.00

1. If you had $7.00 to spend, which restaurant would give you the best choice for your money? Explain.
2. Choose one menu. Find the most expensive and least expensive items. What is the difference in cost between them? How does this compare with the most and least expensive items on the other menus?
3. If you had $30.00 to spend on a meal for your family members, which of these restaurants would you choose? Why? What foods would you order? Estimate the cost as you make up the order. Then find the exact cost and your change, if any.
4. *My Journal:* What did you like best about this activity? Why?

Practise *Your Skills*

Make a chart like this and fill it out.

Dollars	Number of coins			
	Quarters	Dimes	Nickels	Pennies
$ 1.00				
$ 4.00				
$ 6.00				
$10.00				

Cowrie Shell Money

Have you ever wondered what kinds of money systems people used?

In many parts of the world people used beads and shells for money. Sometimes they would string beads and shells and wear money to show their wealth and have it handy.

One of the oldest forms of money dating back to ancient Africa, Asia, and the South Pacific is the cowrie shell. Cowries are china-like oval shells about 4 cm long. The word cowrie comes from the Hindu *kauri,* meaning pearl.

In 17th century Africa 500 cowries bought a goat and 2 bought a chicken. In the early 19th century a house in India cost 16 million cowrie shells. Although cowrie shells are no longer used for money, they are still worn as jewellery and as decorations for clothes and hair.

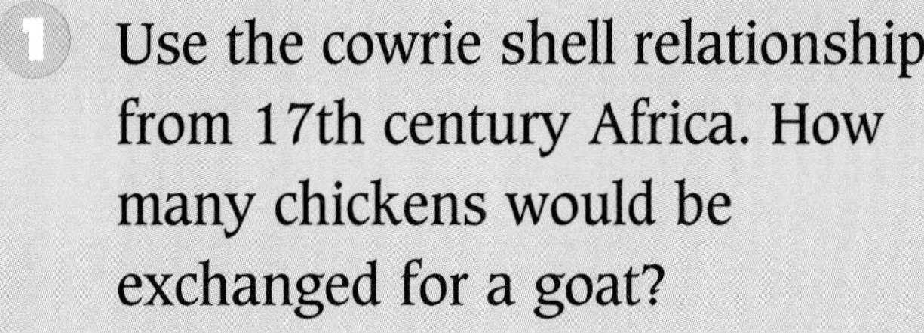

1. Use the cowrie shell relationship from 17th century Africa. How many chickens would be exchanged for a goat?

2. What do you think the seller of the house in 19th century India did with 16 million cowrie shells?

How Much Does a Sandwich Cost?

$0.89

Children like
peanut butter-and-jelly sandwiches!
Have you ever thought about how to make them?
How much they cost? How you could pay for them?

Here's your job!
How much do you think it would cost
to make 100 peanut butter-and-jelly sandwiches?

- Figure out the cost.
- Write about how you decided this.
- Show several ways to pay for the ingredients.

Check YOURSELF

Great job! You have figured out the cost of making the sandwiches. Your report includes an explanation of how you decided the costs. You have shown many ways to pay for the sandwiches.

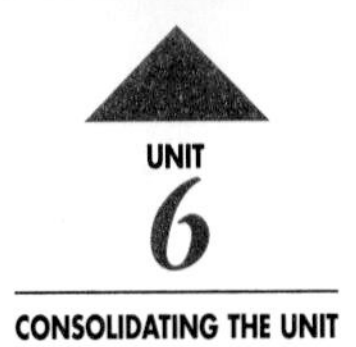

1. Sunil has 68¢. What is the smallest number of coins he could have? What other combination of coins might he have?

2. Noa emptied her piggy bank and sorted the coins. This is what she found.

a. About how much money do you think she has? How can you find out exactly?

b. She wants to trade coins to get as many loonies as possible. How many loonies would she have after trading coins?

3. You earn 50¢ for each chore you do. How many chores must you do to have enough for a kite?

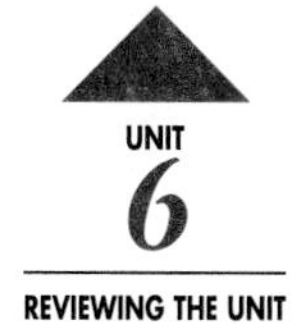

1. Find two ways to make each amount.
   a. 55¢ **b.** 85¢ **c.** $1.28 **d.** $0.98

2. Which is more, 7 nickels or 4 dimes? Tell how you decided.

3. **a.** Liliana wants 6 beads. She has $5.00. Does she have enough money? Explain.
   b. Phinjo has $2.00. He buys 2 beads. What is his change?
   c. How many beads can you buy with $4.00? Explain.

CUMULATIVE REVIEW

1. Write directions for each.
   a. going from the monkeys to the lions
   b. going from the zebras to the elephants

2. Explain where the giraffes are. Use as many of the other animal locations as you can.

3. Multiply or divide. Draw a picture for each.
   a. 4 x 2 **b.** 7 x 7 **c.** 24 ÷ 3 **d.** 36 ÷ 6

UNIT

7

Describing and Relating Measures

How can we measure it?

DESCRIBING AND RELATING MEASURES

STARTING OUT

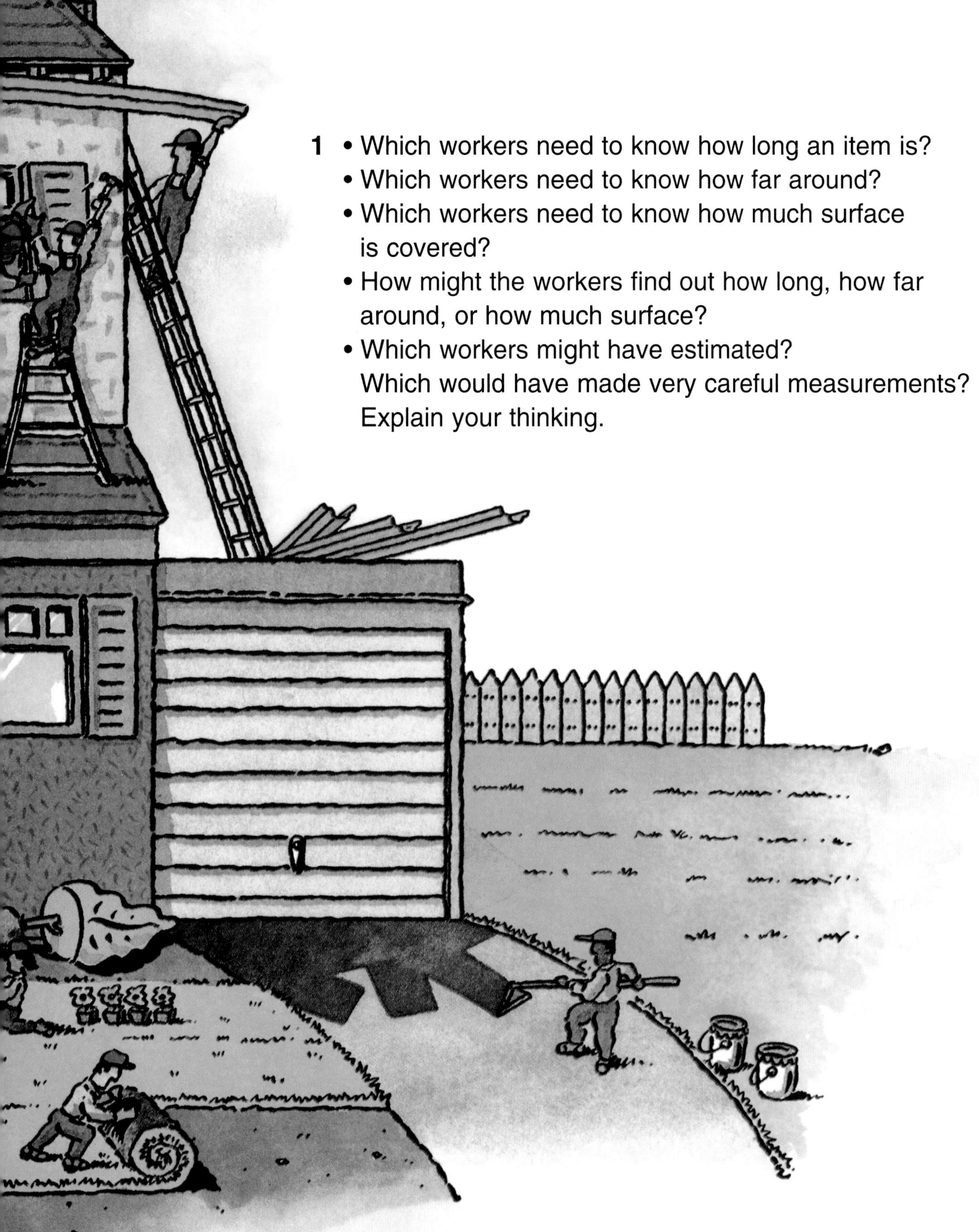

1 • Which workers need to know how long an item is?
- Which workers need to know how far around?
- Which workers need to know how much surface is covered?
- How might the workers find out how long, how far around, or how much surface?
- Which workers might have estimated? Which would have made very careful measurements? Explain your thinking.

My Journal: Tell about some situations where you might measure how long, how far around, or how much surface.

DESCRIBING AND RELATING MEASURES

STARTING OUT

2 • In which pictures was this measured:
  - length?
  - the distance around?
  - the amount of space something covered?
  - mass?
  - how much a container holds?
• Draw and write about another situation that you could add to this page.

My Journal: What interesting things do you know about measuring that you would like to tell someone?

UNIT 7 ACTIVITY 1

Estimating and Measuring Length

How can you find the length of your arm span?

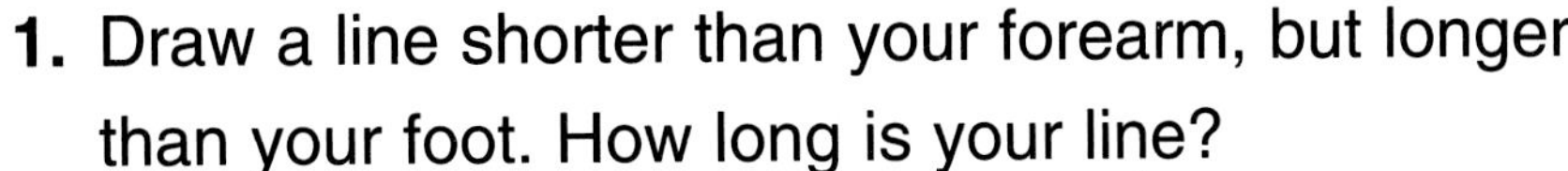

1. Draw a line shorter than your forearm, but longer than your foot. How long is your line?

2. Design a rectangular postcard. Make the sum of the lengths of the sides equal to 30 cm. What other ways can you find? Which would you choose? Why?

3. How many children, lying on the floor and placed head to foot, would stretch from one end of your classroom to the other? Write how you would solve the problem without asking anyone to lie on the floor.

4. Decide which is longer. Write to share your reasoning.
   - **a.** 5 chalk erasers placed end-to-end or the length of your desk
   - **b.** 10 paper clips placed end-to-end or your foot
   - **c.** the height of the door or the height of two classmates

5. ***My Journal:*** What have you learned about estimating length?

Practise *Your Skills*

1. Here are the heights of 5 children.
Order them from shortest to tallest.
Raji: 130 cm Tamika: 137 cm Wilson: 129 cm
Hsiao: 141 cm Jennifer: 132 cm

2. What can you find that is
- **a.** between 1 cm and 10 cm long
- **b.** between 10 cm and 30 cm long
- **c.** longer than 50 cm and shorter than 100 cm

3. Measure each line to the nearest centimetre.
a. ________________ **b.** __________
c. __________________________

Selecting Measures

▶ You have one minute to make a chain.
How long do you think your chain will be?
Measure it.

Units to Know

One centimetre (1 cm):
The width of your little finger is about 1 cm.

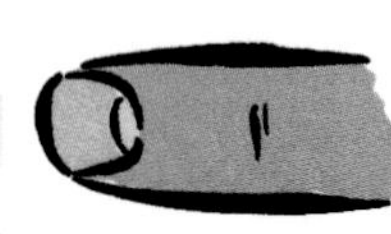

One metre (1 m):
1 m = 100 cm
The height of a door knob above the floor is 1 m.

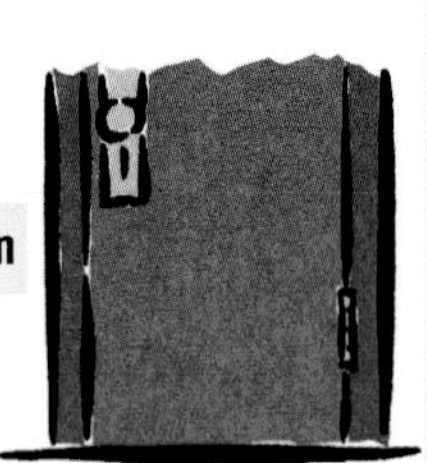

One decimetre (1 dm):
1 dm = 10 cm;
10 dm = 1 m
The length of a computer disk is about 1 dm.

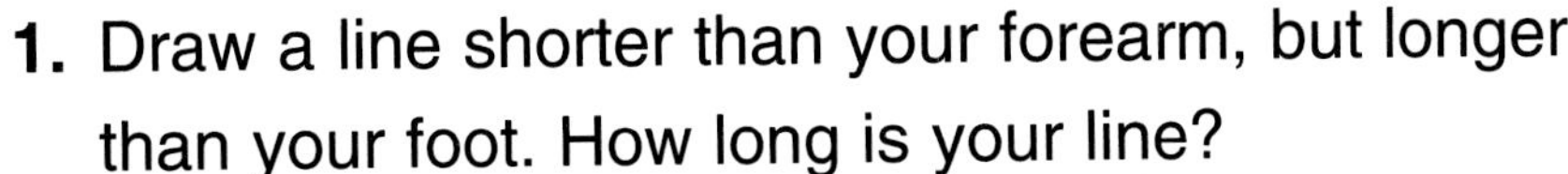

1. Draw a line shorter than your forearm, but longer than your foot. How long is your line?

2. Design a rectangular postcard. Make the sum of the lengths of the sides equal to 30 cm. What other ways can you find? Which would you choose? Why?

3. How many children, lying on the floor and placed head to foot, would stretch from one end of your classroom to the other? Write how you would solve the problem without asking anyone to lie on the floor.

4. Decide which is longer. Write to share your reasoning.
   a. 5 chalk erasers placed end-to-end or the length of your desk
   b. 10 paper clips placed end-to-end or your foot
   c. the height of the door or the height of two classmates

5. *My Journal:* What have you learned about estimating length?

Practise Your Skills

1. Here are the heights of 5 children. Order them from shortest to tallest.
   Raji: 130 cm Tamika: 137 cm Wilson: 129 cm
   Hsiao: 141 cm Jennifer: 132 cm

2. What can you find that is
   a. between 1 cm and 10 cm long
   b. between 10 cm and 30 cm long
   c. longer than 50 cm and shorter than 100 cm

3. Measure each line to the nearest centimetre.
   a. ______________ **b.** __________
   c. ________________________

Selecting Measures

- You have one minute to make a chain. How long do you think your chain will be? Measure it.

Units to Know

One centimetre (1 cm):
The width of your little finger is about 1 cm.

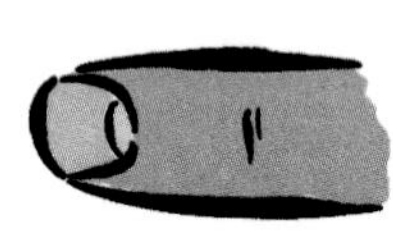

One metre (1 m):
1 m = 100 cm
The height of a door knob above the floor is 1 m.

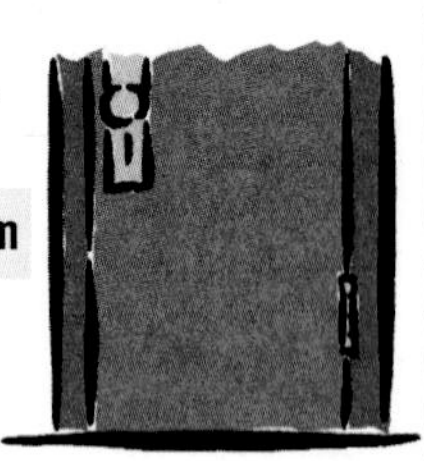

One decimetre (1 dm):
1 dm = 10 cm;
10 dm = 1 m
The length of a computer disk is about 1 dm.

1. Measure and record your giant step in centimetres. Is it longer or shorter than 1 m?

2. Cut a string 1 m long. Use a ruler and crayons to mark it in decimetres. (Remember, a decimetre is 10 cm.) Use your string to measure five objects in the classroom. Record your measures to the nearest decimetre.

3. Measure the arm spans of family members. Order the measures from shortest to longest.

4. ***My Journal:*** When would you use centimetres to measure? Decimetres? Metres?

Practise Your Skills

1. Measure the length of your hand. How long is it?

2. Use your hand to estimate. About how long is:
- **a.** your leg
- **b.** your arm
- **c.** your giant step

3. What can you find that is
- **a.** about 1 cm long
- **b.** about 1 dm long
- **c.** about 1 m long

Introducing the Kilometre

We measure long distances in kilometres.

You can walk 1 km in about 15 minutes.

You can make 1 km of paper using about 3500 sheets.

You can ride a bike 1 km in about five minutes.

Units to Know

One kilometre (1 km):
1 km = 1000 m
We use kilometres to measure distance.

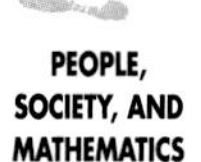

PEOPLE, SOCIETY, AND MATHEMATICS

At Arm's LENGTH

Have you ever wondered how people measured before tools and instruments like we use were available?

People around the world used what was readily available. The Egyptians used units based on finger, hand, and arm lengths.

Centuries ago people in England used a system much like the Egyptian one. It too was based on finger, hand, and arm lengths. Both systems were based on tens. The chart shows some of the units.

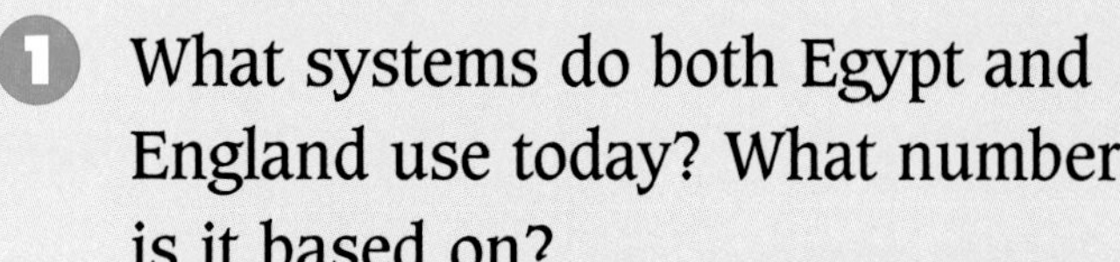

1. What systems do both Egypt and England use today? What number is it based on?

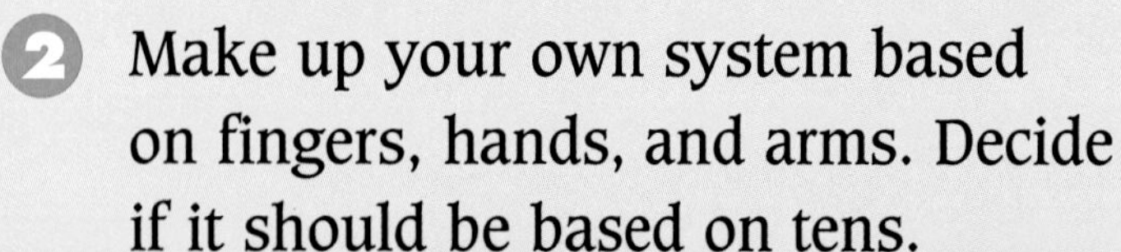

2. Make up your own system based on fingers, hands, and arms. Decide if it should be based on tens.

Measure	Egypt	England
fingerwidth	zebo	fingerwidth
ten zebos or fingerwidths	span	span of length
ten spans	nent	armstretch or fathom
ten nents or fathoms	khet	chain

Exploring Area and Perimeter

Words to Know

Perimeter is the distance around a shape.

Area is the amount of space a shape covers.

1. Choose three books. Measure and record the perimeter of the cover of each. Write the measurements in order. How does the perimeter of the cover of this math book compare?

2. Draw two different shapes, on grid paper, with perimeters of 24 cm. How many squares does each shape cover?

3. How would you measure the perimeter of the classroom? Write a plan and then measure. What did you find?

4. ***My Journal:*** When might you need to measure perimeter? When might you need to measure area?

Exploring Area

What is the area of each shape? Tell how you decided.

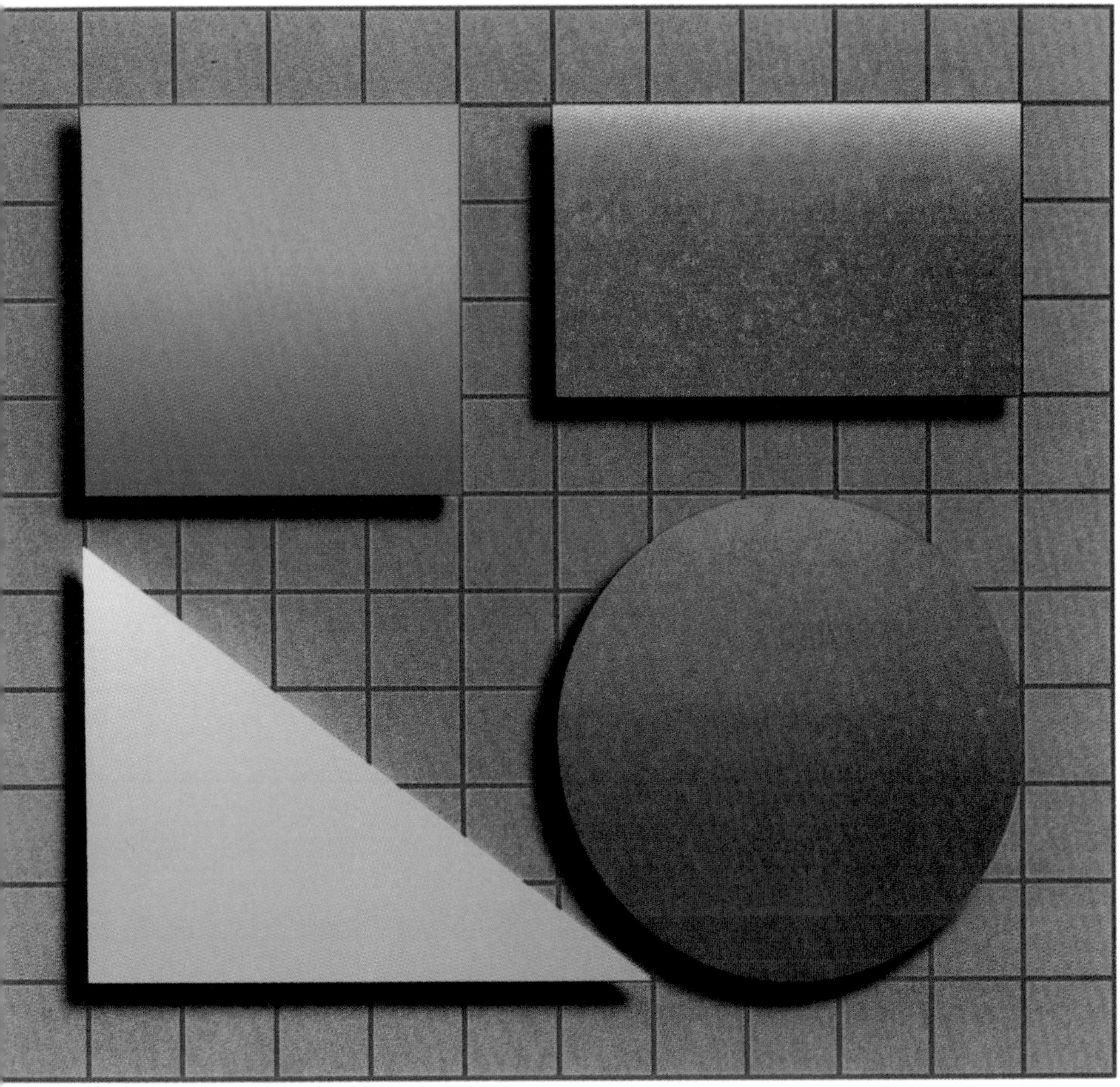

Find the area and perimeter of each design.

1. 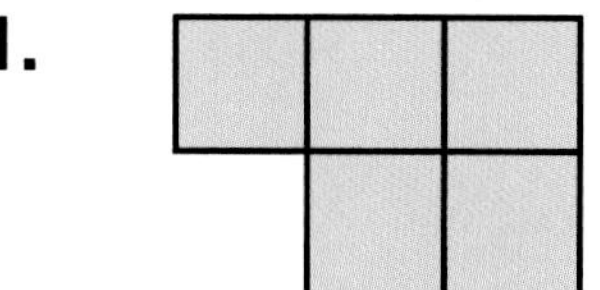

2. 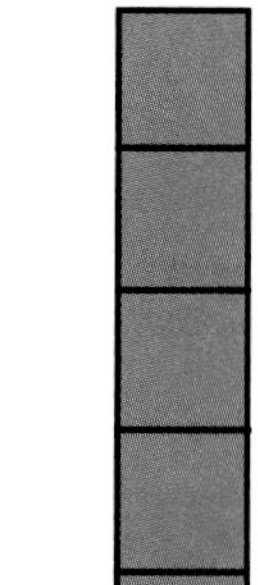

3. 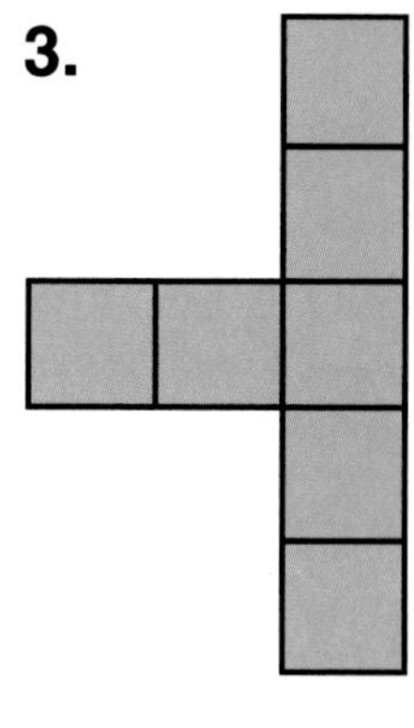

4. 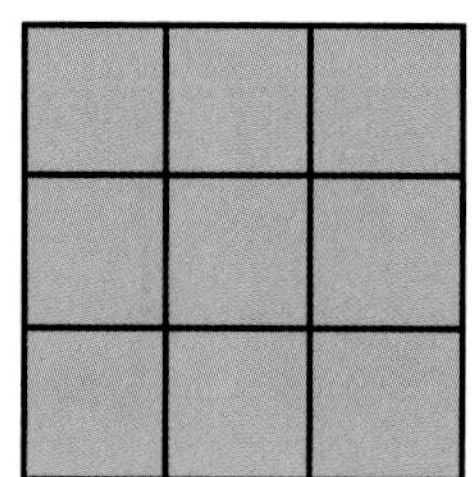

5. ***My Journal:*** How are perimeter and area related?

Practise Your Skills

1. Would you use centimetres, decimetres, metres, or kilometres to measure:
   - **a.** the distance between cities
   - **b.** the length of a necklace
   - **c.** the length of your classroom
   - **d.** the length of your baby finger

2. Name two things longer than
   - **a.** one centimetre
   - **b.** one decimetre
   - **c.** one metre
   - **d.** one kilometre

3. Find the perimeter.

4 cm

2 cm

Exploring the Litre

Units to Know

One litre (1 L)
One litre fills about four glasses.

1. How many glasses of liquid do you drink each day? About how many litres is that? Explain your estimate.

2. 

Here is your supply of lemonade. You want to sell 80 glasses. Do you have enough lemonade? Explain your thinking.

3. Look for containers at home. List them in a chart like this one.

Less than 1 L	1 L	More than 1 L

4. *My Journal:* How would you describe a one-litre container to someone who couldn't see it?

Estimating and Measuring Mass

▶ About how heavy is this child?

Units to Know

One gram (1 g):
One gram is about as heavy as a jellybean.

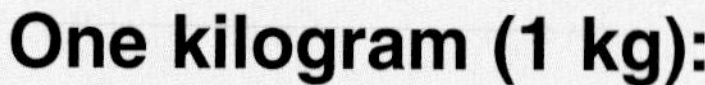

One kilogram (1 kg):
1 kg = 1000 g
One kilogram is about as heavy as this math book.

1. Your Math textbook has a mass of about 1 kg. How many books would be about equal to your mass? Explain how you would find out.

2. A market sells apples in bags these size. In what different ways can you buy 20 kg of apples?

3. *My Journal:* What do you know about measuring mass?

Practise Your Skills

1. Write the mass of each object in kilograms.

Have an Amazing
BEAN OLYMPICS
You and your group will try each of these events. Work together to decide on an estimate and to do the measuring. Keep a record sheet of your results for all the events.
Event 1: ROW OF BEANS
Look carefully at a lima bean. How far do you think 1000 beans will reach? Record your estimate. Make a plan and carry it out. What did you find?
Event 2: BEAN COVER-UP
Look at your bean again. About how many do you think it would take to cover your math book? Record your estimate. Make a plan and carry it out. What did you find?

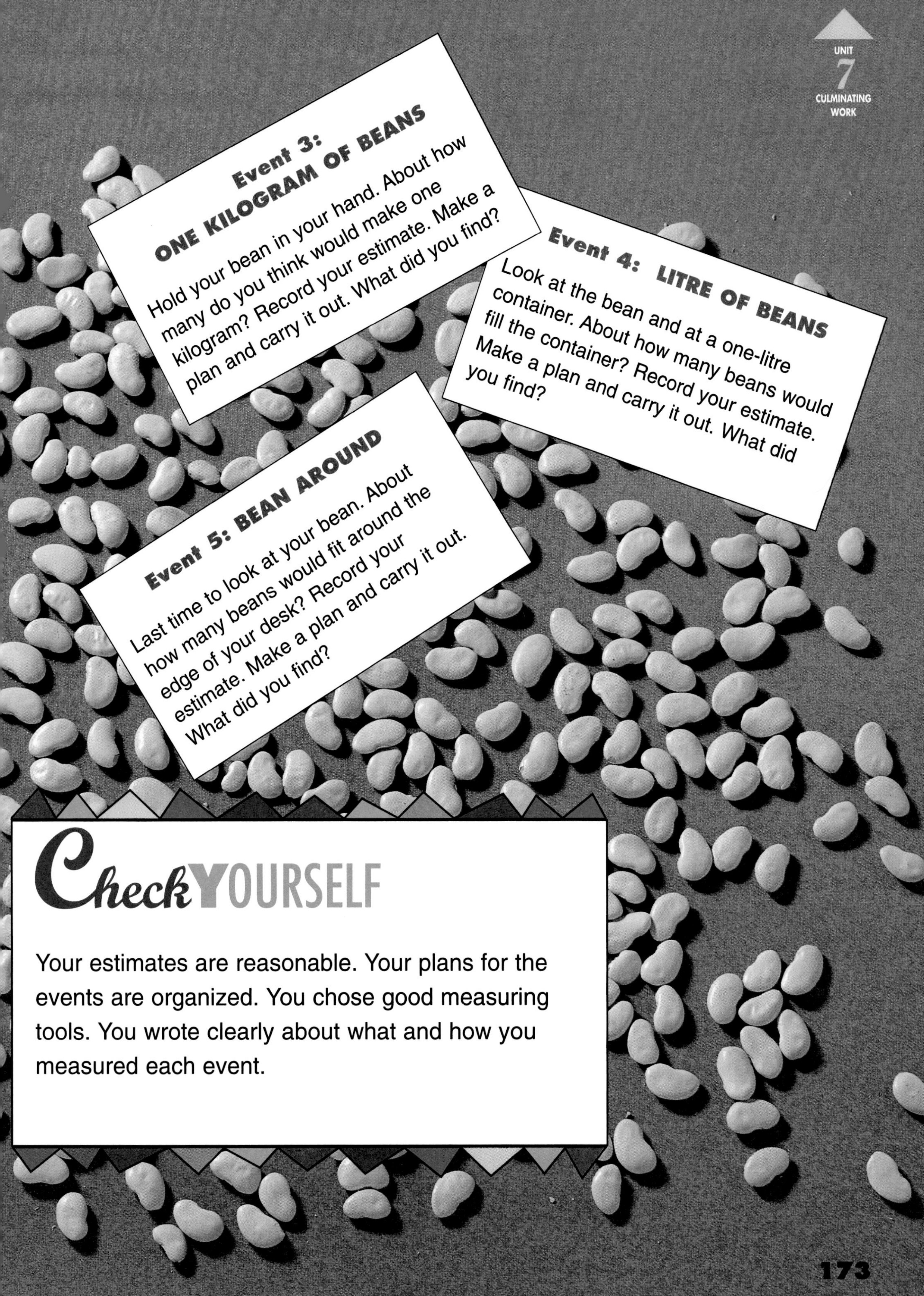

Check YOURSELF

Your estimates are reasonable. Your plans for the events are organized. You chose good measuring tools. You wrote clearly about what and how you measured each event.

PROBLEM BANK

1. Work with a partner to estimate and then measure to the nearest centimetre:
a. how high you can jump off the floor
b. how long your longest step is
c. how far you can throw a cotton ball
d. how wide you can spread your fingers
e. how tall you can reach toward the sky.

2. Start in the middle of a sheet of paper. Begin to draw a spiral like this:

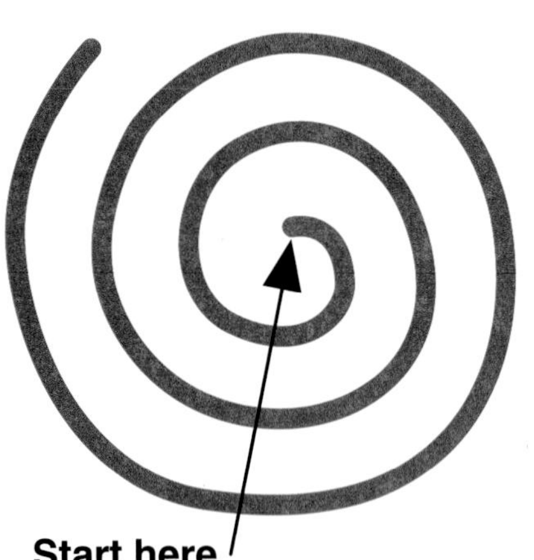

Stop when you think you have travelled 50 cm. Lay a string along the line and cut it to equal the length. How long is your line? How much longer or shorter is it than 50 cm?

3. Human hair grows about 1 cm a month. Suppose you had never had a haircut. How long would your hair be now:
a. in centimetres
b. in decimetres
c. in metres

4. You need 4 m of ribbon to wrap presents. You have 350 cm of ribbon. Do you have enough? Explain.

5. Colour squares on grid paper to show an area of 12 square units. Find many ways to do this. What is the perimeter of each shape?

6. Make this arrangement with colour tiles.

Add one more tile so that the area is 6 square tiles and the perimeter is still 12.

7. About how much liquid do you think you drink in one day? In one week? In one month? Remember: one litre fills about four glasses.

8. The average mass of a grizzly bear is about 360 kg. About how many grade 3 children together have the mass of a grizzly bear? Explain your thinking.

1. Order these lengths from shortest to longest.
   20 cm 1 m 15 cm 1 dm 65 cm

2. Would you use centimetres, decimetres, metres, or kilometres to measure:
   a. the distance from your home to your school
   b. the length of a worm
   c. the length of a baseball bat
   d. the perimeter of your classroom

3. How many square units is each shape?

a. 

b. 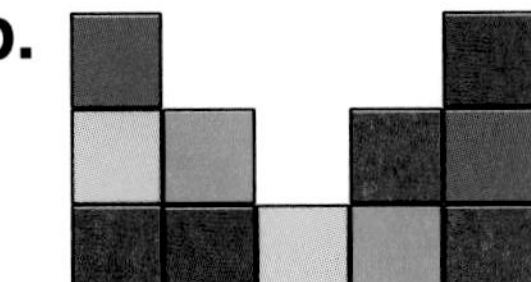

c. 

4. A school needs 10 L of juice at snack time. Here are the containers. Is there enough?

5. Write the mass of each animal in kilograms.

a. 

b. 

1. Draw a picture for each.

a. 4 groups of 5 **b.** 3 + 3 + 3 + 3 + 3 + 3 **c.** 2 x 7

2. Copy this picture for 3 x 6.
Change it to show 3 x 8.
Write what you did.

3. Write two multiplication sentences and two division sentences for each array.

a. 

b. 

c. 

4. Write a problem for each of these number statements.
Solve your problems.

a. 2 x 9 **b.** 7 x 5 **c.** 15 ÷ 5 **d.** 21 ÷ 7

5. You have 7 dimes and 2 nickels. Your friend has 8 nickels and 3 dimes.

a. Who has more?

b. How much more does that person have?

6. 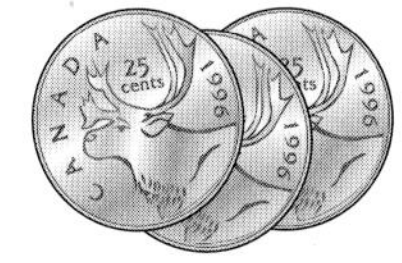 

a. How much money is shown?

b. Show this amount two other ways.

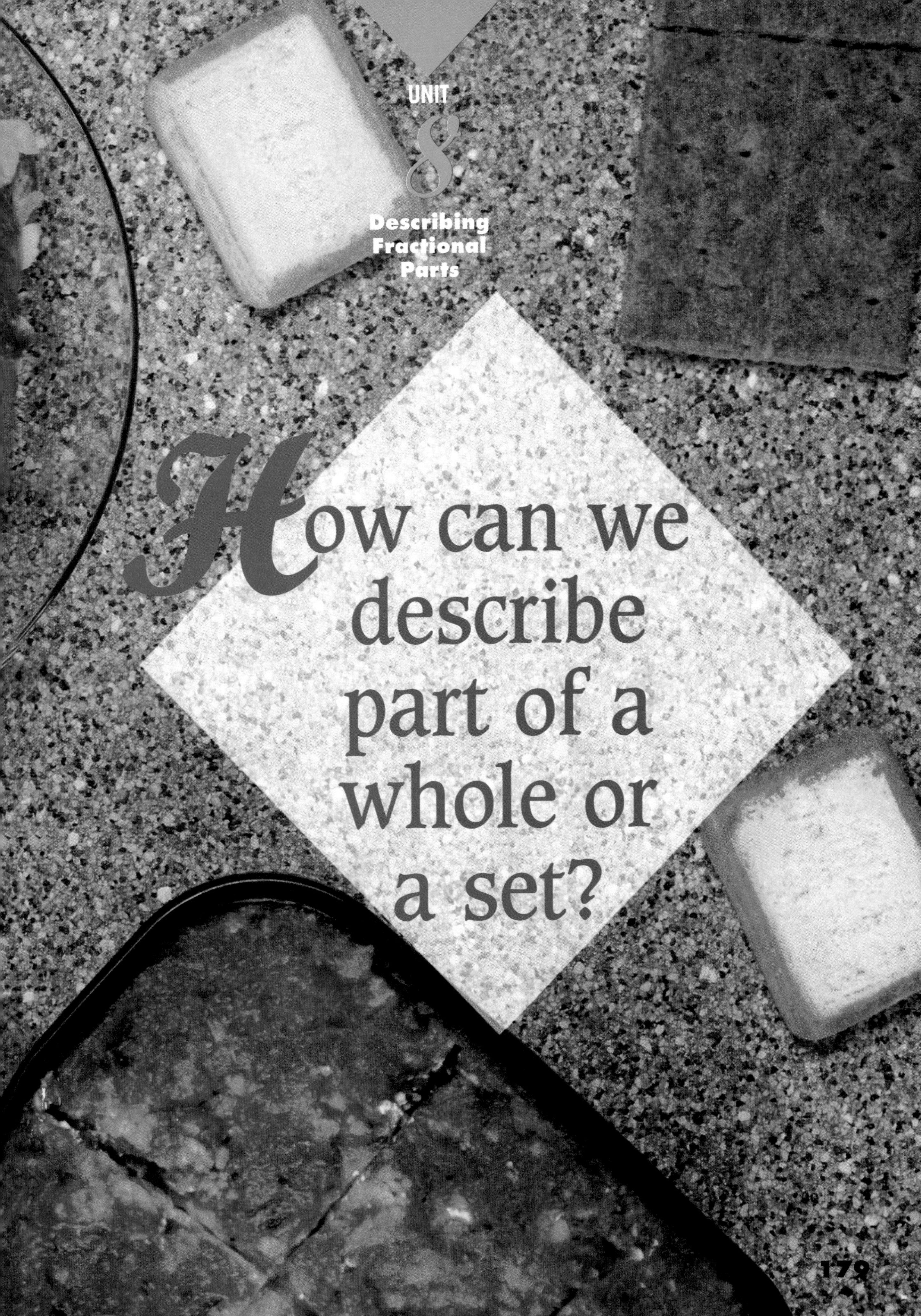
UNIT
8
Describing
Fractional
Parts
How can we describe part of a whole or a set?

DESCRIBING FRACTIONAL PARTS

STARTING OUT

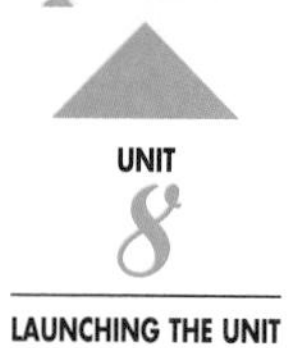

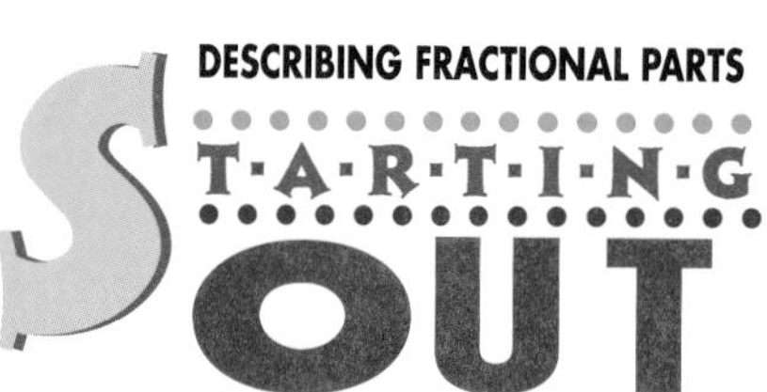

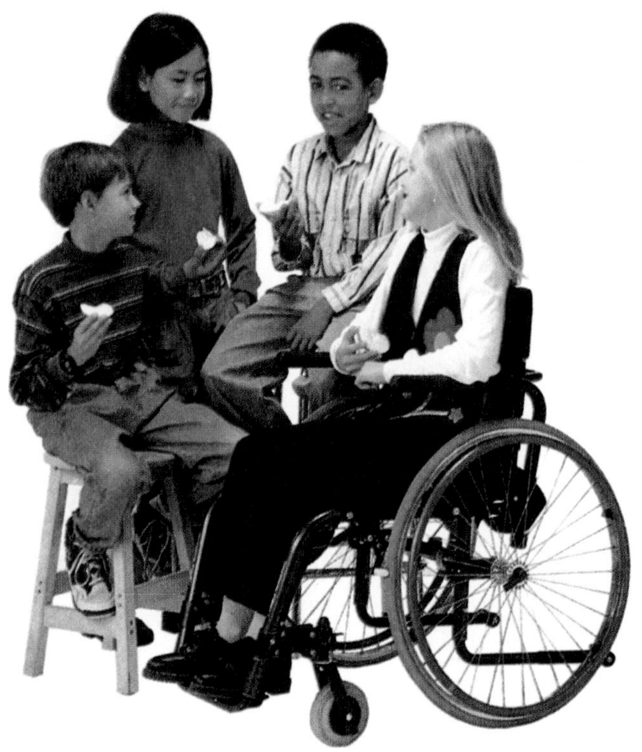

1 • What is happening in each of these pictures?
• How can the children make sure that each will get an equal share of the snack?
• Tell about some times when you shared a snack.
• How did you make sure you shared fairly?

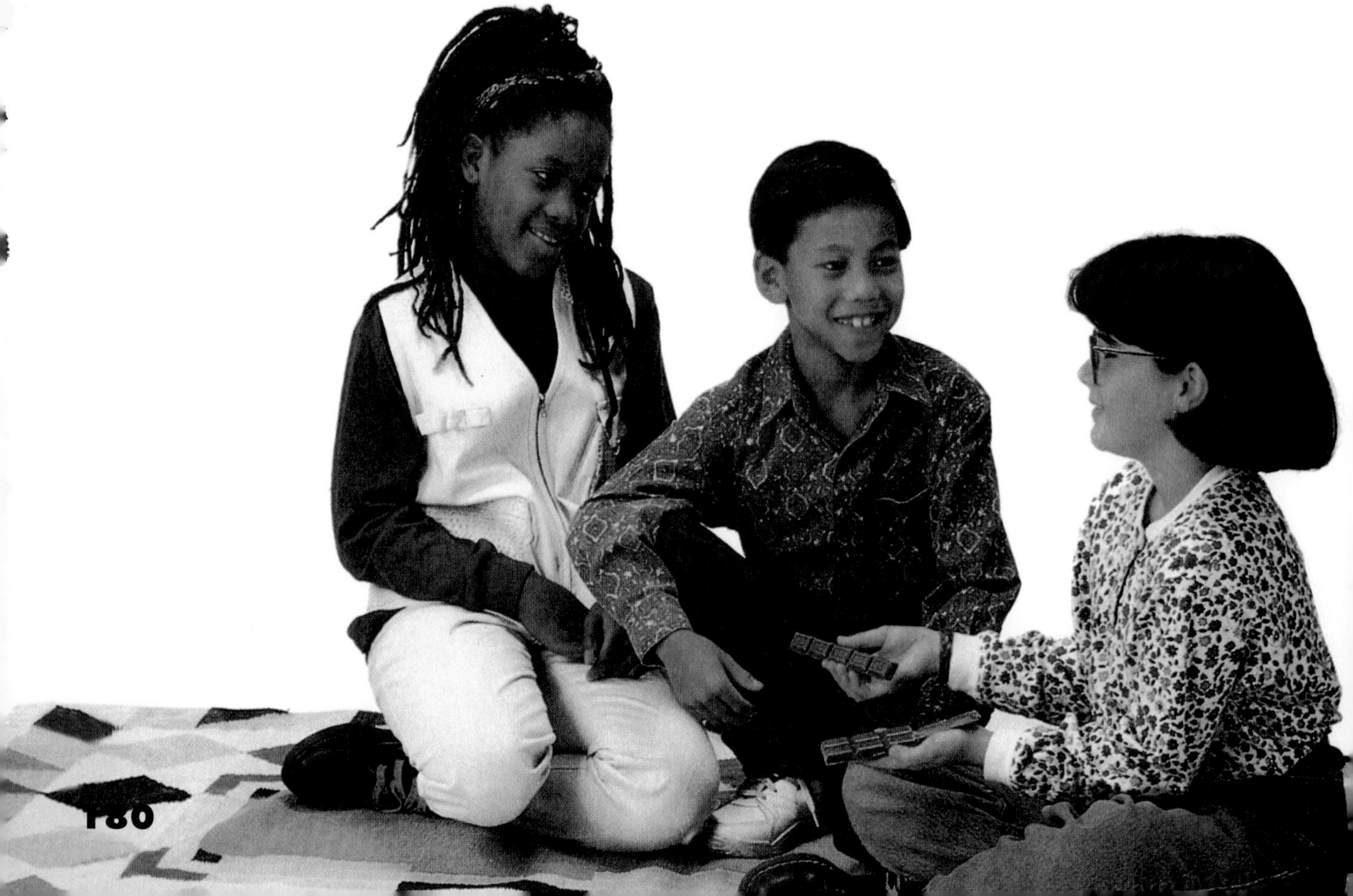

My Journal: When is it easy to divide a snack into equal shares? When is it difficult?

DESCRIBING FRACTIONAL PARTS

STARTING OUT

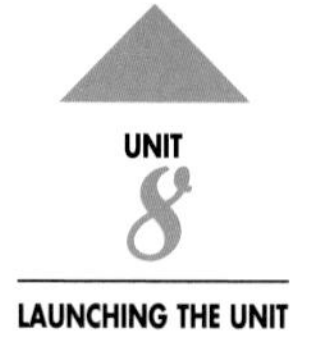

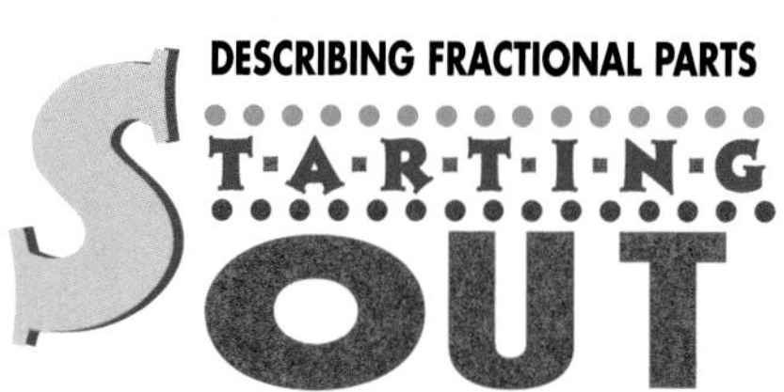

2 • Find things in the picture that show a whole divided into equal parts.
- How many equal parts is each divided into?
- What fractions can you use to describe the equal parts of each whole?
- Describe some situations where you or your family has divided a whole into equal parts.

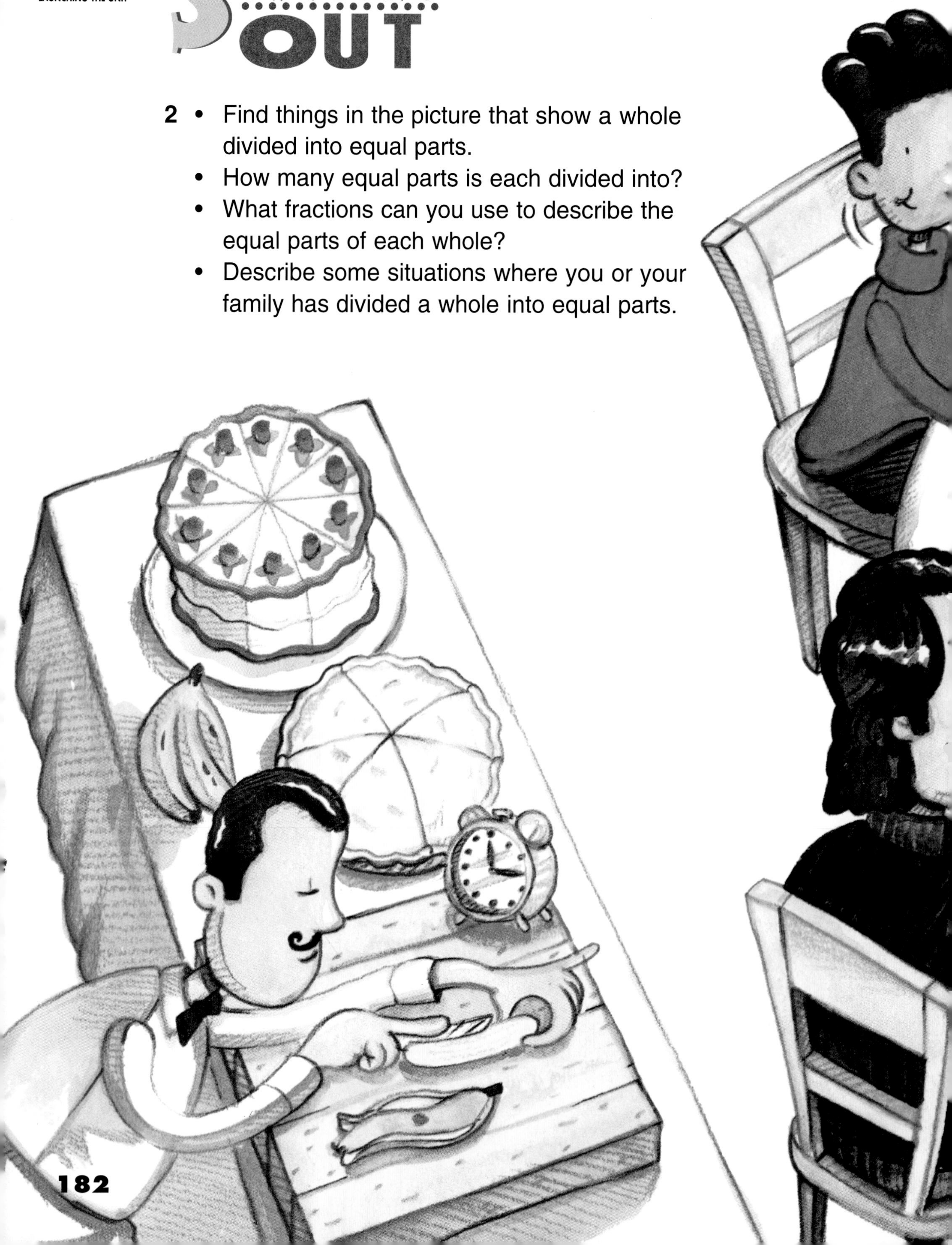

My Journal: Why do you think we use fractions?

Exploring Fractions

Fractions name equal parts of wholes.
How many pieces are in each pie? Compare the sizes of the pieces.

Fractions around the World

1:4
2:4
Germany

1/4; 1-4; $\frac{1}{4}$
2/4; 2-4; $\frac{2}{4}$

Egypt

Exploring Unit Fractions

Which block can be used repeatedly to cover this shape?

Can you find another block that can be used to cover the shape completely?

- Try to cover each shape below with as many different types of blocks as possible. Use only one colour at a time. For each type that you use, write a fraction that describes what part of the whole each block covers.

1

2

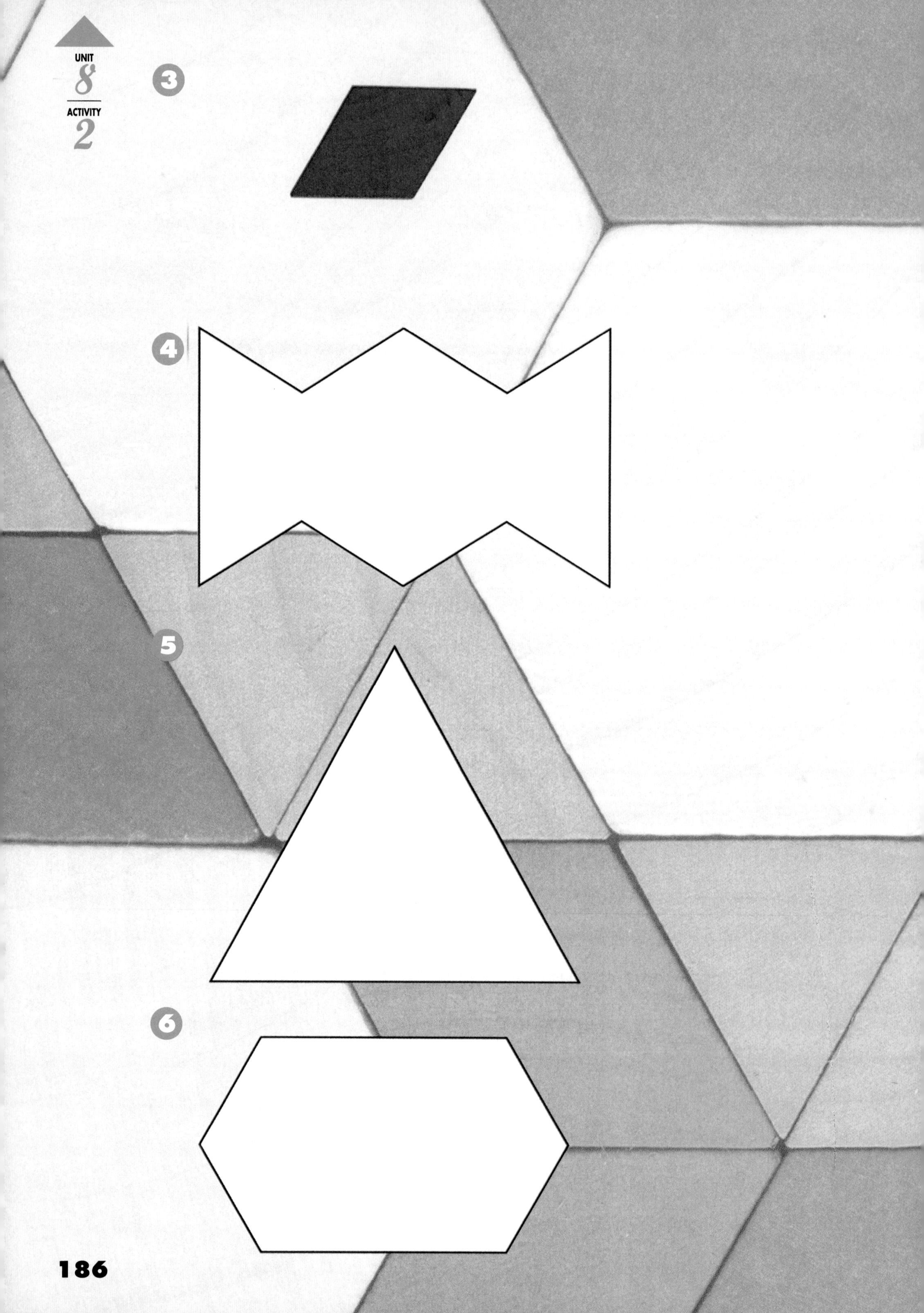
3
4
5
6

1. The shape below represents $\frac{1}{4}$ of the whole. Draw a picture that shows what the whole might look like.

2. Use the same shape as in Problem 1 but now let it represent $\frac{1}{3}$. Draw a picture that shows what the whole might look like.

3. Make any design using Pattern Blocks or Power Polygons. Write and tell what fraction each type of block is of the whole.

4. *My Journal:* What did you learn that was new?

Practise *Your Skills*

Use fractions to tell how each object is divided.

1.

2.

3.

4.

How much of each picture is shaded?

5.

6.

Relating Fractional Parts

- How many ways can you make a half?
  Compare the halves you have made.

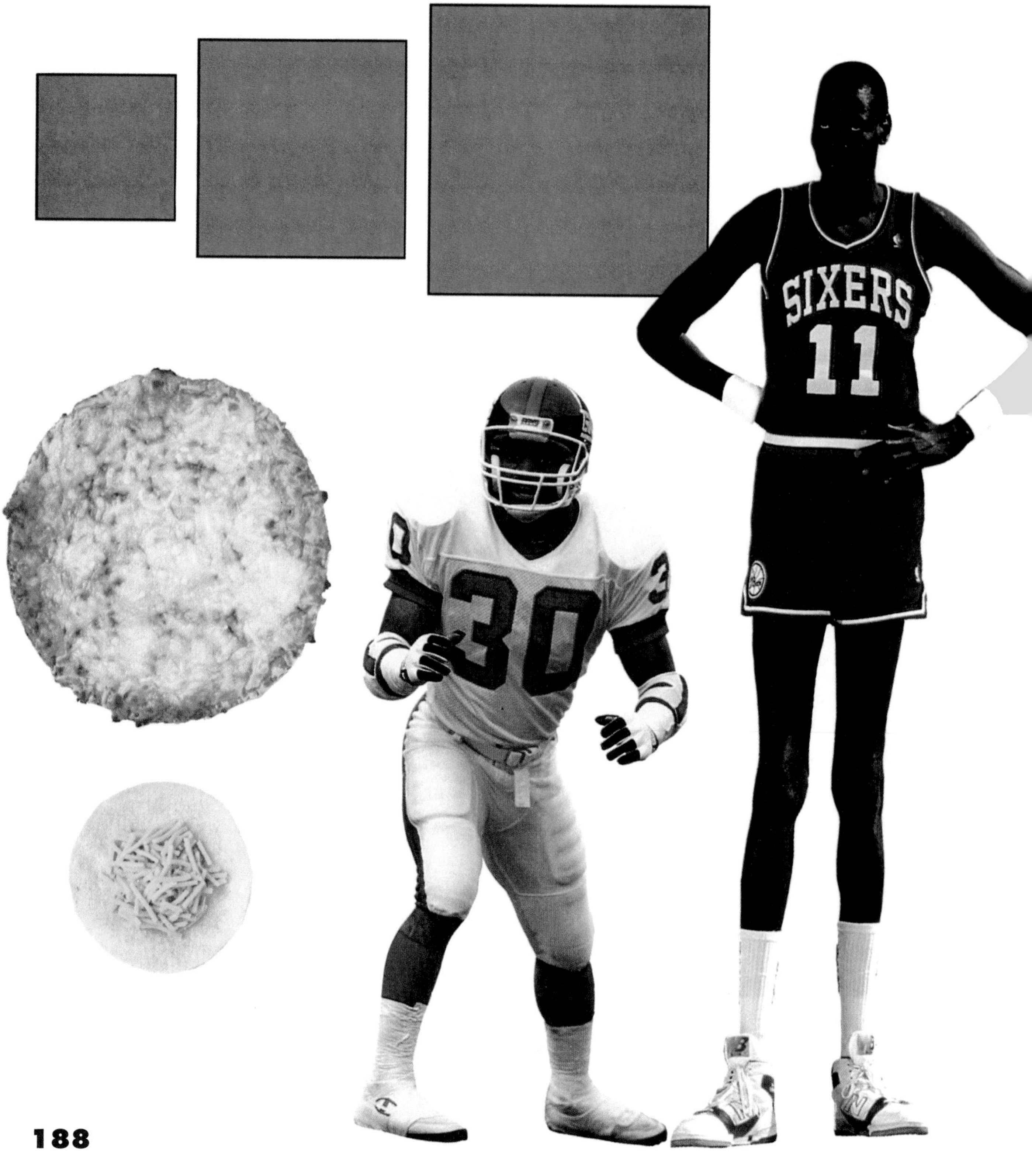

SIXERS
11

30

LOOK TO THE TREES

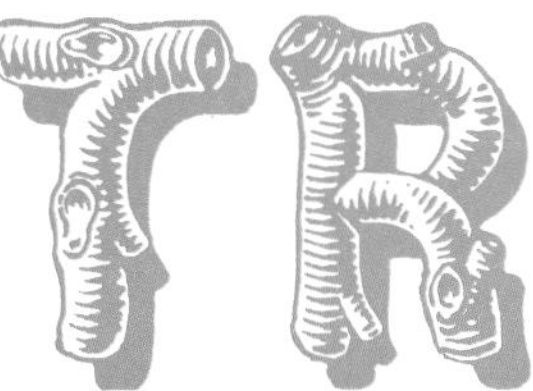

Did you ever wonder where in the real world you would find fractions?

Just look at some trees around you. The branches, buds, and flowers are arranged in circular spirals. The fraction tells you how far around the branch to go. Scientist Boris A. Kordemsky recorded the fractions for certain trees.

linden and elm	$\frac{1}{2}$
beech	$\frac{1}{3}$
oak and cherry	$\frac{2}{5}$
poplar and pear	$\frac{3}{8}$

Notice that the circles spiral up.

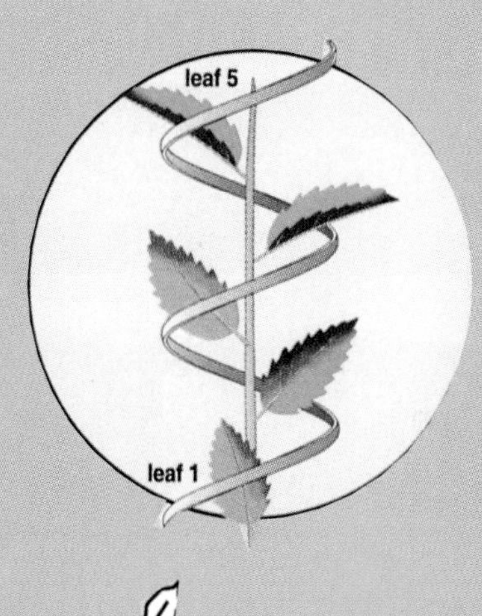

$\frac{1}{2}$

1. Draw a circular diagram for the leaves on a beech or an oak tree.

2. Look at a tree branch with leaves in a circle. Write a fraction for the part of the circle between two leaves.

Making Fraction Strips

▶ Folding Halves

1.

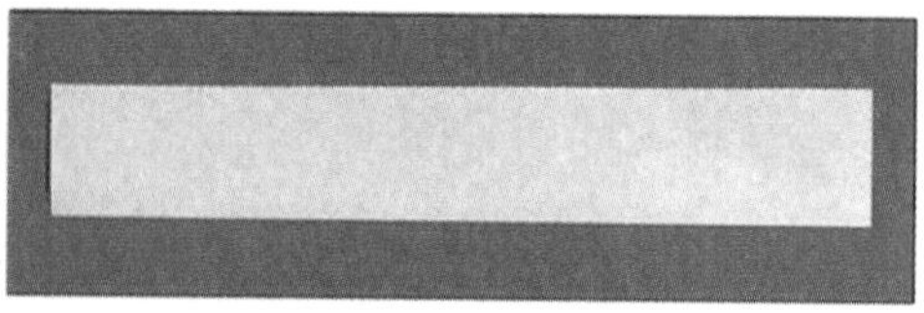

2.

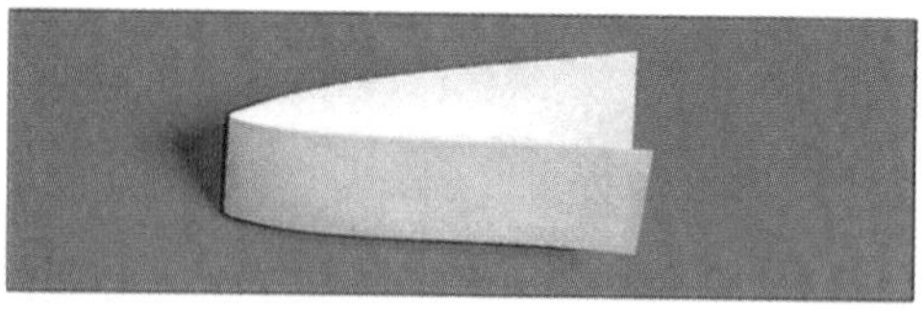

3.

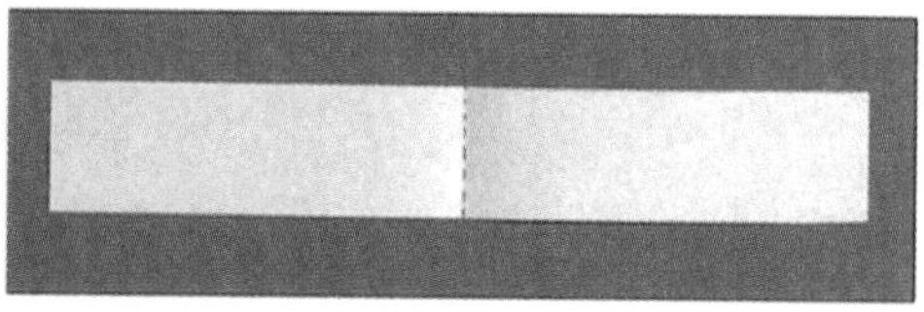

4. $\frac{1}{2}$ $\frac{1}{2}$

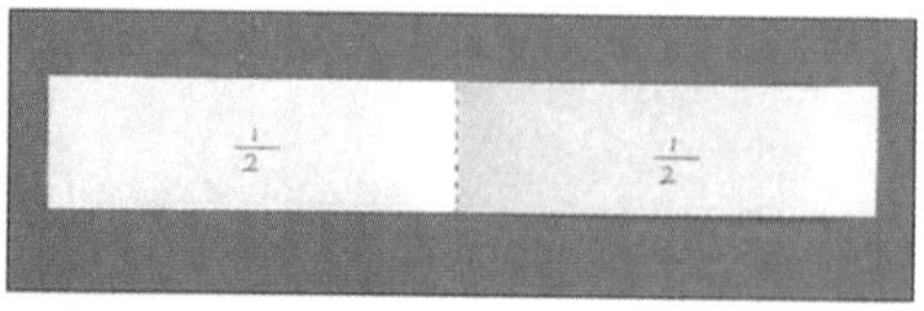

▶ Folding Fourths

1.

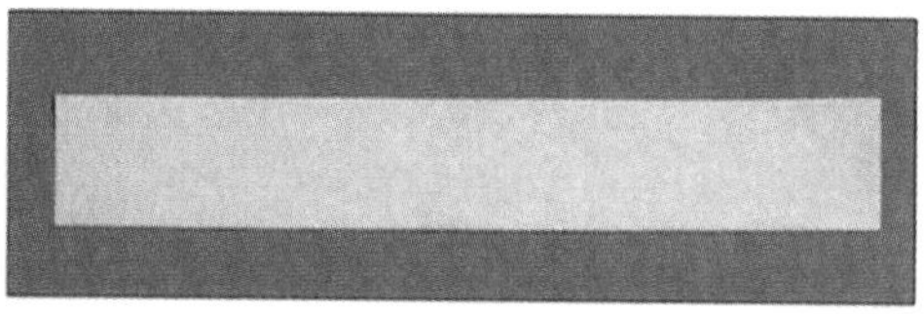

2.

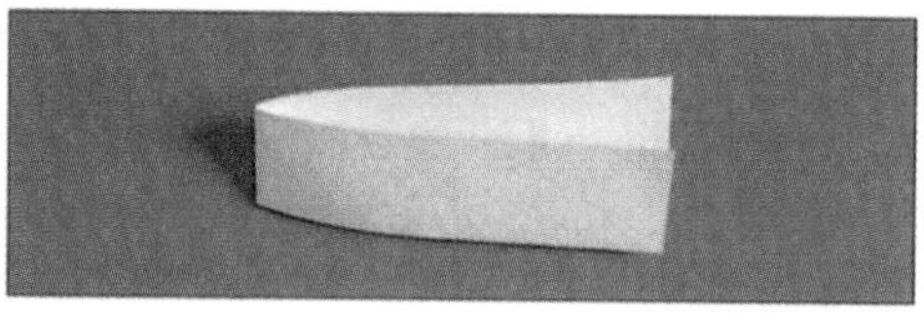

3.

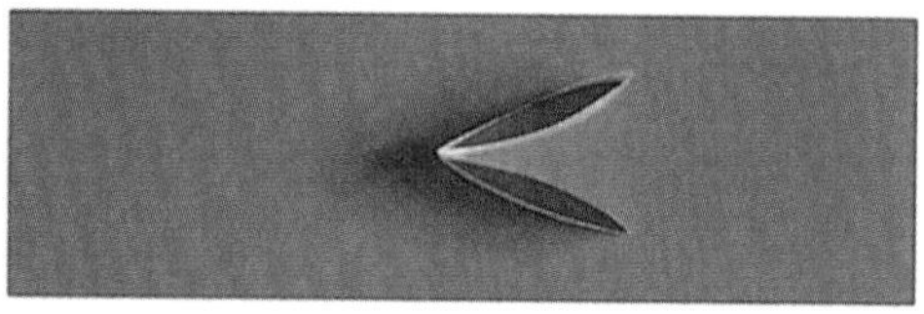

4.

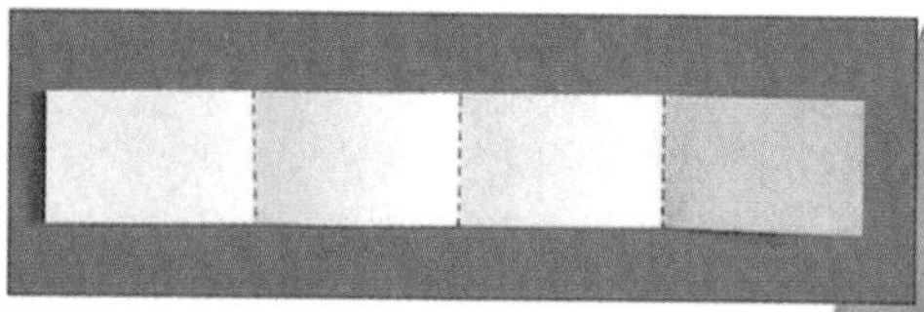

5. $\frac{1}{4}$ $\frac{1}{4}$ $\frac{1}{4}$ $\frac{1}{4}$

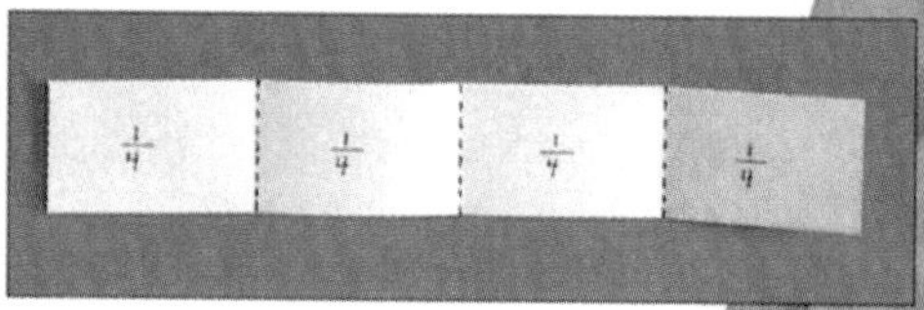

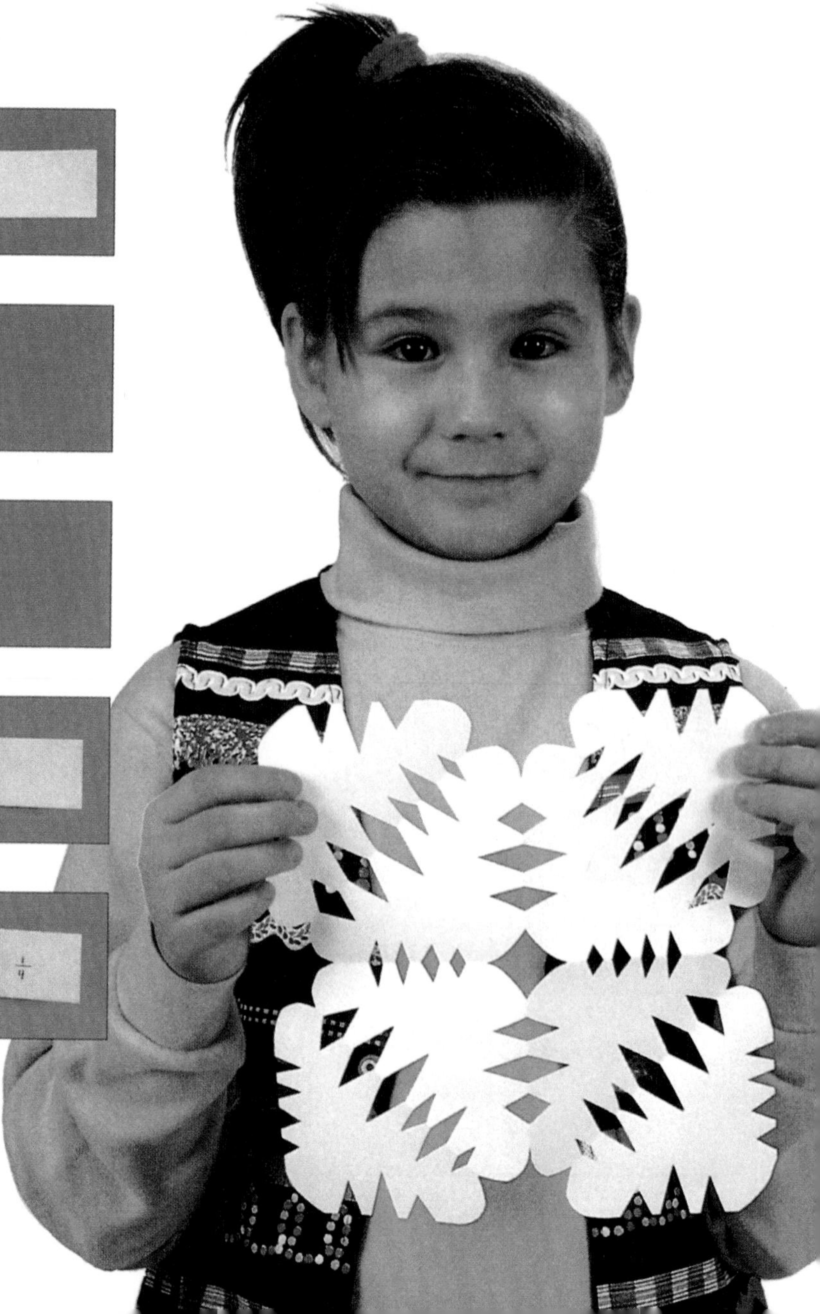

Fractions of a Set

What fraction of each chain is red?

What fraction of each chain is blue?

Solve these problems.

1. You have 5 apples. $\frac{1}{5}$ are red, $\frac{2}{5}$ are yellow, and the rest are green. Draw a picture of your apples.

2. There are 10 children in the yard. $\frac{1}{10}$ are playing ball and $\frac{4}{10}$ are skipping. Draw a picture. How many are not playing ball or skipping?

3. You have 8 coins. $\frac{1}{2}$ are nickels, $\frac{1}{4}$ are pennies, and the rest are dimes. Draw a picture of your money. How much money do you have?

4. *My Journal:* What questions do you have about fractions of a set?

Using Fractions of a Set

Can you follow the clues to make the mystery set?

1. There are 20 shapes in all.
2. $\frac{1}{10}$ of the shapes are hexagons.
3. There are 4 more squares than hexagons.
4. The rest of the shapes are triangles.

1. Look at the picture of the dogs.
   a. What fraction of the dogs is brown?
   b. What fraction of the dogs is black?
   c. What fraction of the dogs has spots?

2. What fractions can you use to tell about each picture?

b.

c.

d.

3. *My Journal:* What have you learned about fractions of a set?

Practise *Your Skills*

1. Draw a set of circles to show each statement.
   a. $\frac{2}{5}$ of the circles are red.
   b. $\frac{1}{10}$ of the circles are red.
   c. $\frac{3}{10}$ of the circles are red and $\frac{2}{10}$ of the circles are blue.

2. Write a fraction to tell what part of each set is blue.
   a. ◆ ◆ ◆ ◆ ◆
   ◆ ◆ ◆ ◆ ◆
   b. ♥ ♥ ♥
   ♥ ♥
   c. ☾☾☾☾☾
   ☾☾☾☾☾

Making
MATCHES

Which pictures show the same fraction?

Choose any fraction. Create as many ways as you can to show your fraction.

Check YOURSELF

Your display is attractive and creative. It shows many different pictures of the fraction you chose. You explained clearly in writing how each picture shows your fraction.

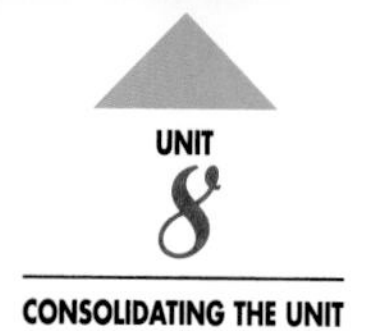

1. Use fractions to tell what part of this quilt is red. Use fractions to tell what part of it is blue.

2. Eight friends were having a picnic. There were 12 sandwiches to share. How much did each person get if everyone got an equal share? Draw pictures and write to explain your solution.

3. Find an object that is about half as long as another object. Explain how you know that one is about half as long as the other.

4. Make a design with colour tiles. Make $\frac{1}{2}$ of the design red and $\frac{1}{10}$ of it blue. Use green and yellow tiles in your design too. Describe the green and yellow tiles as fractions of the whole design.

5. Use colour tiles to build a rectangle that is $\frac{1}{6}$ green, $\frac{2}{6}$ blue, and $\frac{3}{6}$ red. Record your solution on squared paper and label the regions with fractions.

6. This Power Polygon piece represents $\frac{1}{5}$ of a whole. Use Power Polygons to show what the whole might look like. Find another way to do the same thing.

7. Lila drew the picture below. She said that the picture shows that halves and thirds are the same. Is she correct? Explain your ideas in writing.

$\frac{1}{2}$	$\frac{1}{2}$

$\frac{1}{3}$	$\frac{1}{3}$	$\frac{1}{3}$

8. Describe this chain using fractions.

9. You have 5 marbles. $\frac{2}{5}$ are red, $\frac{1}{5}$ are blue. The other marbles are yellow. Draw a picture to show your marbles. Use fractions to tell about your yellow marbles.

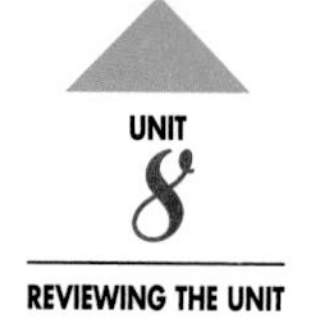

1. Write a fraction to tell what part of each shape is shaded:

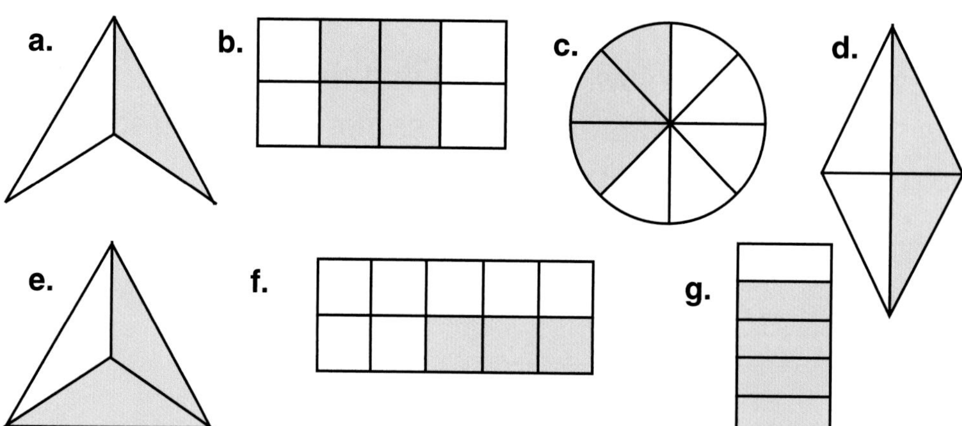

2. Draw a square and colour it to show each fraction.
   a. $\frac{1}{2}$ of the square is red. b. $\frac{1}{4}$ of the square is blue.

3. Draw a set of circles to show each situation.
   a. $\frac{1}{2}$ of the circles are red. b. $\frac{2}{5}$ of the circles are blue.
   c. $\frac{1}{10}$ of the circles are green. d. $\frac{4}{10}$ of the circles are yellow.

4. Write a fraction to tell what part of each set is shaded.

a.

b. c.

5.

a. What fraction of the stamps are 45¢ stamps?

b. What fraction of the stamps are not 45¢ stamps?

SKILL BANK

LOOKING BACK

1. a. What is the total cost for the eraser and pen?
   b. You have $5. Can you buy the pen and the markers? Explain.
   c. How much more do the markers cost than the coloured pencils?
   d. How much would 4 pens cost?

2. Total these receipts.

   a. $2.87, $3.15

   b. $1.40, $1.40, $1.40

   c. $5.65, $0.55, $2.30

   d. $0.89, $0.99, $1.99, $2.99

3. Here are plans for different swimming pools. Find the perimeter of each.

   a.

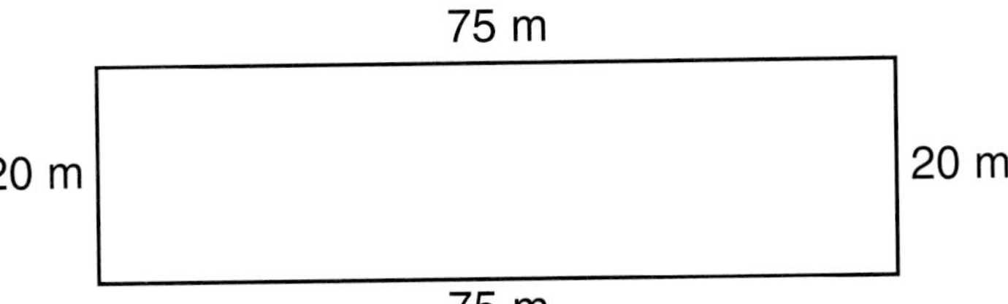

   b.

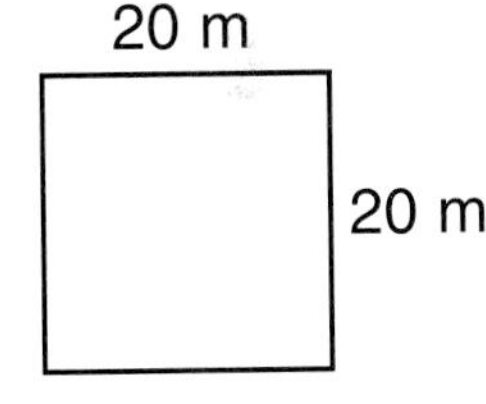

   c.

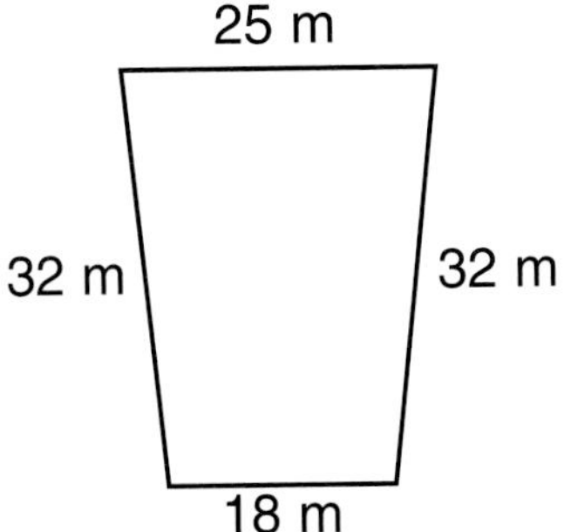

4. Which would you rather have? Explain your choice.
   a. 150 cm or 2 m of quarters placed in a row
   b. 250 g or 1 kg of your favourite candy
   c. 1 L or 10 L of milk to drink in a day

UNIT

9

Exploring Symmetry

How do we know it has symmetry?

EXPLORING SYMMETRY

STARTING OUT

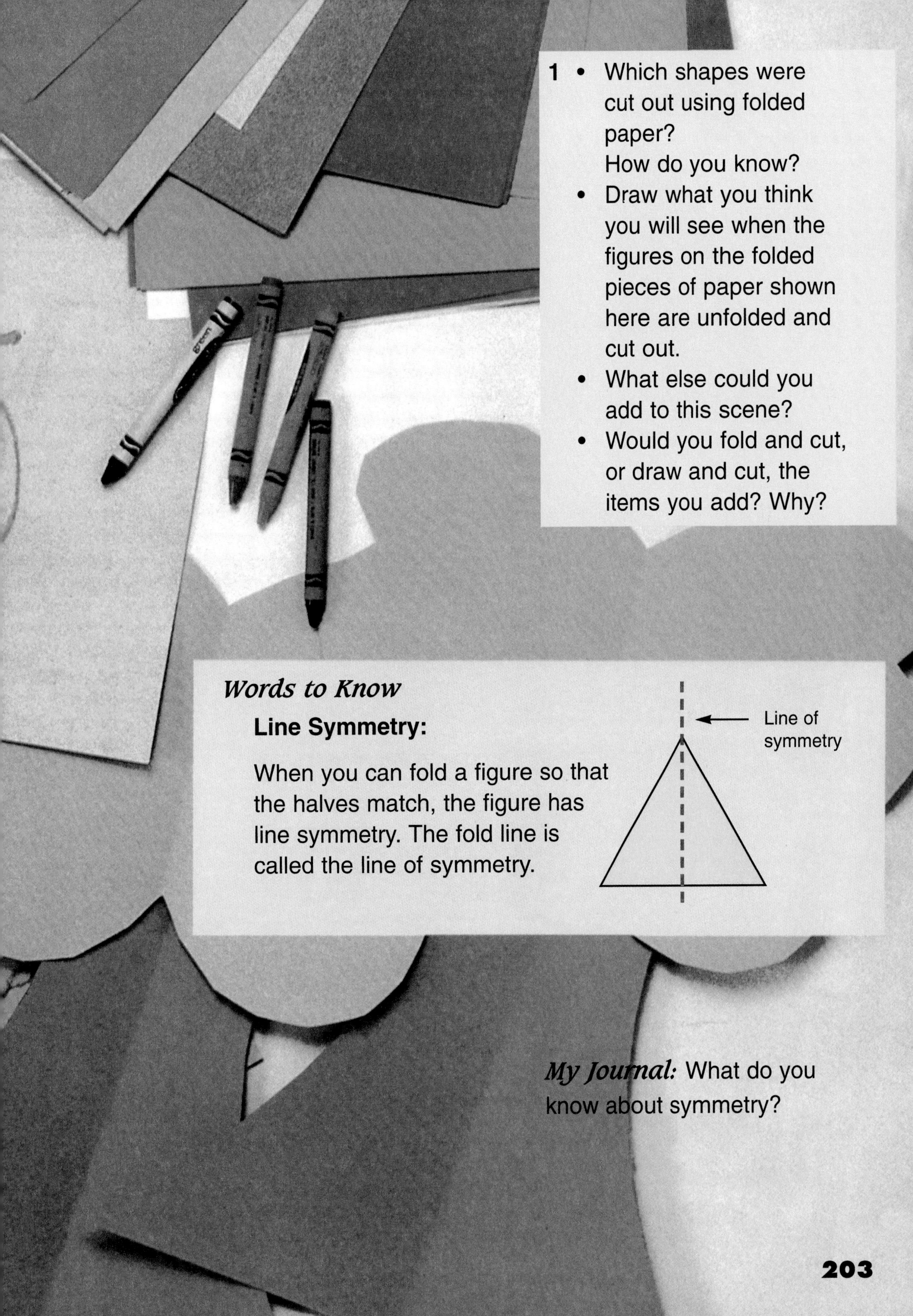

1
- Which shapes were cut out using folded paper? How do you know?
- Draw what you think you will see when the figures on the folded pieces of paper shown here are unfolded and cut out.
- What else could you add to this scene?
- Would you fold and cut, or draw and cut, the items you add? Why?

Words to Know

Line Symmetry:

When you can fold a figure so that the halves match, the figure has line symmetry. The fold line is called the line of symmetry.

My Journal: What do you know about symmetry?

UNIT 9 ACTIVITY 1

Lines of Symmetry

▶ Which pictures show line symmetry?

1. Think about objects that have line symmetry. Why do you think many things people build are designed to have line symmetry?

2. Do the numbers from 0 to 9 have line symmetry? Make a chart to show what you discover. Are the findings true for the kind of digits used in a calculator display? Explain.

3. *My Journal:* Tell what you know about line symmetry. Draw pictures to support your ideas.

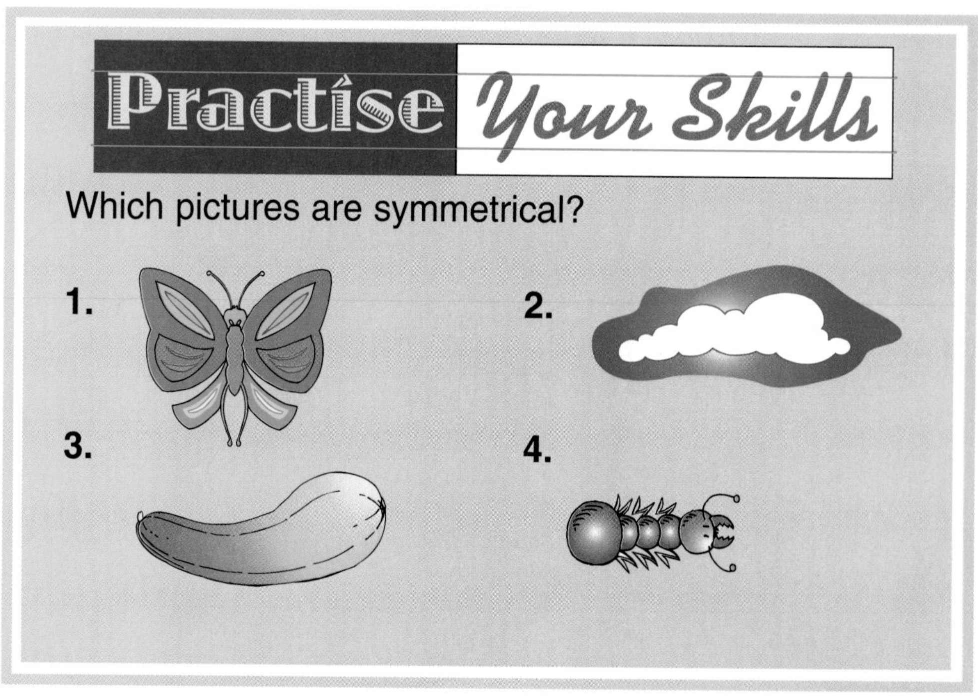

Creating Symmetrical Designs

UNIT 9 ACTIVITY 2

▶ Copy and complete the designs so that they are symmetrical.

UNIT 9

ACTIVITY 2

1. Follow the steps to make Happy Hound. You need 2 square pieces of paper.

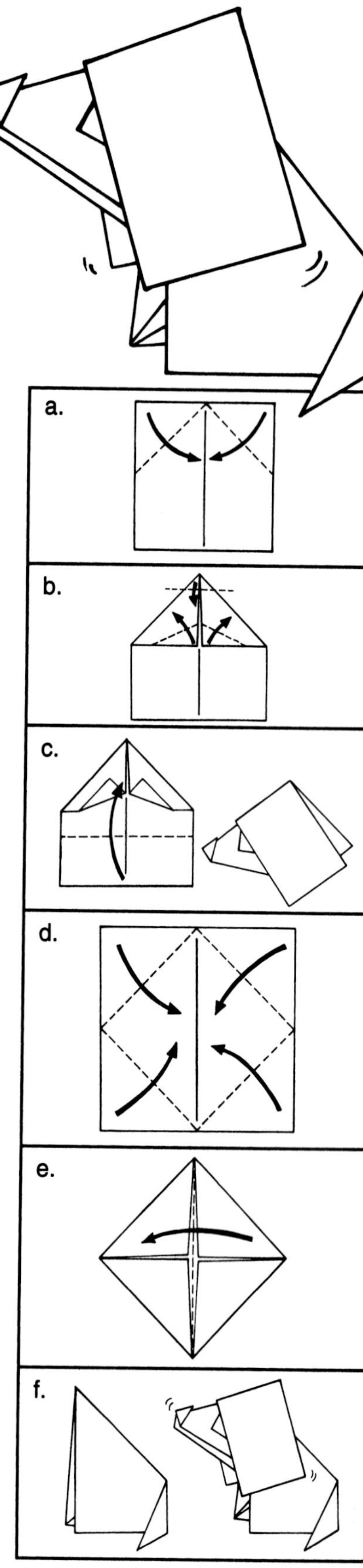

- First make Happy Hound's head. Start with one square of paper.

  a. Fold the paper in half the tall way. Unfold. Now fold each top corner to the middle.

  b. Fold up the centre corners a little. This makes eyes. Fold down the top centre corner a little. This makes a nose.

  c. Fold the bottom up to the folded eyes. Fold the head in half. Do you see the ears, nose, and eyes? Put the head aside for now.

- Next make Happy Hound's body. Use the other square of paper.

  d. Fold the paper in half the tall way. Unfold. Now fold each corner to the middle.

  e. Fold the new shape in half along the first fold you made in step d.

  f. Fold in the bottom corner to make a tail.

  Balance the head on top of the pointed neck. Gently pet Happy Hound. Watch her head bounce!

2. Copy each figure onto dot paper. Then complete each one so that when you unfold the paper, the figure is symmetrical. The fold is the line of symmetry.

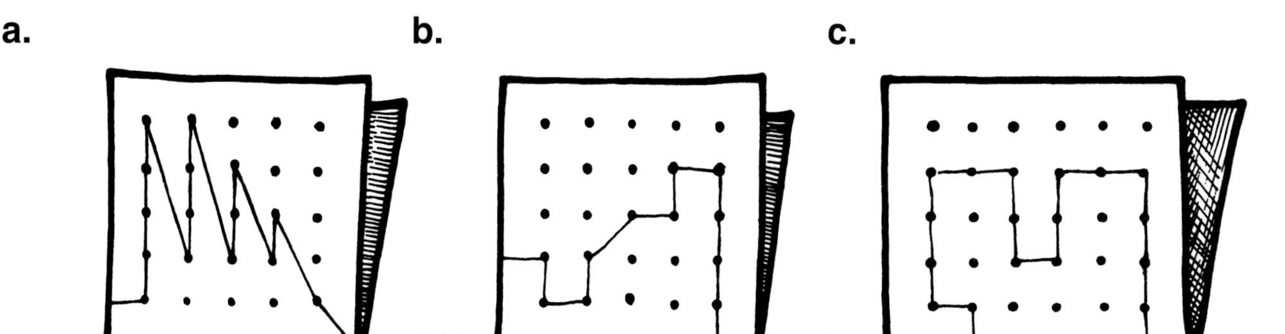

3. Use dot paper or grid paper. Create a design as complicated as you wish, with one or more lines of symmetry.

4. ***My Journal:*** Describe line symmetry in your own words. Tell why it is important.

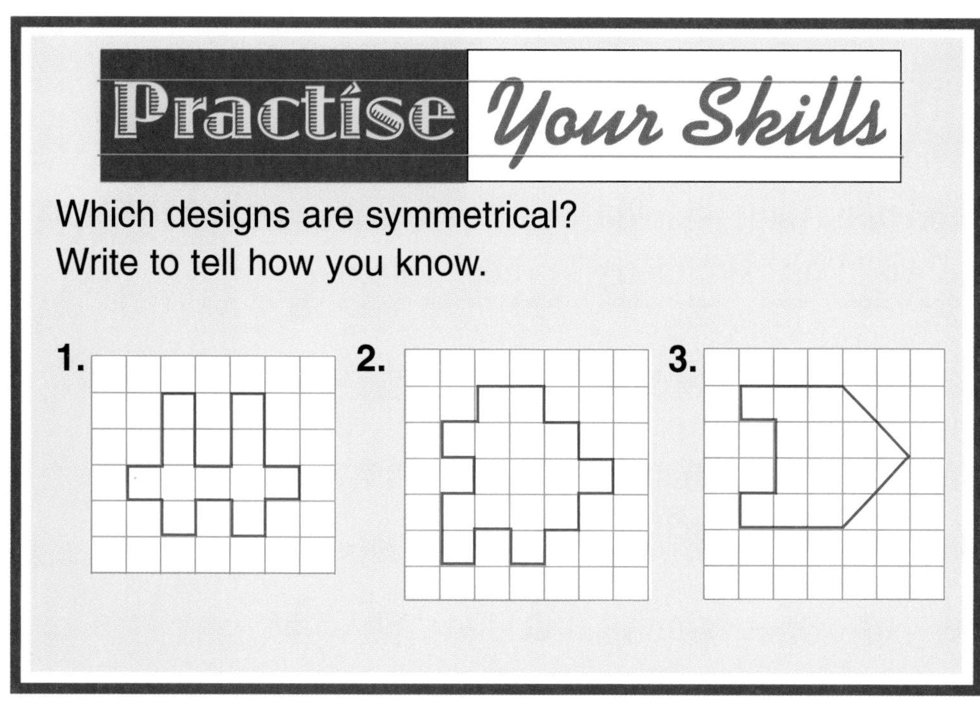

Repeat YOURSELF

Did you ever wonder how people use symmetry?

Symmetry is in designs of all kinds in nature and in designs people have made.

Some examples of symmetry in nature are:

Cactus
Many lines of symmetry

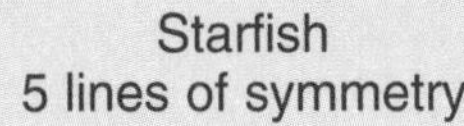

Starfish
5 lines of symmetry

Rubber Plant Leaf
1 line of symmetry

Symmetrical designs made by people include:

Aztec Goddess
1 line of symmetry

Persian Rug
2 lines of symmetry

1. Why do you think people from different parts of the world use symmetry in their designs?

2. Find some symmetrical designs that interest you in objects in your home, fabrics, pictures in magazines, or in nature. Tell how many lines of symmetry each example has.

3. Make your own symmetrical design. Tell what you would use it for.

Symmetrical Designs

- Which designs have one or more lines of symmetry?

UNIT 9
ACTIVITY 3

ON YOUR OWN

1. Use any materials you have at home to create a symmetrical design with at least two lines of symmetry. Bring it to class. Ask a classmate to find the lines of symmetry.

2. Find three objects in your home that have line symmetry. Describe or draw each and tell where to find its lines of symmetry.

3. Find three objects in your neighbourhood that have line symmetry. Describe or draw each and tell where to find its lines of symmetry.

4. Look at the thunderbird. You can find this symbol in some First Nations art, especially in the Pacific Northwest. Does it have symmetry? If so, how many lines of symmetry are there? Describe what you see.

5. Design a symbol to stand for yourself, your school, your town, or your family. Make it have one or more lines of symmetry.

6. ***My Journal:*** In what situations might you be interested in using line symmetry? Explain.

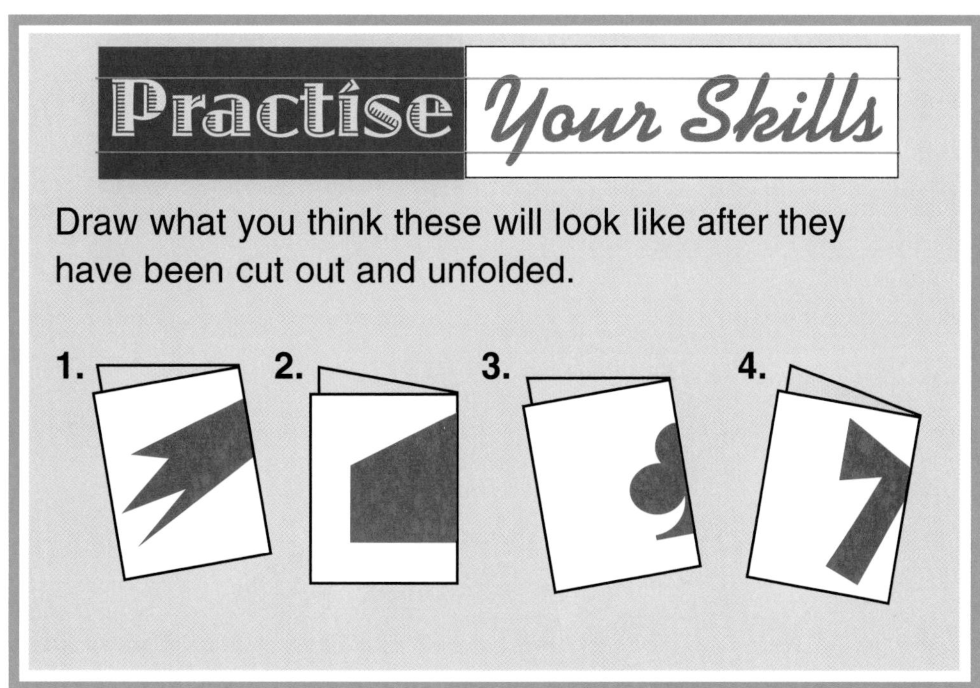

Practise *Your Skills*

Draw what you think these will look like after they have been cut out and unfolded.

PUZZLING STEPS

Follow these steps.

1. Design two Power Polygons puzzles. Make one that has no lines of symmetry and another that has 1 or more lines of symmetry. Put each puzzle together on a sheet of paper.

2. Trace just the outline of each puzzle on the paper. Below each puzzle, tell how many lines of symmetry the puzzle has, and describe where the lines are. Include other clues if you want.

3. On another sheet of paper, record the way you used the pieces to make your puzzles.

4. Exchange puzzles with a classmate. Try to use the Power Polygons pieces to make the puzzle.

5. When you think you have solved the puzzle, ask the puzzle maker to check. If you find a correct, but different, solution, record it to share later, and try again. Keep trying until you find the original solution.

Use these 4 pieces to make this puzzle.
There are no lines of symmetry.

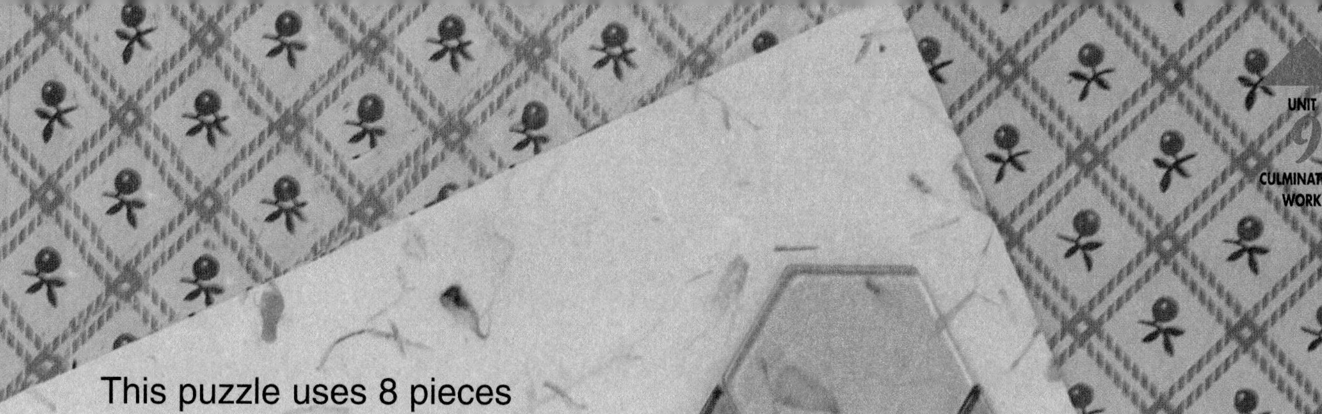

This puzzle uses 8 pieces and has 1 line of symmetry.

Checklist for making a puzzle	Checklist for solving a puzzle
• How many lines of symmetry will your puzzle have? • Is your puzzle interesting and challenging? • How many pieces will you use? • How can you record your puzzle? • What clues can you give the solver?	• How many lines of symmetry must you think about? Where can they be? • What other clues did the puzzle maker give you? • What do you know about the pieces that can help you? • What other hints would help?

Check YOURSELF

You created two good puzzles, one without symmetry and one with at least 1 line of symmetry. Your clues were helpful, but did not give too much away. You wrote to explain how you used symmetry and various shapes to make your puzzle.

1. How could you cut this fruit so Sam and Kisha will have the same amount? Explain whether your cut would be along the line of symmetry. Draw what you would see.

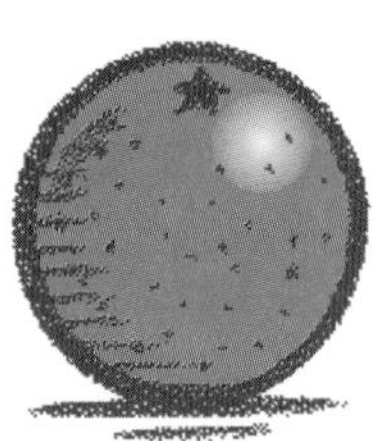

2. What parts of this bicycle are symmetrical?

3. Create a design using Power Polygons. Describe, but don't show, your design to a friend. Challenge your friend to try to create the same design. When you put the two designs together are they symmetrical? Explain.

1. Print these letters. Draw lines to show the lines of symmetry.

2. a. Which of these shapes have lines of symmetry?
How do you know?

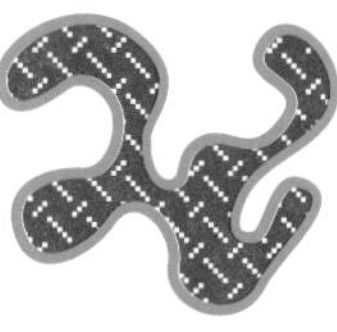

b. How many lines of symmetry does each shape have?

CUMULATIVE REVIEW

What fraction of each figure is coloured?

1. 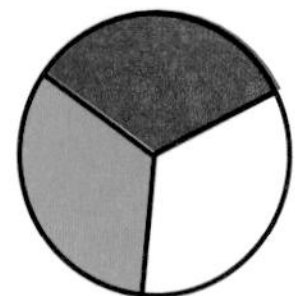 **2.** 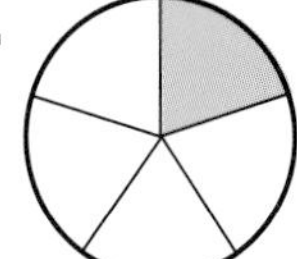 **3.** 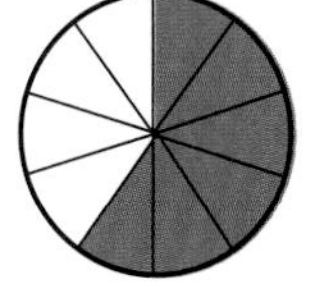 **4.** 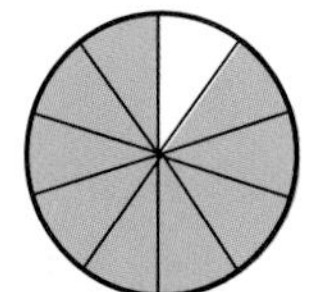 **5.** 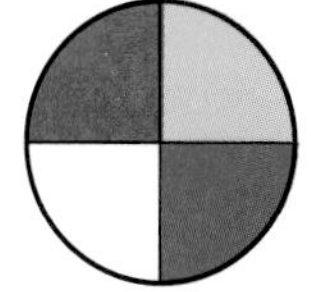

What fraction of each set is red?

6.  **7.**  **8.** 

UNIT

10

Examining Shapes and Solids

How can we combine shapes and solids?

EXAMINING SHAPES AND SOLIDS

1 • What shapes can you find in these buildings?
  • Which shapes seem to appear often? Not often?
  • Why do you think that buildings are constructed to look so different?
  • What type of building would you like to add to this page?

My Journal: What shapes and solids do you find interesting? Why did you choose these?

Describing and Sorting Solids

▶ How do we describe solids?

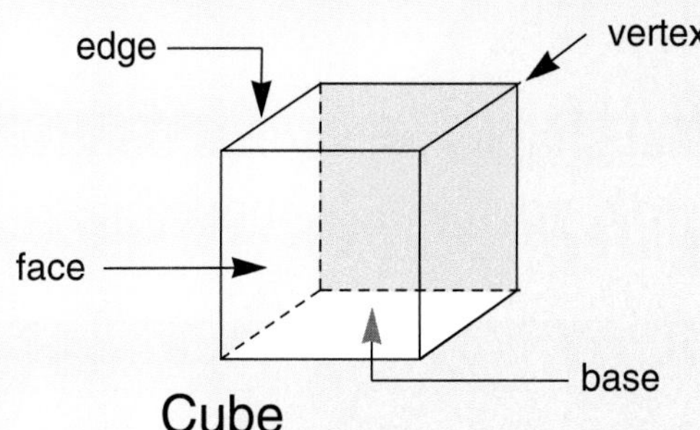

Cube

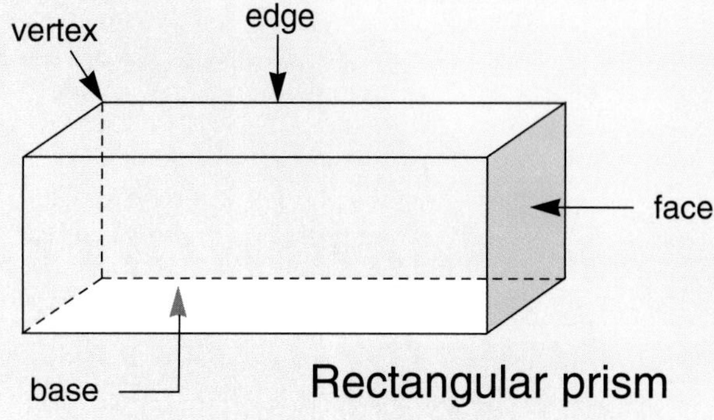

Rectangular prism

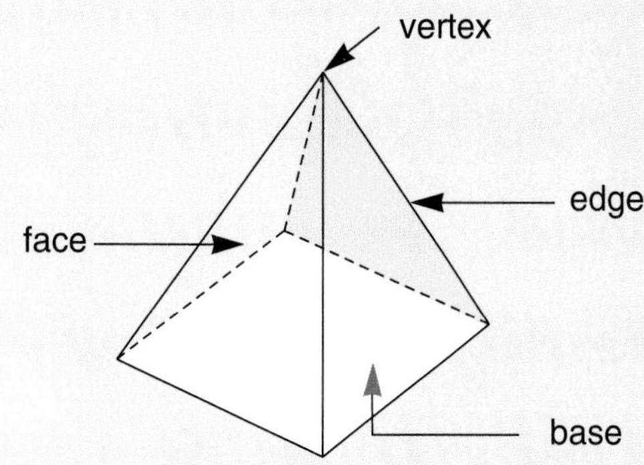

Pyramid

Words to Know

Face:
A flat surface of a geometric solid

Edge:
The line segment where a pair of faces meet

Vertex:
A point where 2 or more edges meet

Base:
The face that is the bottom of a solid

1. How are these solids alike?
   How are they different?

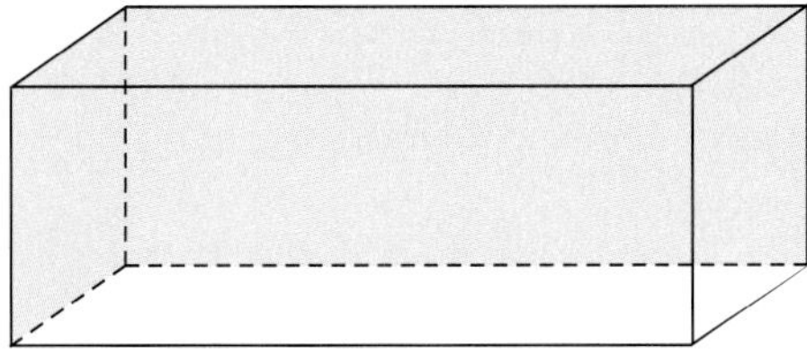

Rectangular prism

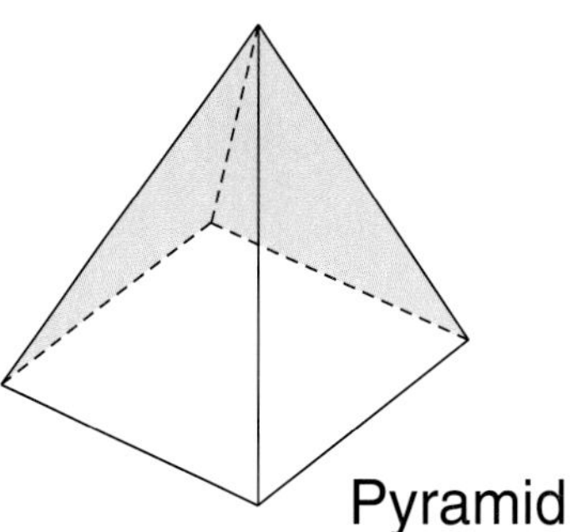
Pyramid

2. Choose a solid.
   Describe it in as much detail as you can.

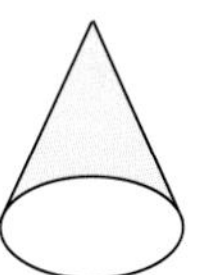 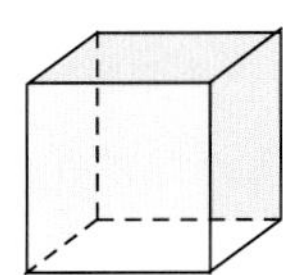 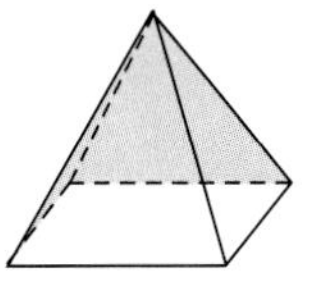 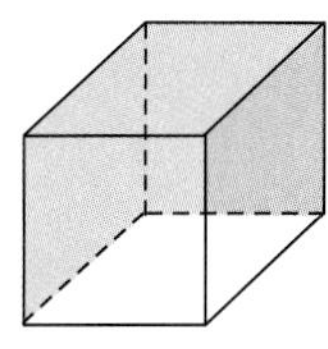

3. **a.** What is the sorting rule?

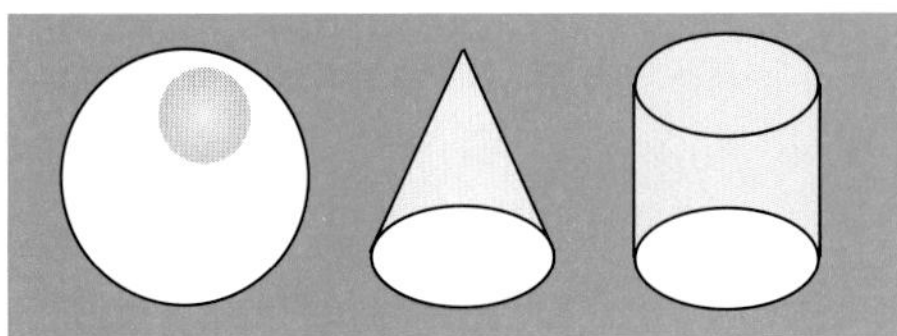 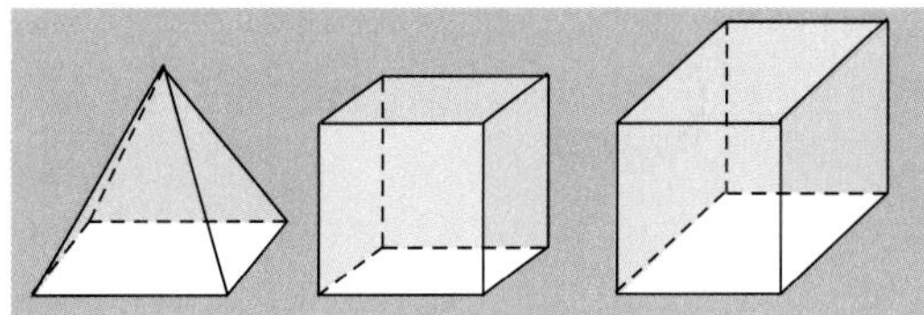

   b. In which set does this belong?

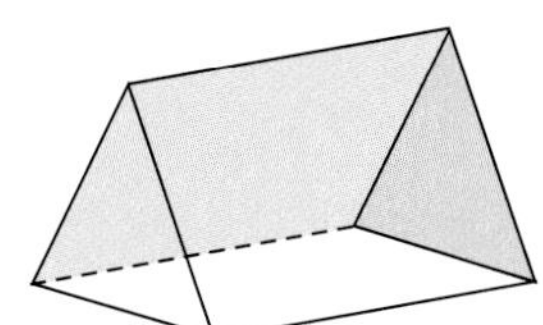

4. ***My Journal:*** What questions do you have about shapes and solids?

Make and complete this table.

Solid	Number of faces
Cube	
Pyramid	
Rectangular prism	
Triangular prism	

IDENTIFYING SOLIDS
The Yes-No Game

Group

2 players

Materials

Geometric solids

Game Rules

1. One player secretly thinks of a solid.
2. The other player asks questions to try to guess the solid. The questions must be ones that can be answered by "yes" or "no."
3. Keep track of the number of questions a player has to ask before guessing the solid.
4. Talk about the kinds of questions you think are good ones for guessing the secret solids.

Words to Know

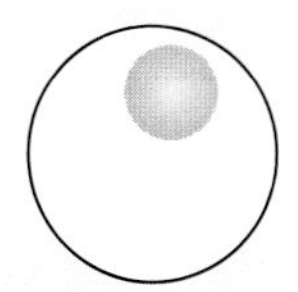

Sphere

Cube

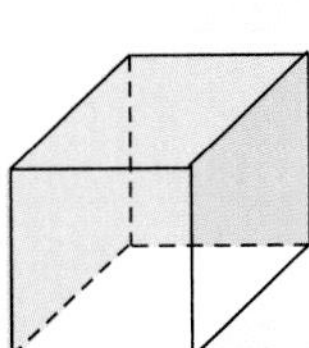

Rectangular prism

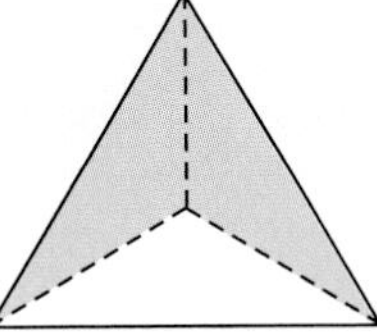

Pyramid

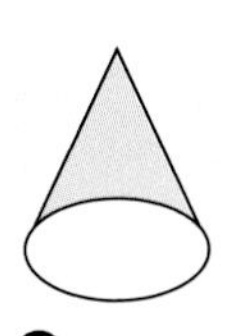

Cone

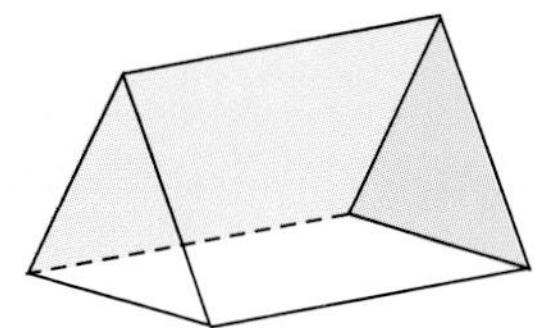

Triangular prism

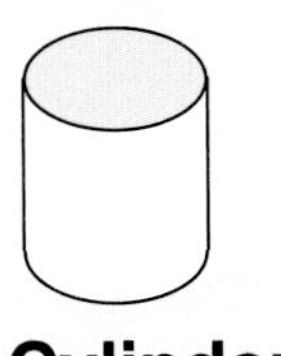

Cylinder

STAMPING Shapes

In many countries, plants, shellfish, and insects are boiled to create dyes that are used to colour yarn or cloth.

Here is a recipe for dye. The colour depends on the plants you use. Dandelion heads make yellow, spinach makes green, and blackberries make blue. You will need an adult to help you make the dye.

- 15 mL alum *(from the drugstore)*
- 60 mL cream of tartar
- 4 L water
- large amount of plant material, cleaned, dirt and dead leaves removed

Place all the ingredients in a pot on the stove. Bring to a boil. Turn the heat down and let the mixture simmer for 20 minutes. After it has cooled, strain it through a sieve.

You can use this dye, or any paint, to stamp shape patterns on paper, cloth, linens, wood, baskets, and many other things. Stamping with a square block will give you squares. Stamping with a circular sponge will give you polka dots. You can also use fruits and vegetables to create the stamps. If you cut a round fruit, such as an orange, the shape you see on the cut side is a circle. If you cut a star fruit, the shape you see is a star.

1. What is your favourite fruit or vegetable? If you cut it in half, what shape of print could you make? Are there other shapes you could make by cutting your fruit a different way? What are they?

2. What object could you cut to create a stamp that is shaped like a triangle?

3. Decorate your classroom using long strips of adding machine tape. Stamp a pattern of your choice onto the tape. You can use blocks, sponges, cut fruit, or anything else you can think of, to stamp your pattern.

UNIT 10
ACTIVITY 3

Describing and Comparing Faces

▶ What shapes make up these boxes?

Words to Know

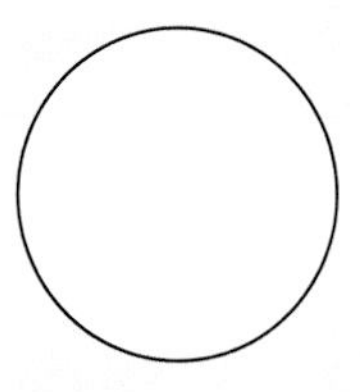
Circle

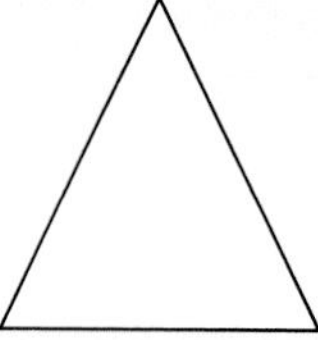
Triangle

Rectangle

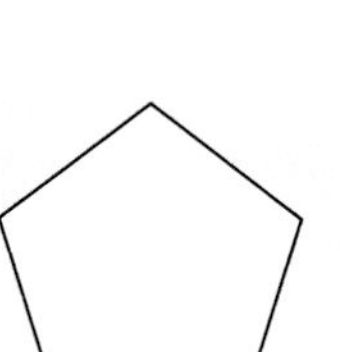
Pentagon

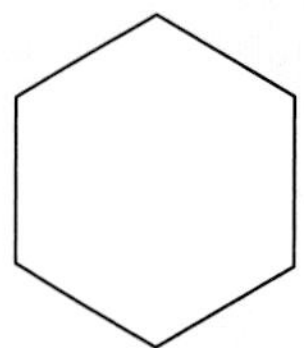
Hexagon

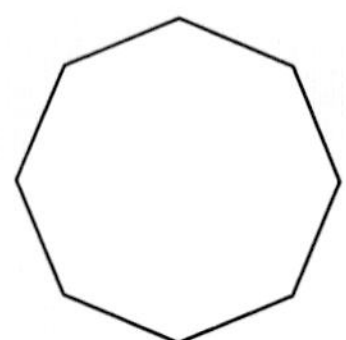
Octagon

1. Find 2 boxes at home. Trace the largest face on each. How do they compare?
2. Take a look at as many cereal boxes as you can. What do they all have in common? How are they different?
3. Why do you think most cereal is packaged in boxes? Why do you think cans are not as common for packaging cereal?
4. ***My Journal:*** What have you learned about solids that you didn't know before?

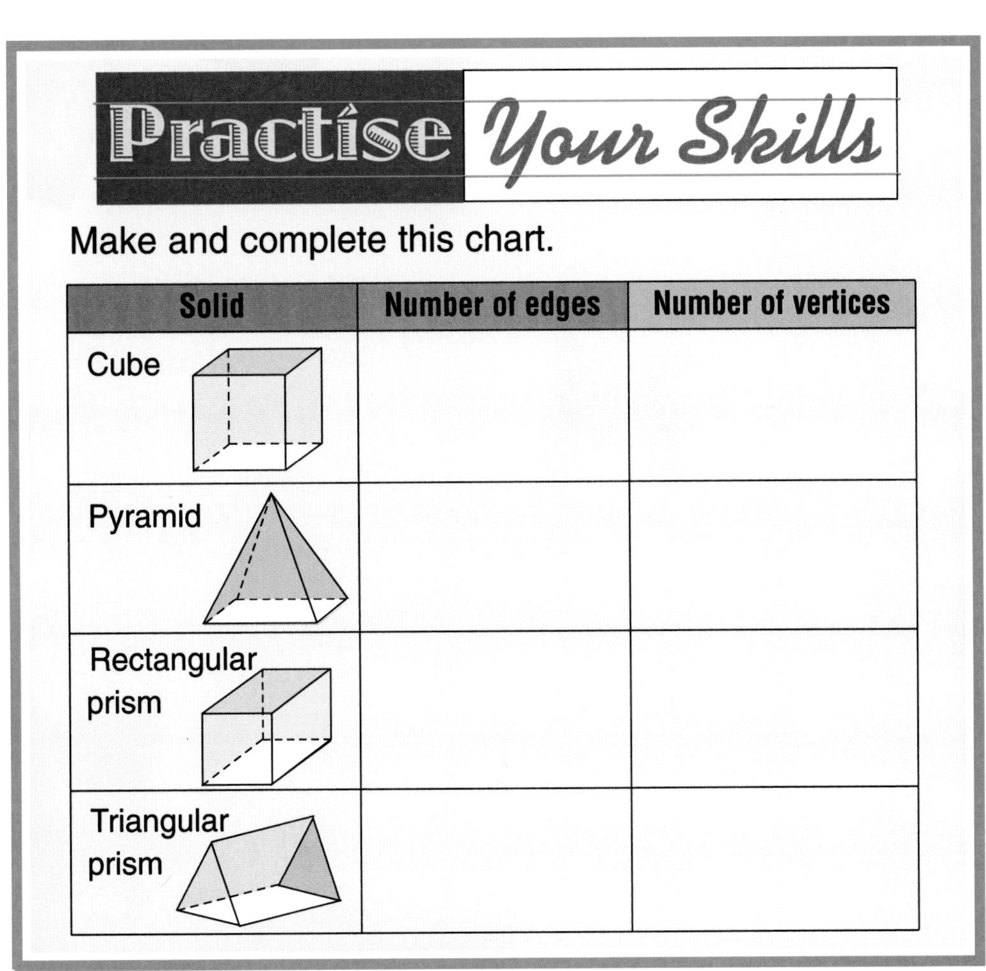

Practise Your Skills

Make and complete this chart.

Solid	Number of edges	Number of vertices
Cube		
Pyramid		
Rectangular prism		
Triangular prism		

Comparing Nets of Boxes

▶ Which nets can be folded to make boxes?

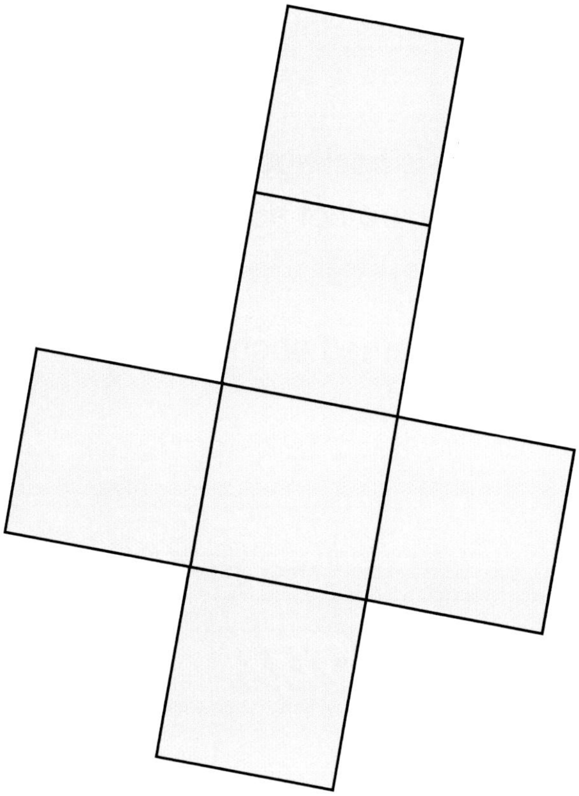

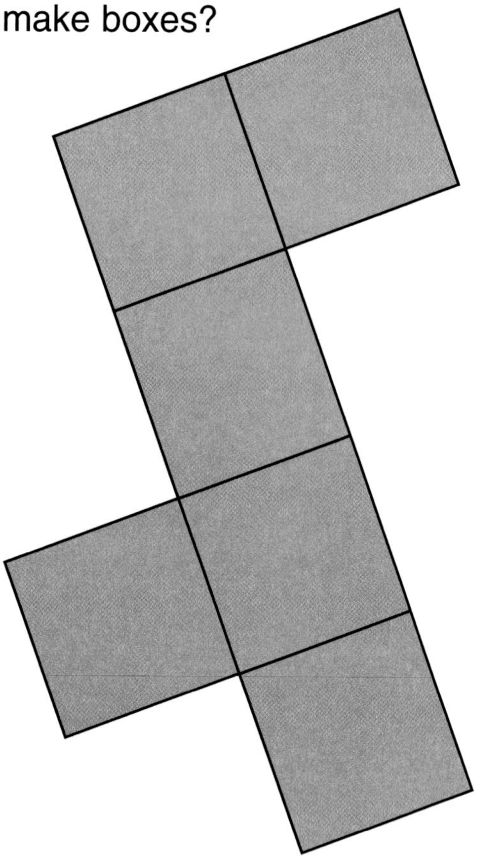

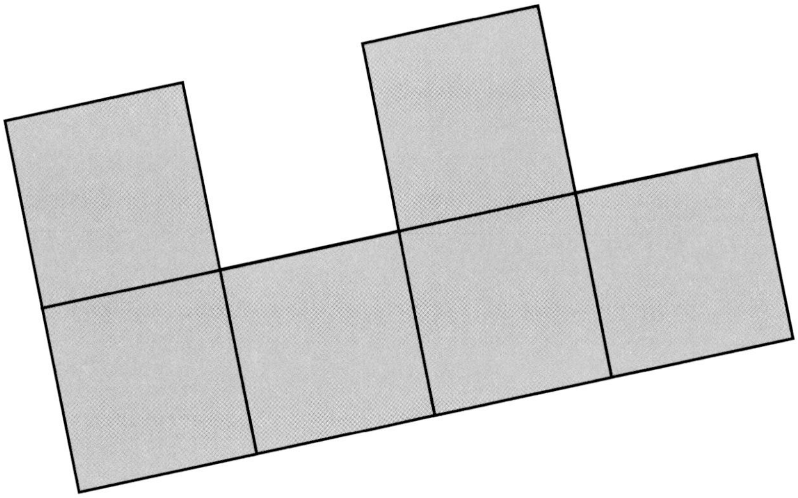

Words to Know

Net: a pattern for a solid

1. Which net made each box?
   Tell how you decided.

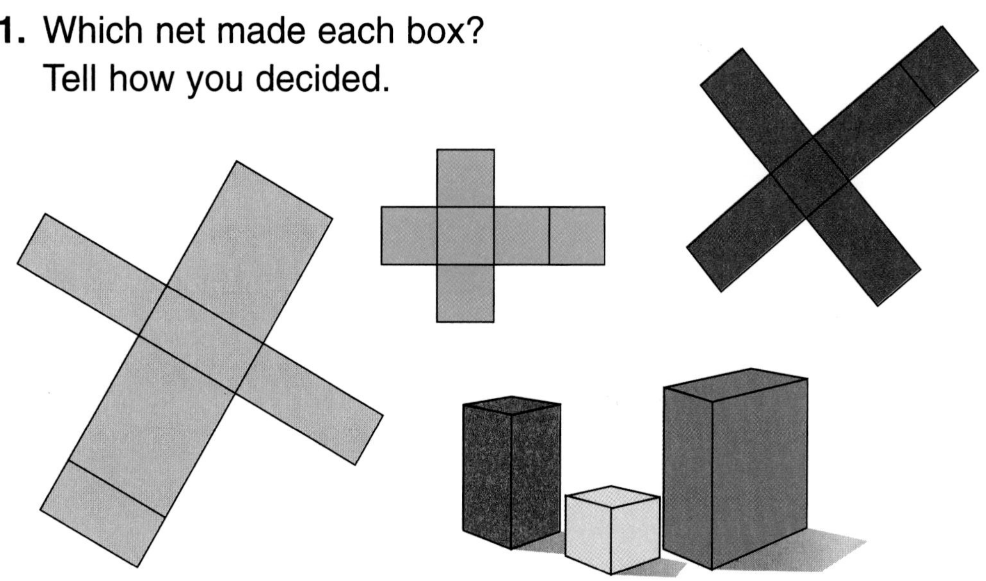

2. How is a rectangular prism like a triangular prism?
   How is a rectangular prism different from a triangular prism?

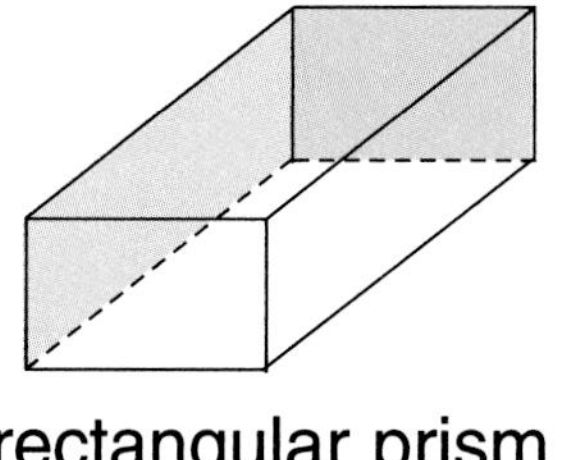

rectangular prism

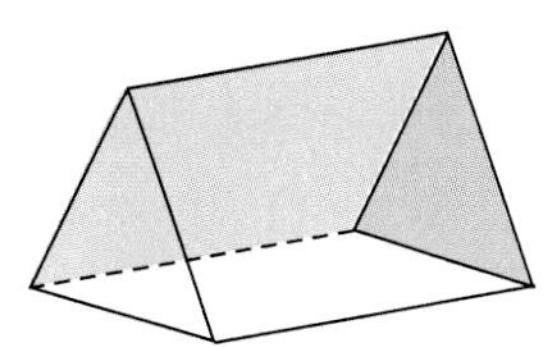

triangular prism

3. *My Journal:* What do you know about nets that make boxes?

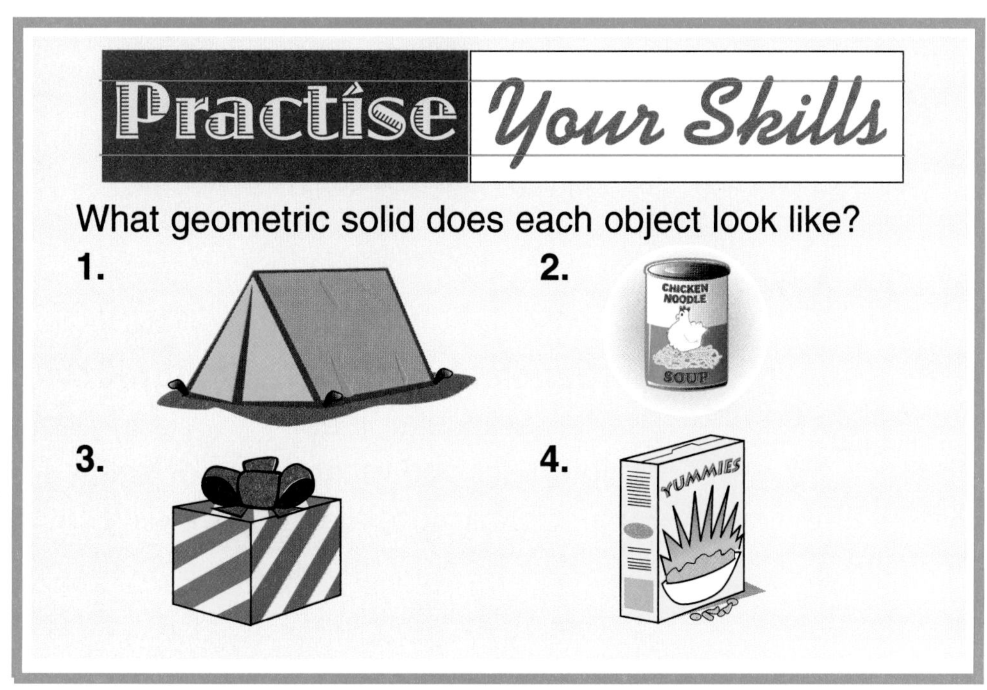

Practise Your Skills

What geometric solid does each object look like?

1.

2.

3.

4.

Making Models

It's time to make a box.

- Use a piece of cardboard.
  Think of what you know about nets.
  Get to work!

Words to Know

Parallel:
Parallel lines do not intersect. They are a fixed distance apart.

Perpendicular:
Perpendicular lines intersect and make a square vertex.

Congruent:
Congruent shapes or solids match exactly in size and shape.

1. Look at this net. Now look at the cube.

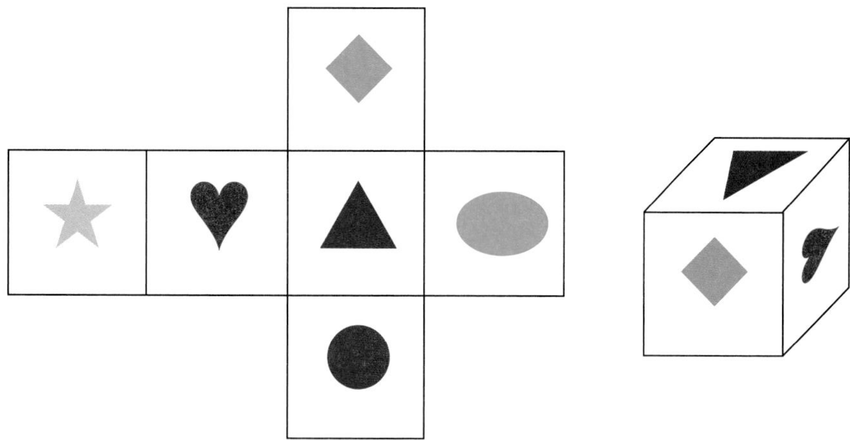

   a. Which picture is on the base?
   b. Which picture is opposite the diamond?
   c. Which picture is opposite the heart?

2. Use grid paper. Make a net for a cube. Make a design on each face. Describe the cube. Tell which faces are opposite one another.

3. *My Journal:* What do you know about opposite faces of a rectangular prism?

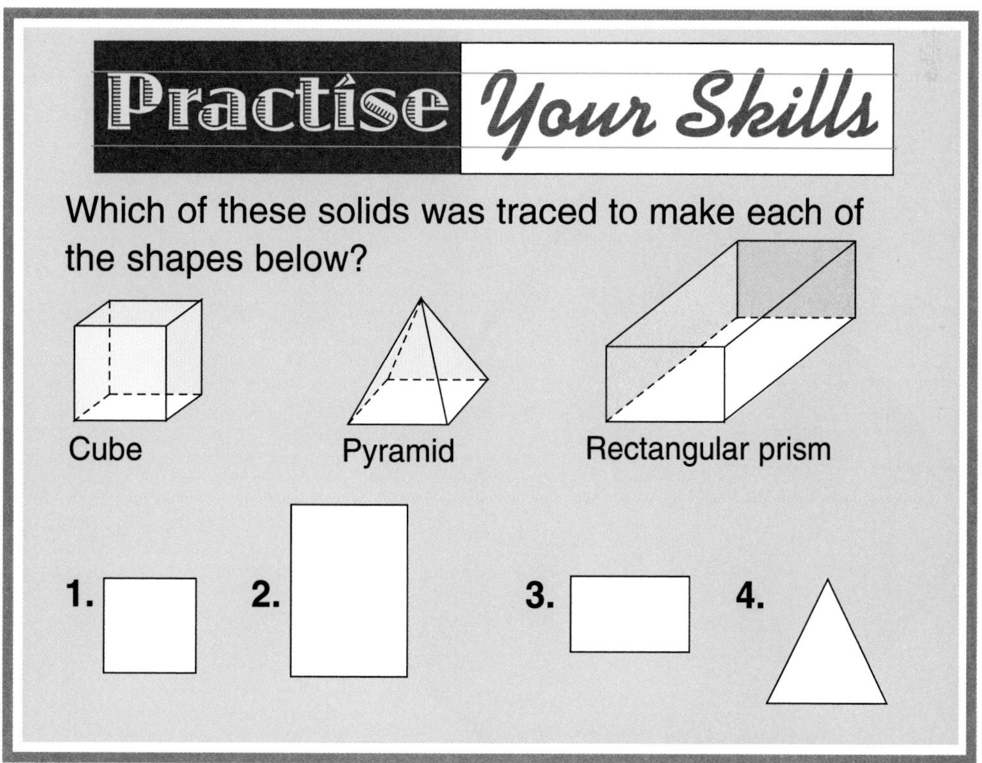

Practise *Your Skills*

Which of these solids was traced to make each of the shapes below?

Making Model Pyramids

▶ What do you think makes a pyramid a pyramid?

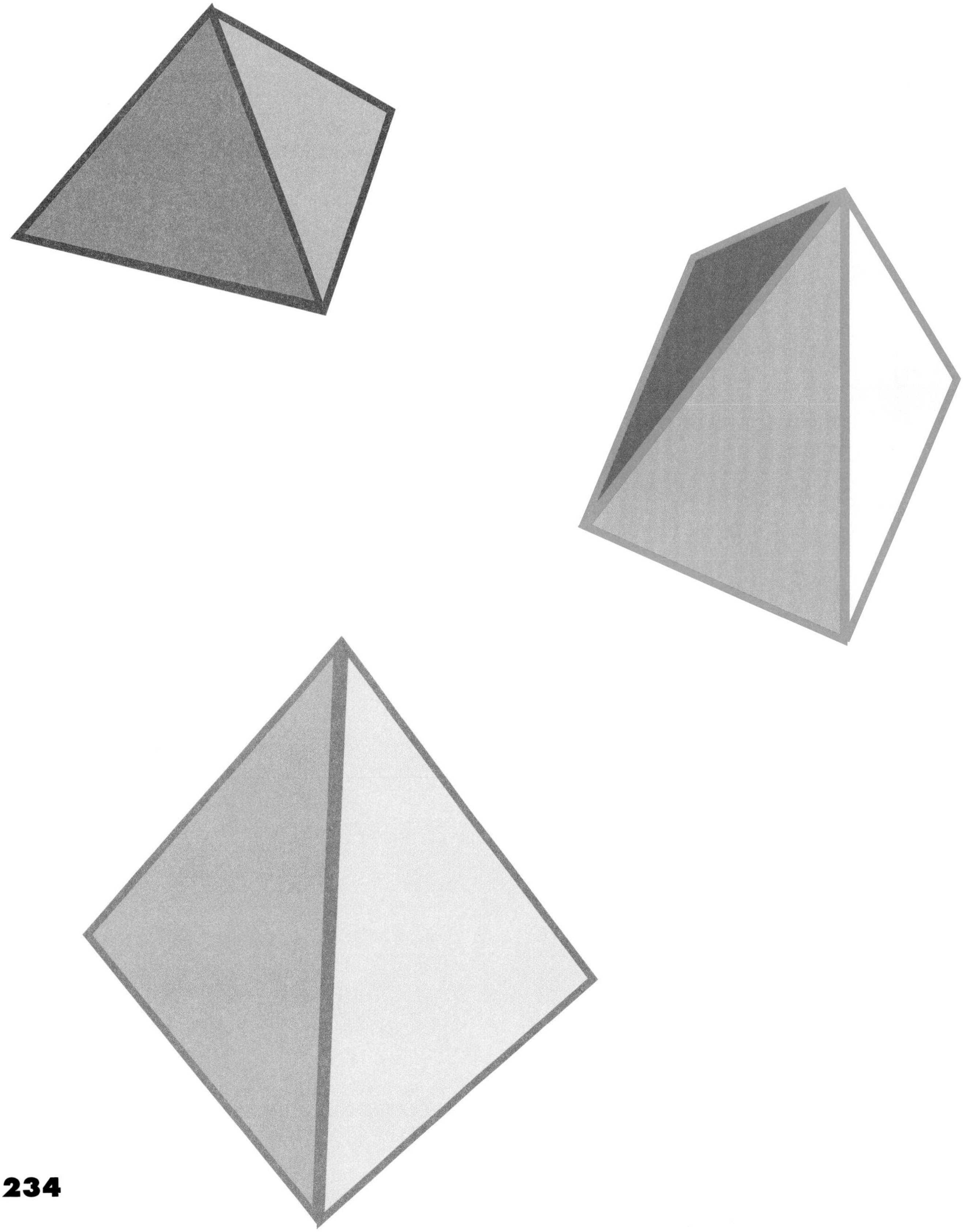

1. Design a pyramid-shaped box for a new game or puzzle. What will you print and draw on each face? Draw each face to show your ideas.

2. How are pyramids different from prisms? How are they the same?

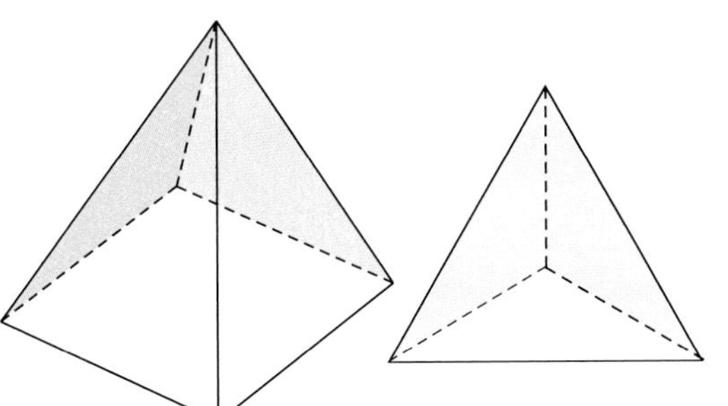

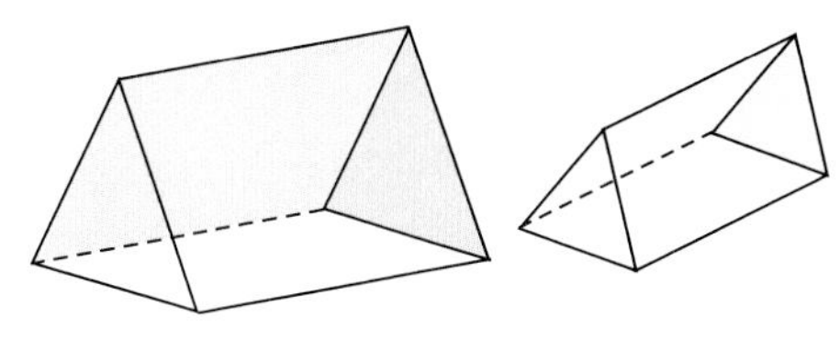

3. *My Journal:* What have you learned about pyramids?

Practise *Your Skills*

1. How many faces are there?
2. Sketch what each face looks like.
3. How many edges are there?
4. How many vertices are there?

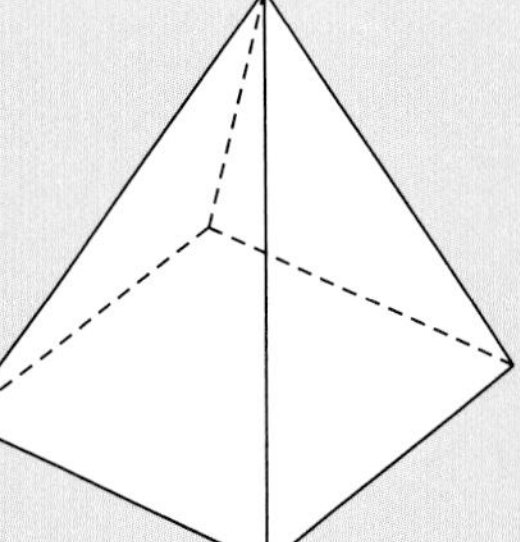

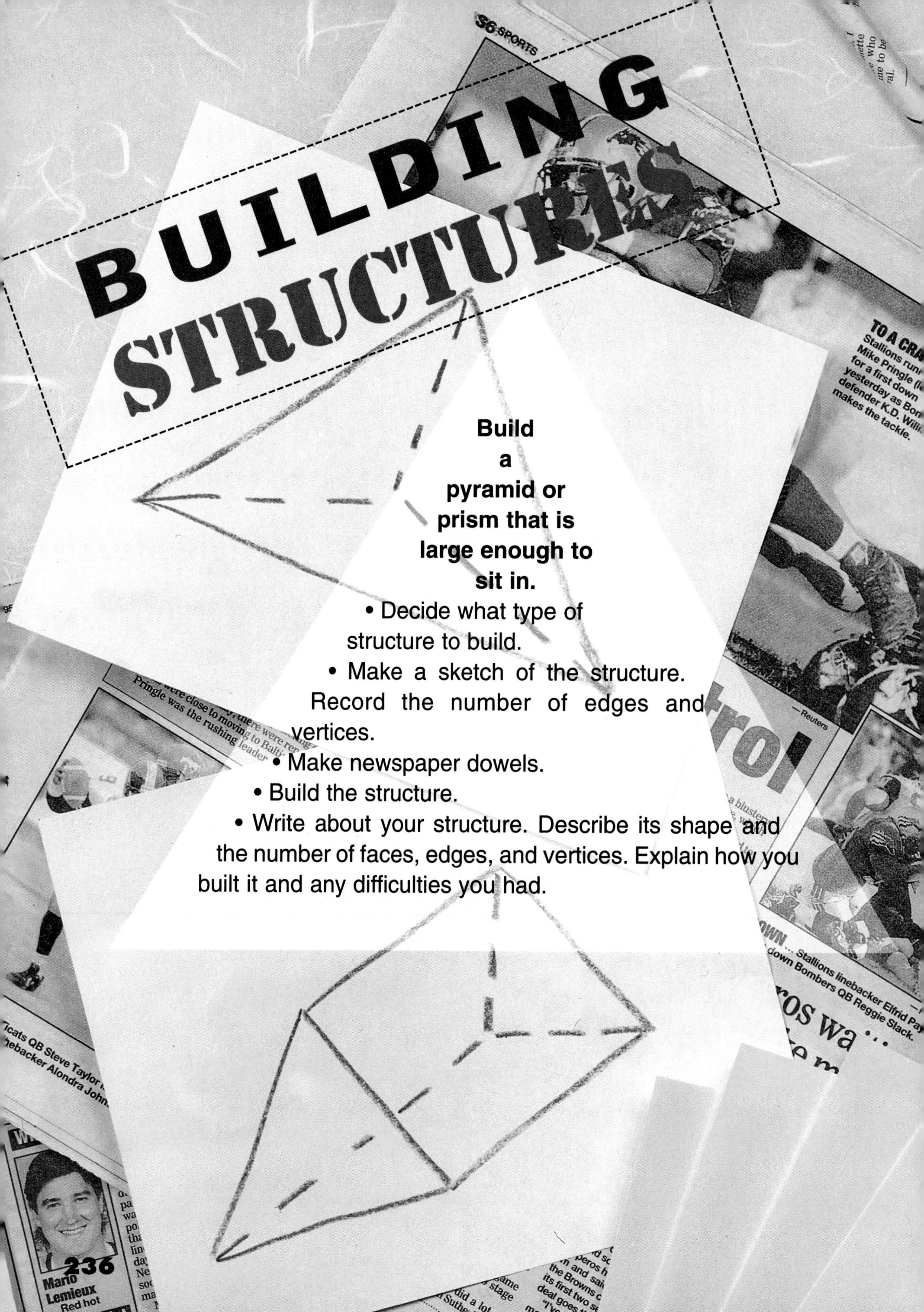

BUILDING STRUCTURES

Build a pyramid or prism that is large enough to sit in.

- Decide what type of structure to build.
- Make a sketch of the structure. Record the number of edges and vertices.
- Make newspaper dowels.
- Build the structure.
- Write about your structure. Describe its shape and the number of faces, edges, and vertices. Explain how you built it and any difficulties you had.

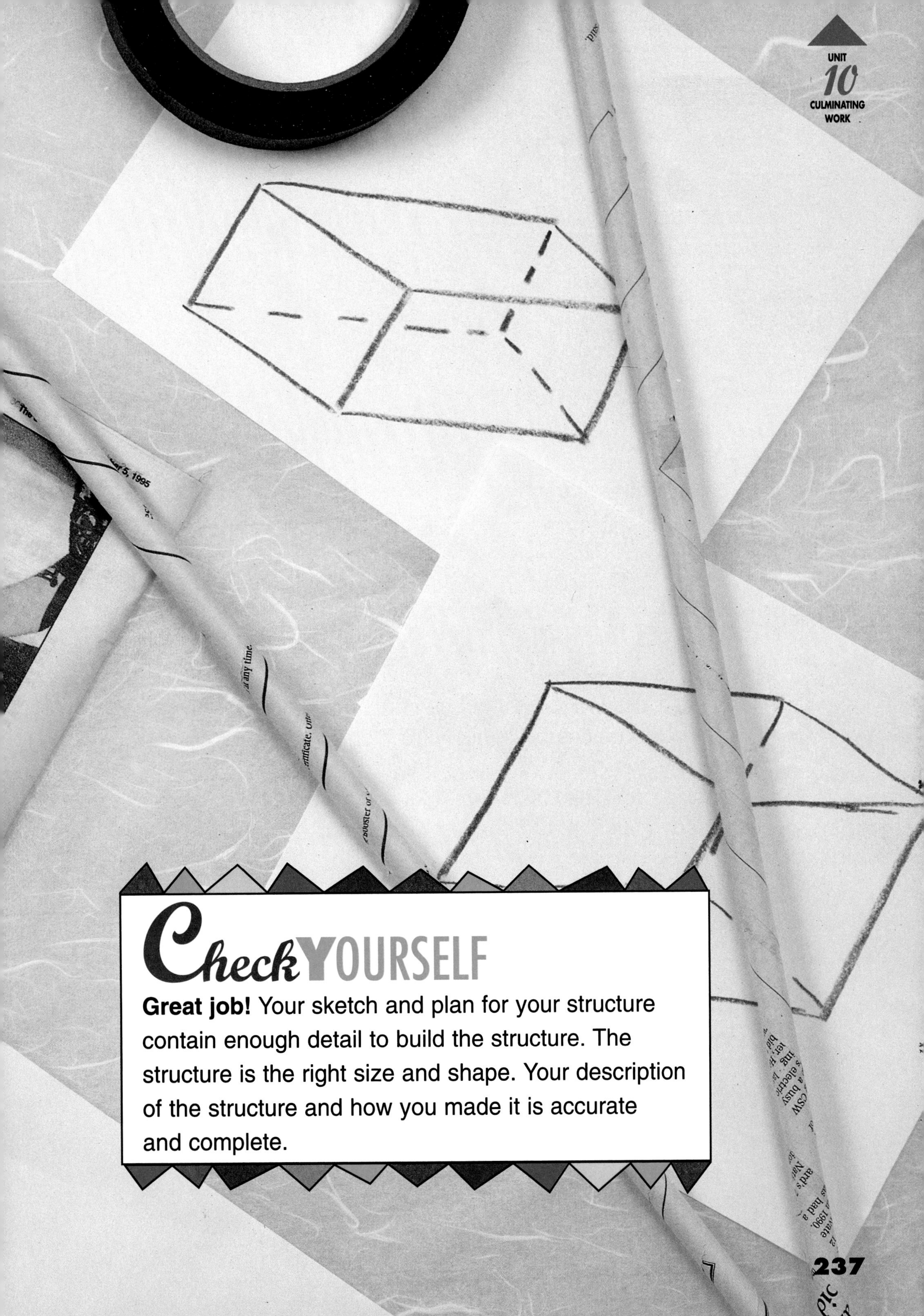

Check YOURSELF

Great job! Your sketch and plan for your structure contain enough detail to build the structure. The structure is the right size and shape. Your description of the structure and how you made it is accurate and complete.

1. How is a cube like a rectangular prism?

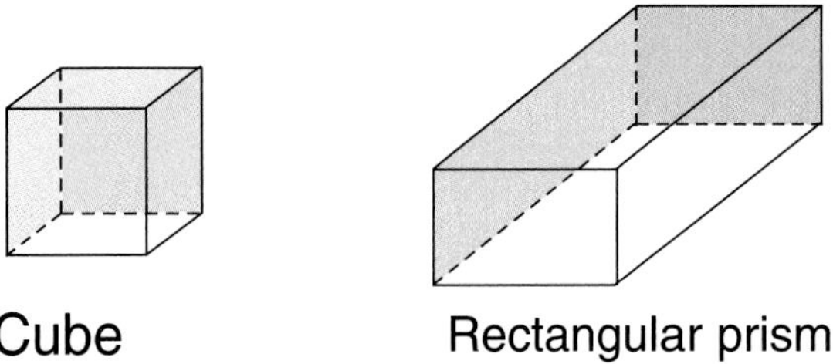

2. Choose one of these solids.

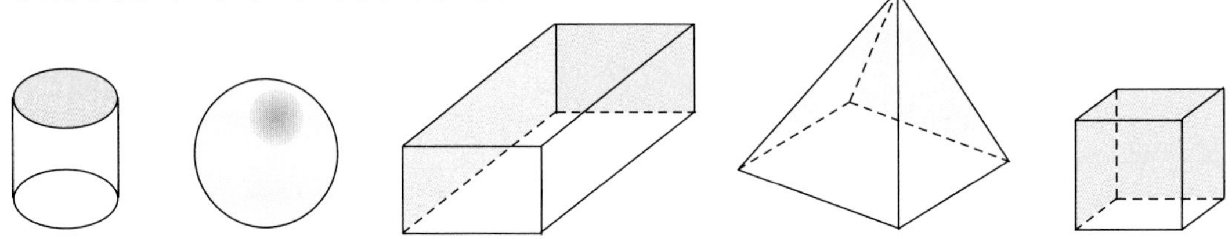

Write a description without naming the solid.
Ask a friend to guess which solid you are describing.

3. Look around the classroom. Make a chart that tells what things you can find that are shaped like these.

Cubes	Rectangular prisms	Pyramids	Cylinders	Spheres

4. Which of these solids was traced to make these faces?

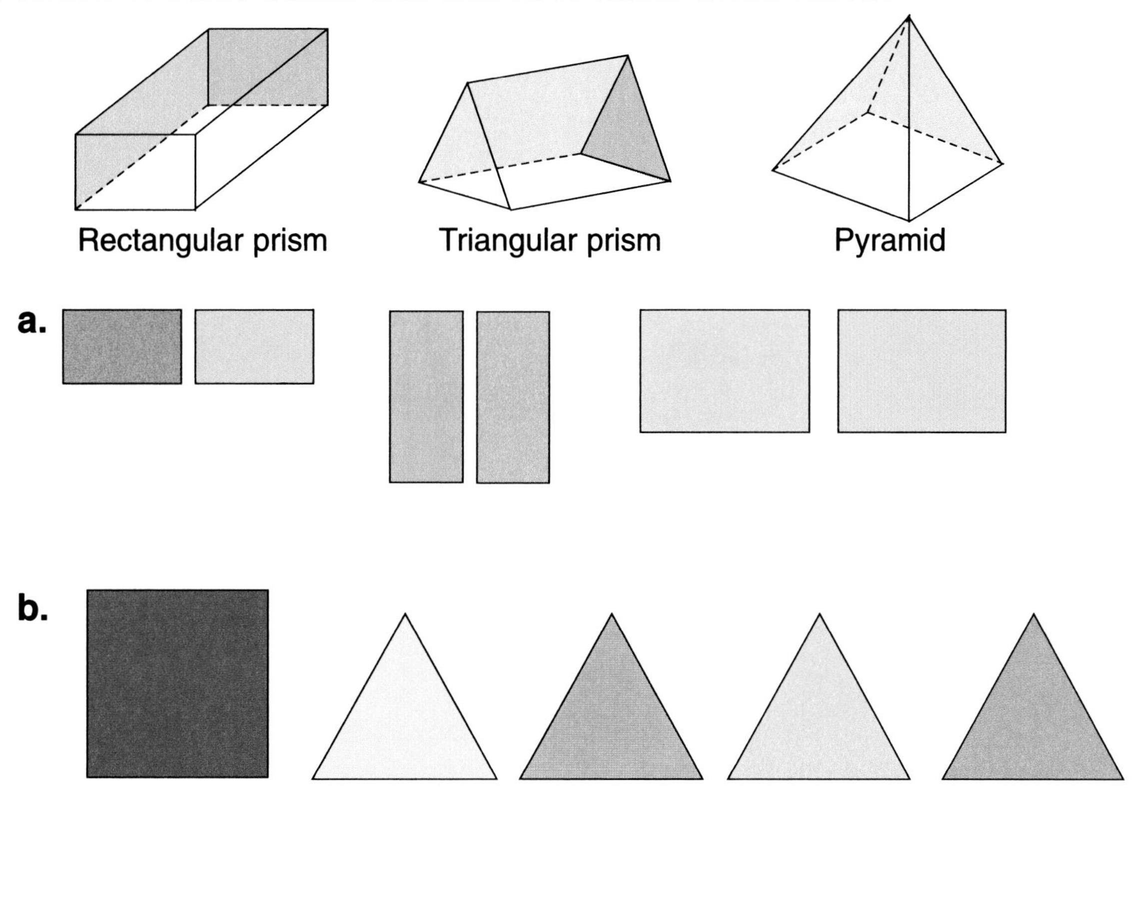

c.

5. Use straws and modelling clay to make a model of a pyramid. Write to tell how many straws and balls of clay you needed.

6. What type of solid can you make using 8 balls of clay and 12 straws? Check your answer by making the model.

1.

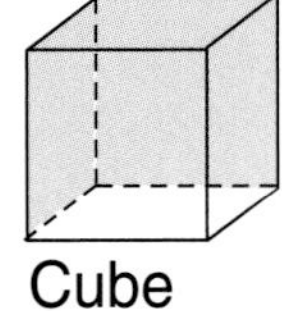
Cube

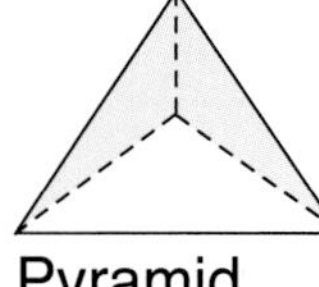
Pyramid

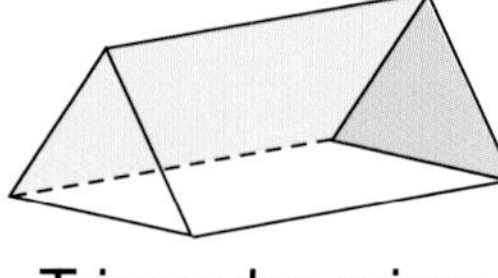
Triangular prism

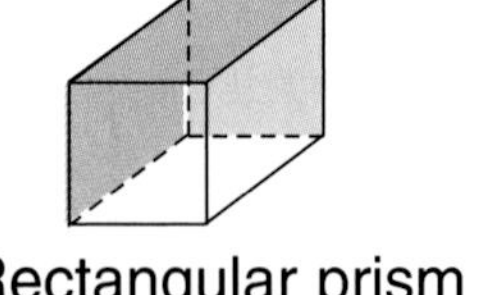
Rectangular prism

Make a chart like the one shown. Record the number and shape of the faces of each solid.

Solid	Number of faces	Shape of faces
Cube		
Pyramid		
Triangular prism		
Rectangular prism		

2. Look at these models. Make a chart to record the number of edges and vertices.

3. Make a chart to tell how many pyramids, rectangular prisms, triangular prisms, and cylinders you see on the shelves.

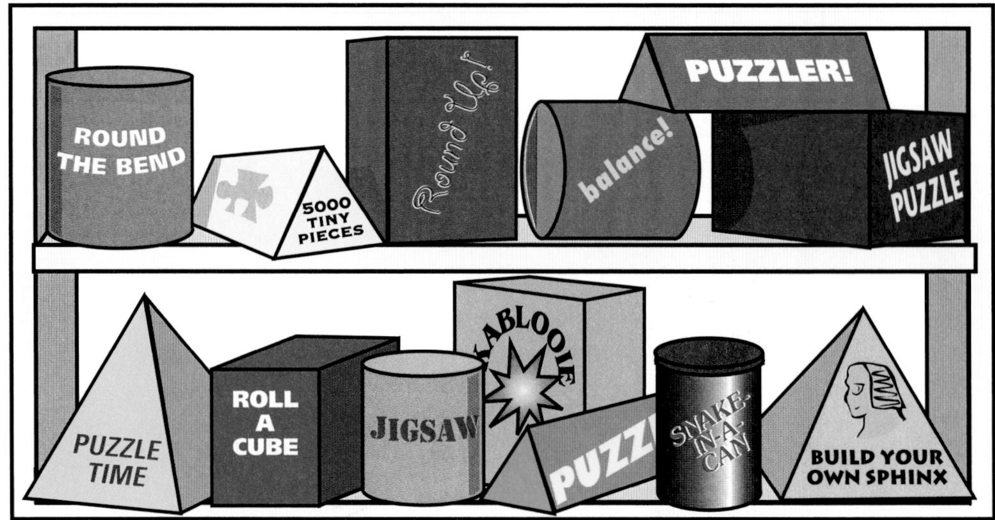

1. Draw these figures. Show the lines of symmetry.

a. 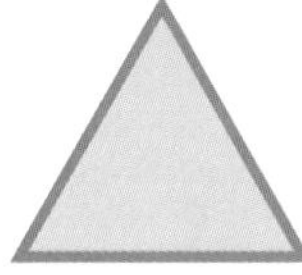

b. 

c. 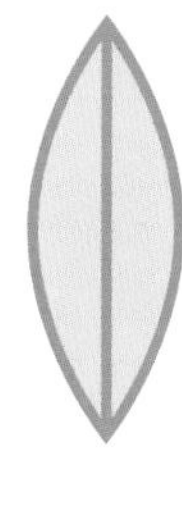

d. 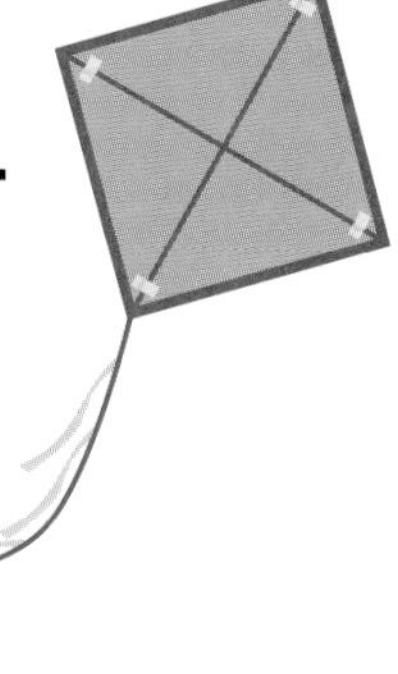

2. Write a fraction for the coloured parts of each figure.

a. 

b. 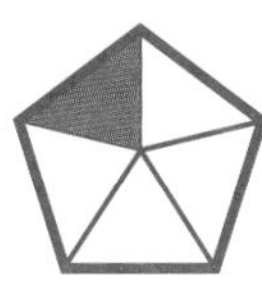

c. 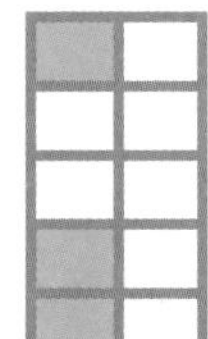

d. 

e. 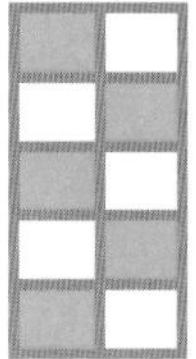

3. Write a fraction for the part of each set coloured blue.

a. 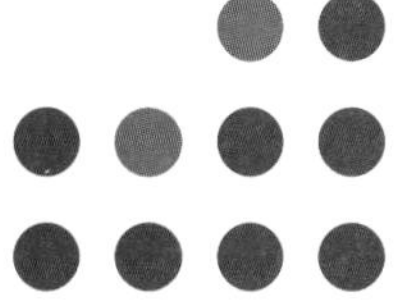

b. 

c. 

4. Each shape is a fraction of a whole.
For each, draw a picture of the whole.

a. 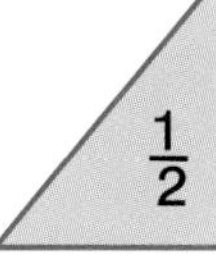

b. 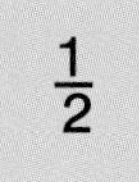

c. 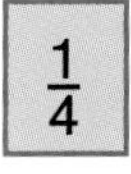

d. 

JEFF
SANDY

UNIT
11
Exploring Chance
What are the chances?
6
2

UNIT
11
LAUNCHING THE UNIT

EXPLORING CHANCE
STARTING
OUT

1 • What is happening in each picture?
• Choose one of the pictures. What do you think your results could be if you did the action in the picture?
• Why do people use things like coin flips, dice, and spinners?

My Journal: Tell about some of the times you and your friends have flipped a coin, rolled dice, used a spinner, or picked a card.

EXPLORING CHANCE

STARTING OUT

2 • Describe what is happening in each picture.
- What determines who wins in each situation?
- In which of these situations would you have a good chance of winning? Why?
- In which could you better your chances of winning? How?
- In which situations would you have little chance of winning? Why?
- What games do you know of that involve chance? How is chance involved in each one?

My Journal: What does the word "chance" mean to you?

Probability Problems

I wonder if it will rain.

Can I throw it so high that it won't come down?

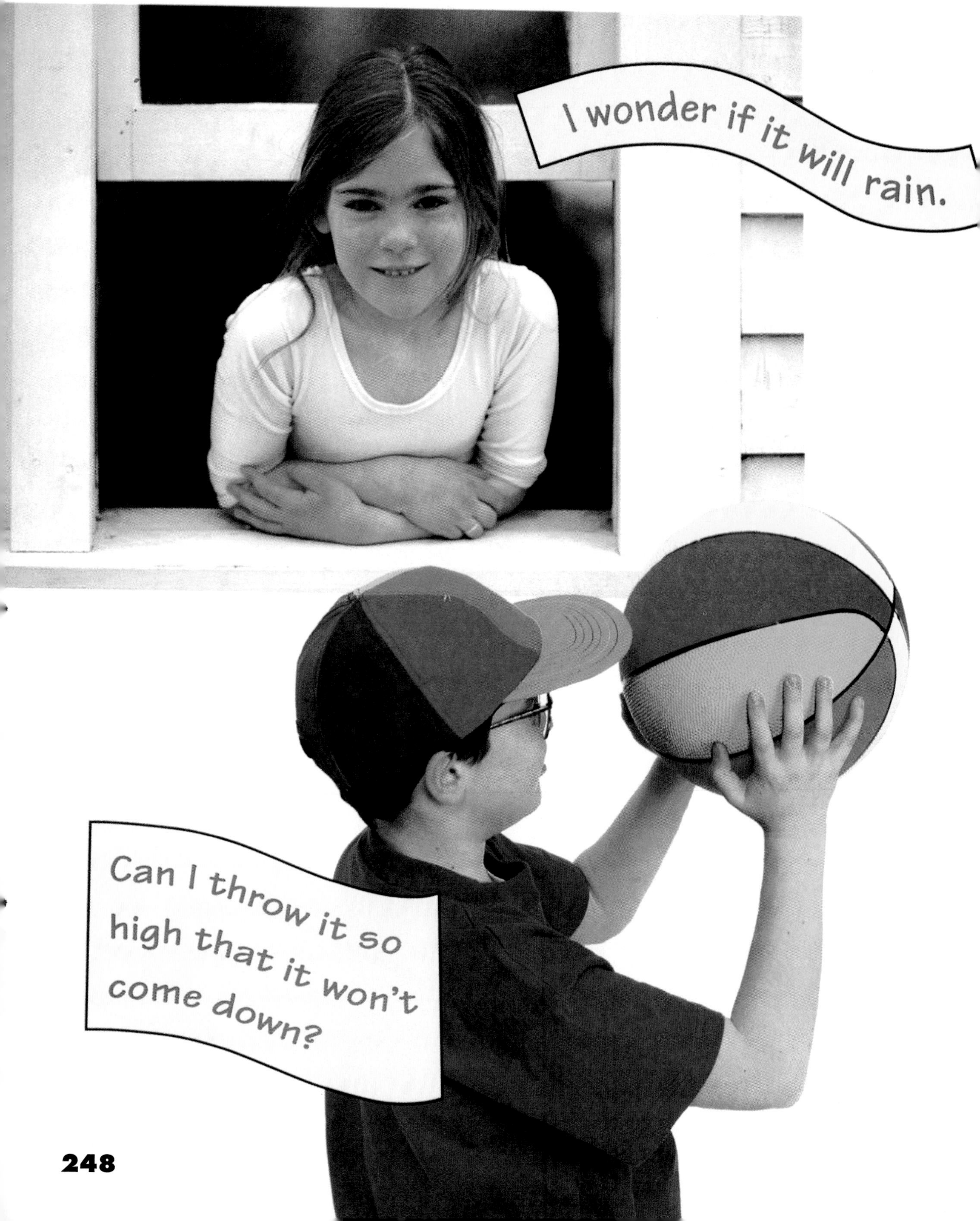

I win if the spin is an even number. You win if it is an odd number.
certain
not in a million years
for sure
likely
unlikely
probably
always
never
uncertain
I need a 12 to win.

UNIT 11 ACTIVITY 2

Using Spinners

▶ Decide for each picture whether the outcome shown is

CERTAIN

IMPOSSIBLE

LIKELY

UNLIKELY

UNCERTAIN

▶ Explain your reasoning.

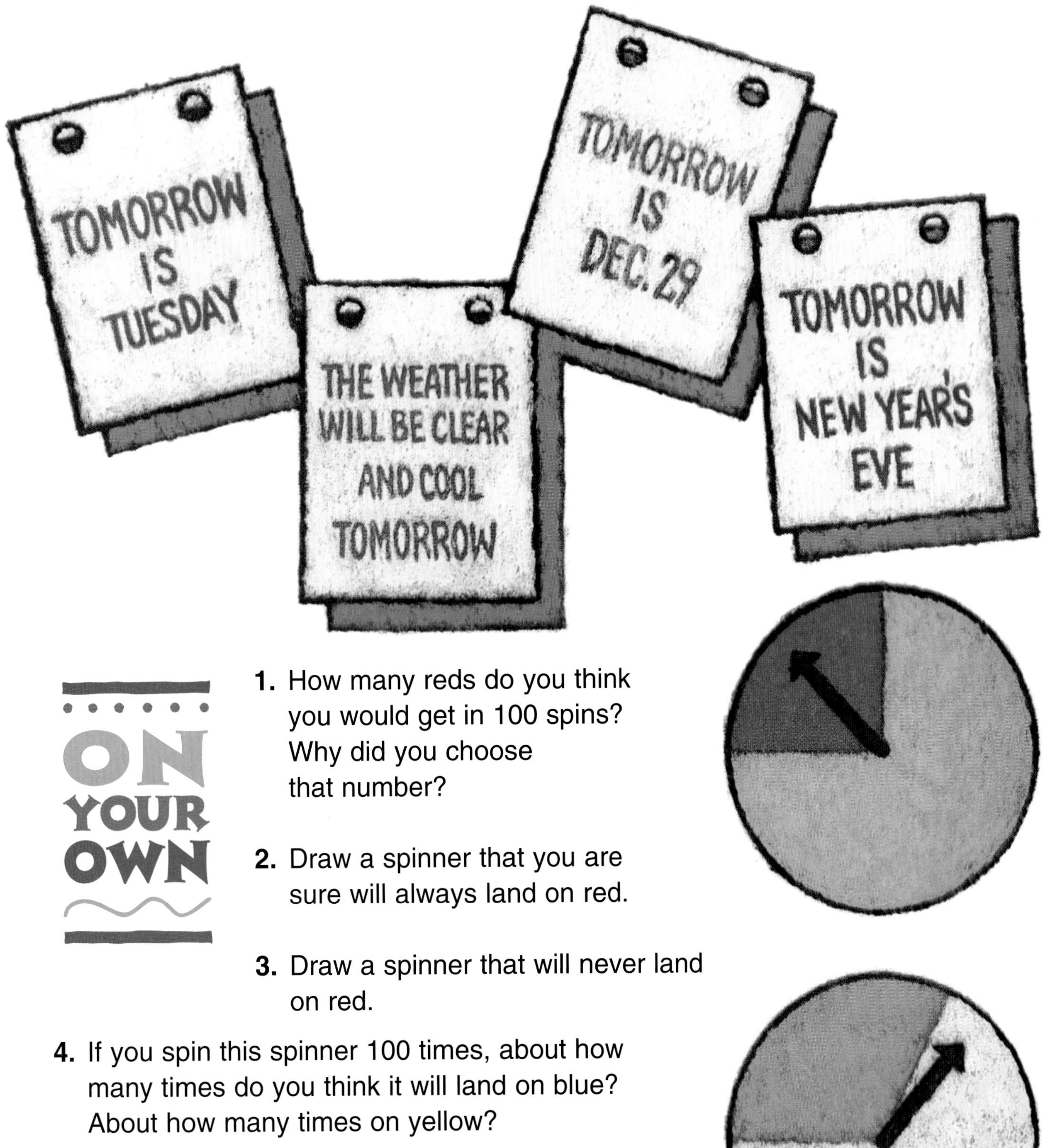

ON YOUR OWN

1. How many reds do you think you would get in 100 spins? Why did you choose that number?

2. Draw a spinner that you are sure will always land on red.

3. Draw a spinner that will never land on red.

4. If you spin this spinner 100 times, about how many times do you think it will land on blue? About how many times on yellow?

5. Draw a spinner that you think will give 90 yellow and 10 red in 100 spins.

6. Draw a three-part spinner that you think will give 50 blue, 25 red, and 25 green in 100 spins.

7. *My Journal:* What did you learn that is new?

UNIT 11
ACTIVITY 3

Probability Experiments

▶ What are the possible outcomes?

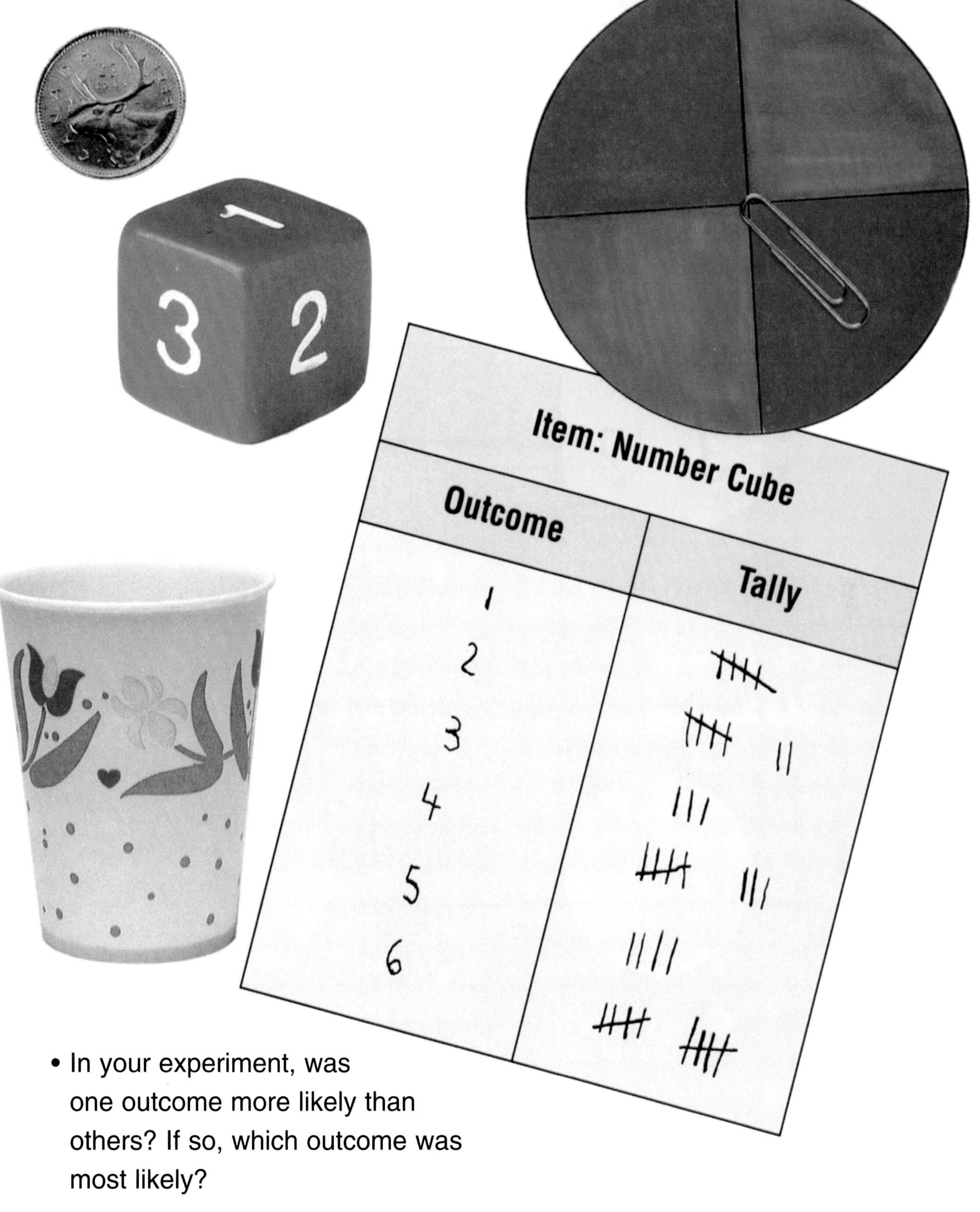

- In your experiment, was one outcome more likely than others? If so, which outcome was most likely?
- Were your predictions close to the actual results of your experiment?
- Was it easy or difficult to make a prediction about your experiment? Why do you think this was so?

For each situation, write Yes if you think the outcomes are equally likely. Write No if you think they are not equally likely. Explain your reasoning.

1.

Outcomes	
Even Numbers	
Odd Numbers	

2.

Outcomes	
Heads	
Tails	

3. *My Journal:* Describe how you feel about chance. Give some examples of when your chances were "good."

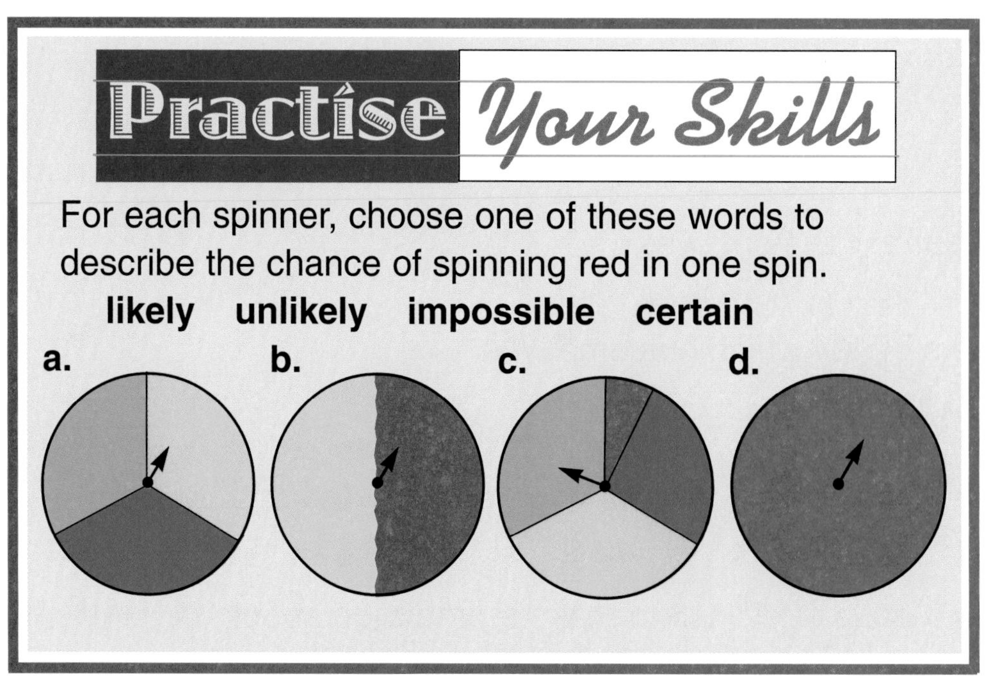

What are the chances of landing in SOUTH AMERICA

Have you ever wondered why South America looks so small on a flat map and looks so much larger on the globe?

Maps show the spherical or ball shape of Earth on a flat sheet of paper, but globes are similar in shape to Earth. They do not change size.

Here is a way to show how flat maps change area.

Use a flat map of Earth and a globe. An inflatable globe ball would be ideal.

Put the flat map on a table or desk. Work with a partner. One person gently slides the map back and forth. The other drops a paper clip gently on the map about 100 times and records where it lands each time.

Then use the globe. Toss it gently 100 times, catch it, and record where the right index finger hits.

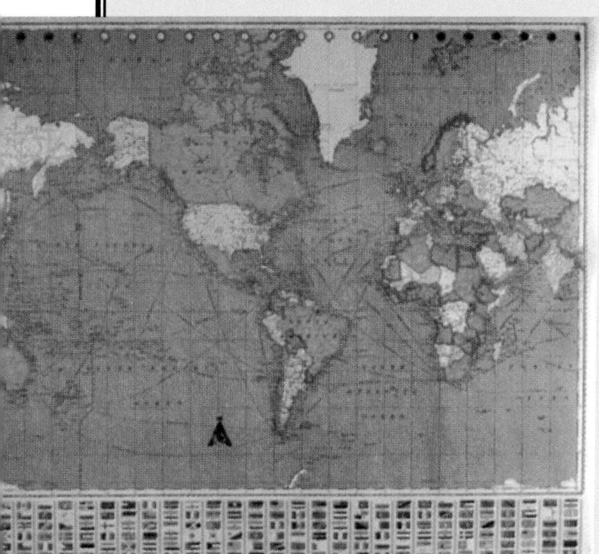

1. Do you have a better chance of landing on South America on the globe or on the map?

2. What can you conclude from your results?

THE PROBABILITY Game

Materials

Two spinners
Recording sheets

Game Rules

1. Decide who will be Player A and who will be Player B.
2. Take turns spinning both spinners.
3. After spinning both spinners, add the numbers that come up.
4. Player A scores 1 point if the sum is 2, 4, 6, or 8. Player B scores 1 point if the sum is 3, 5, or 7.
5. The first player with 10 points wins the round.

Think about each game described below. Then answer these questions:

- Is the game fair?
- If the game is not fair, which player do you think has a better chance of winning?

1. Toss two coins. Player A wins if both are heads or both are tails. Player B wins if there is no match.
2. Spin the spinner twice. Player A wins if the two spins are the same colour. Player B wins if the two spins are different colours.
3. Spin three times. Player A wins if any two spins match. Player B wins if all three spins are different.
4. Roll two 1-to-6 number cubes and add the numbers on the faces. Player A wins if the sum is 7 or greater. Player B wins if the sum is less than 7.
5. *My Journal:* What do you think is important about making a game fair?

MAKING A GAME OF YOUR OWN

Have you ever made up a game of your own? How did you decide on the rules? Was your game fair? Explain how you knew that.

You will have a chance to make up a game of your own. Before you begin, warm up by writing some rules for the Four Colours Game.

THE FOUR COLOURS G

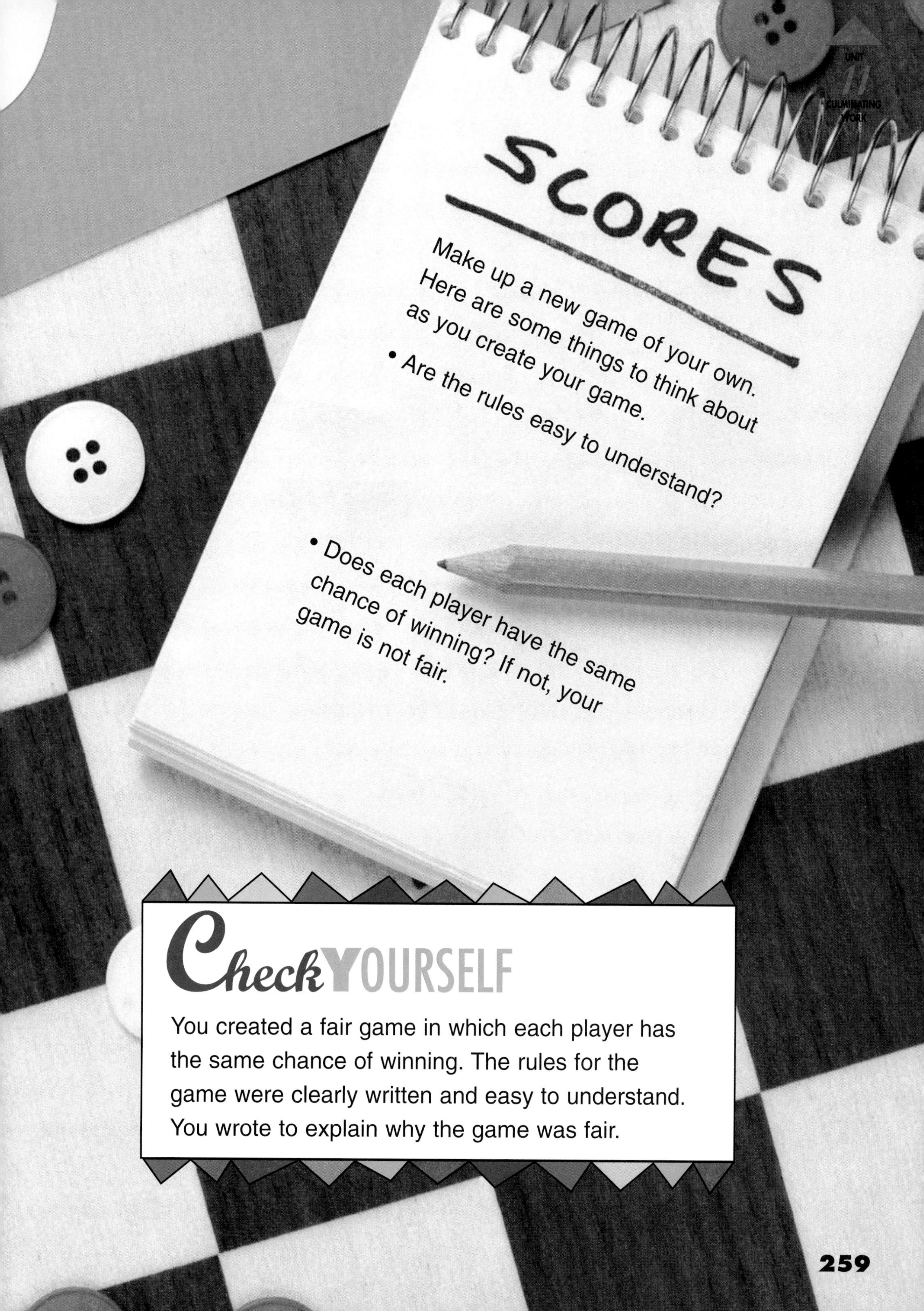

Check YOURSELF

You created a fair game in which each player has the same chance of winning. The rules for the game were clearly written and easy to understand. You wrote to explain why the game was fair.

1. For each of these spinners, decide whether the outcomes are equally likely or not equally likely. Explain your thinking.

a.

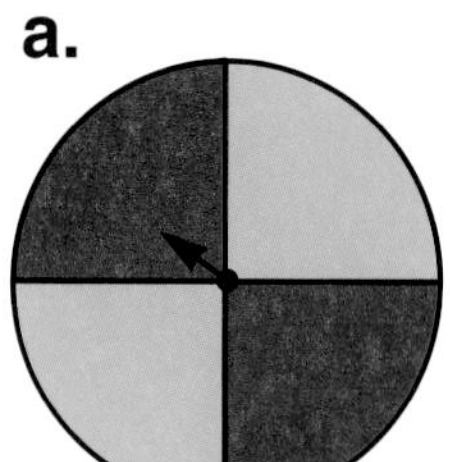

b.

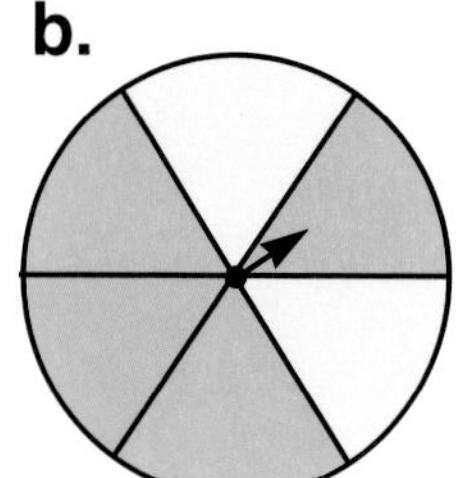

c.

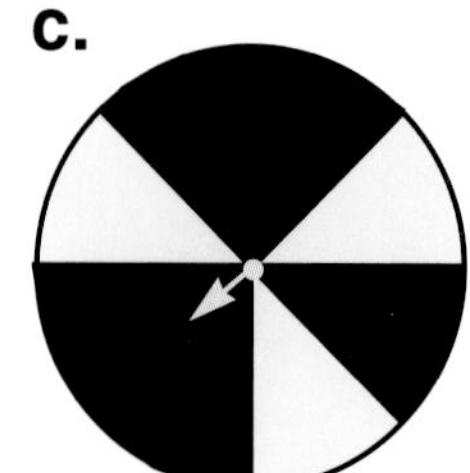

d.

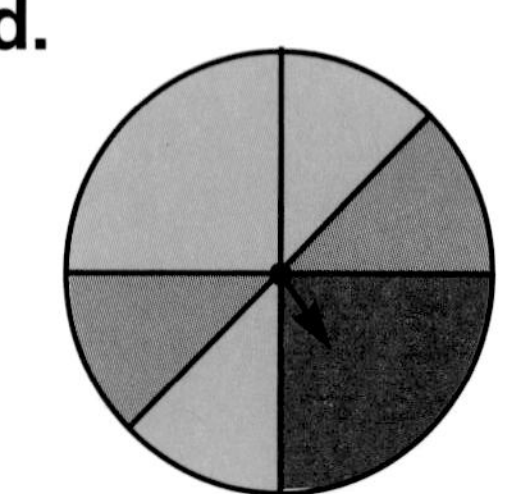

2. About how many times do you think you will get each colour in 100 spins? Explain your thinking.

a.

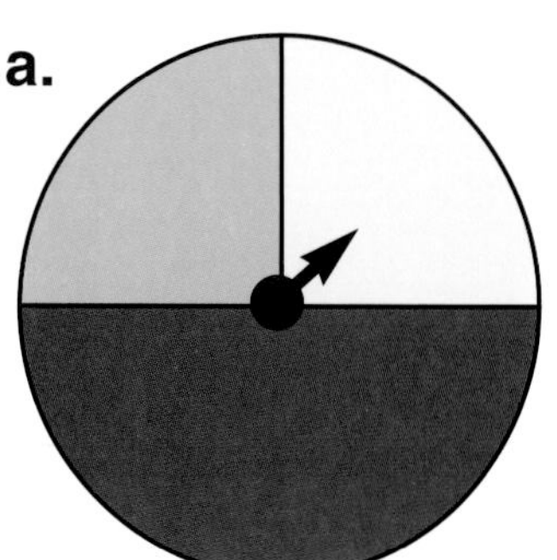

b.

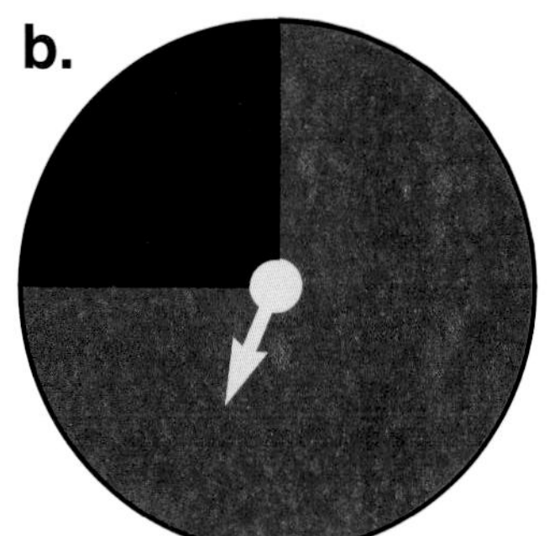

c.

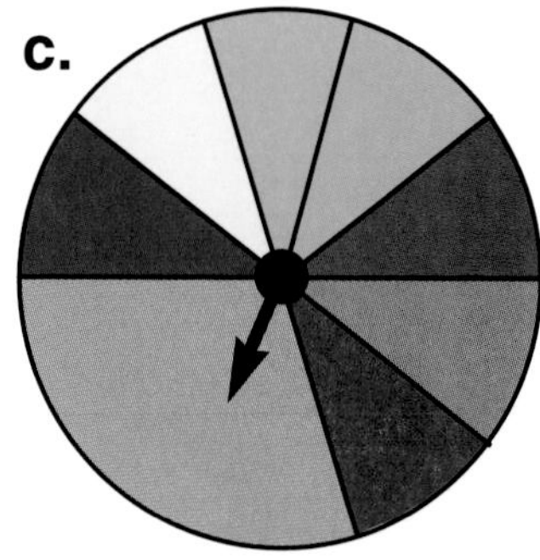

3. Make a spinner that you predict will give about 60 green, 20 red, and 20 orange in 100 spins. Test your spinner to see how close you come to your prediction.

4. Suppose you had two spinners like this:

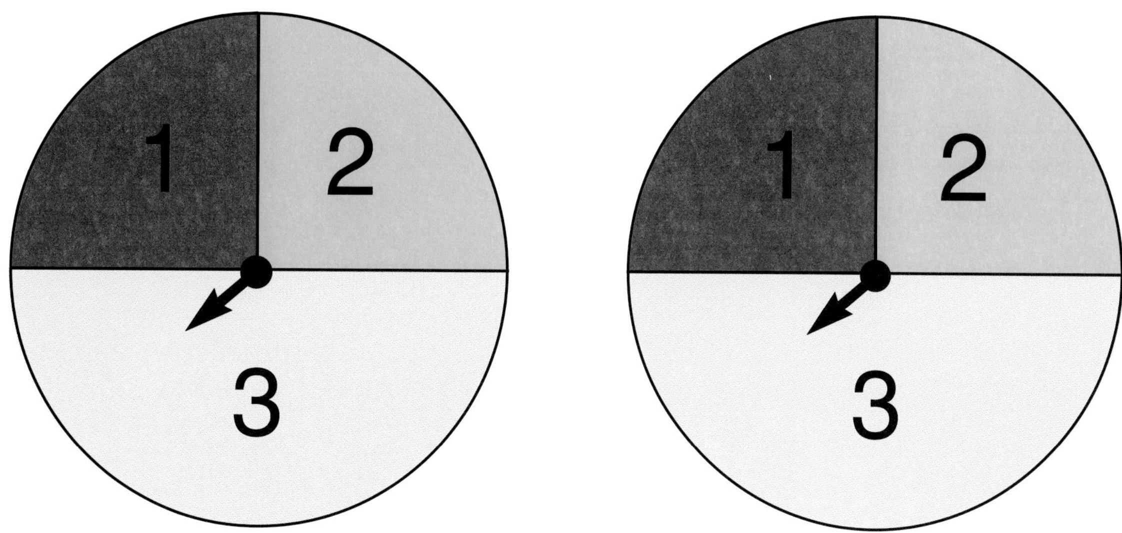

If you were to spin both spinners and add the two numbers, what totals are possible? What total do you think you would get most often? Why do you think so?

5. With a partner, take turns rolling two 1-to-6 number cubes. One player gets a point if the sum of the cubes is even. The other player gets a point if the sum is odd. Play until someone has 25 points. Is this a fair game? Explain your thinking. If it is not fair, how could you make it fair?

1. Make a chart like the one shown.

Unlikely	Likely	Certain

Name at least 5 events that could go in each column.

2. Which of these spinners is likely to land on red more than half the time? Explain your choice.

a. 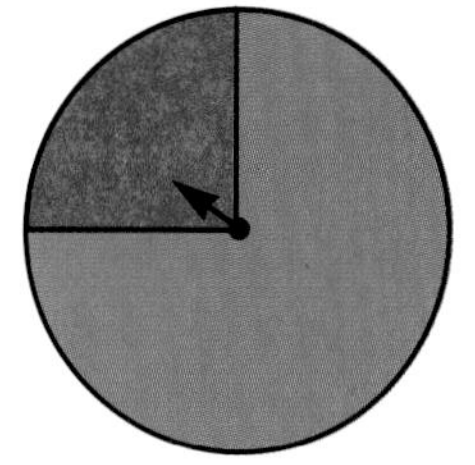

b. 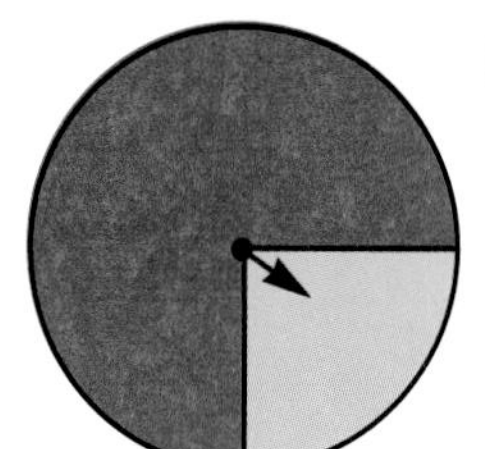

c. 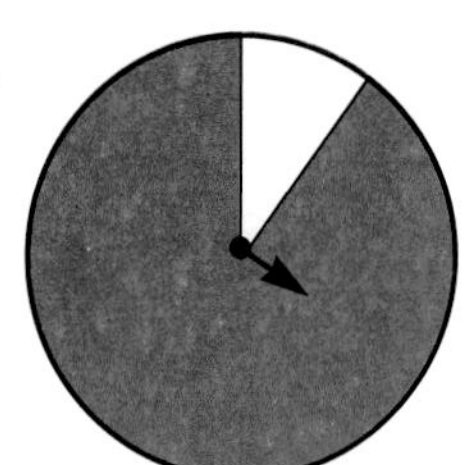

d. 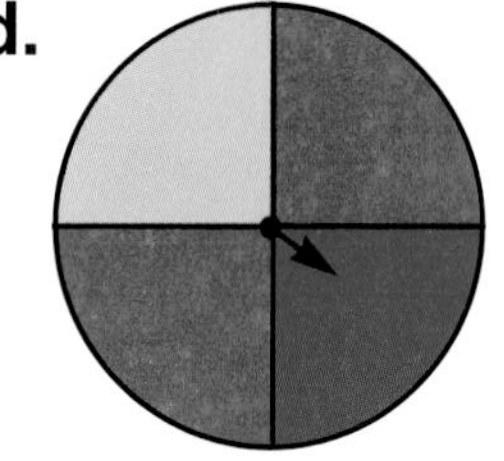

3. Which spinner do you think is most likely to land on yellow at least 50 times in 100 spins? Tell why.

a. 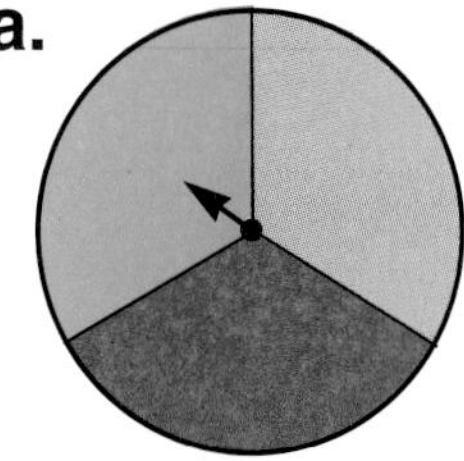

b. 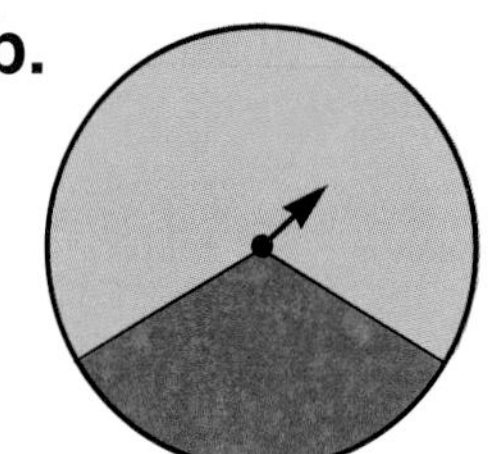

c. 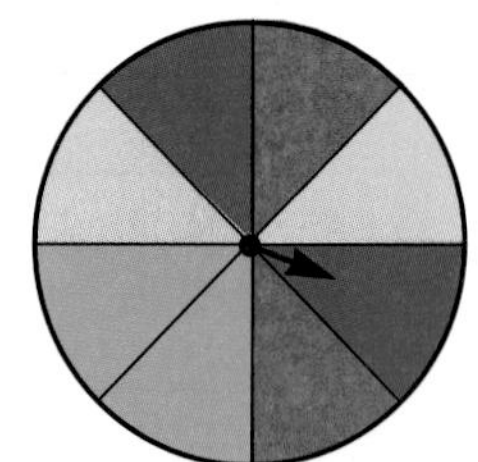

4. Which tally do you think shows how a coin landed in 20 flips? Tell why.

Heads	Tails
卌 ||	卌 卌 |||

Heads	Tails
卌 卌 卌	卌

Heads	Tails
卌 卌 |	卌 ||||

1. Which of these shapes is symmetrical?

a. 

b. 

c. 

2. Draw a rectangle.
Show as many lines of symmetry as you can.

3. How are these solids alike? How are they different?

a.

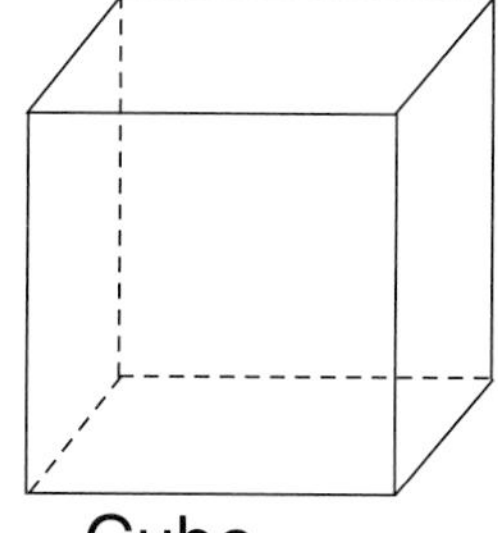

Cube

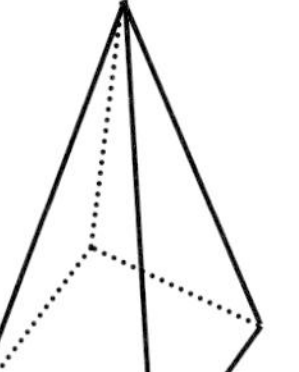

Pyramid

b.

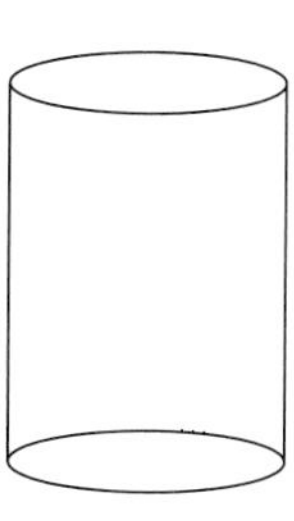

Cylinder

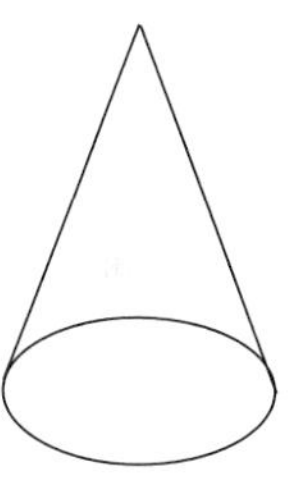

Cone

4. a. How many faces are there?
   b. What shape are the faces?
   c. How many edges are there?
   d. How many vertices does it have?

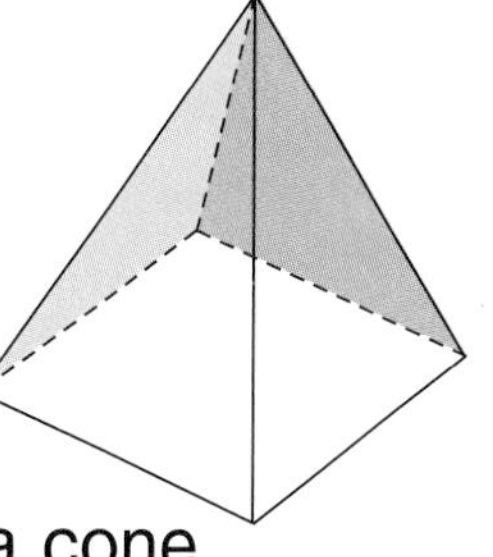

5. Tell whether each object is shaped like a cone, a cube, a pyramid, a rectangular prism, or a cylinder.

a. 

b. 

c. 

d. 

e. 

Index

ILLUSTRATION

Cover Illustration: **Seymour Chwast**

Victoria Allen: 50, 51, 102-103; **Andrea Arroyo:** 122-123; **Kevin Bapp:** 51; **George Baquero:** 167; **Jill Kagan Batelman:** 124-125; **Peter Cook:** 34-35, 55, 56, 76, 118, 139, 145, 177, 231, 239, 240; **Neverne Covington:** 48-50; **Sylvie Daigneault:** 29, 112-113; **Tony Delitala:** 8, 9,10, 36, 84, 85, 106; **Janice Durand:** 256, 257; **Norm Eyolfson:** 156-157; **Henry Fernandes:** 60-61; **Susan Foster:** 128, 129; **Tara Framer:** 122, 132,133; **Barbara Friedman:** 44, 45; **Kristi Frost:** 62-63; **Tuko Fujisaki:** 68, 69; **Tom Gagliano:** 13, 23, 38, 39, 47, 97, 115, 116, 123, 189; **Pamela Harrelson:** 250, 251; **Susan Hartung:** 207, 249, 252, 253; **Margaret Hathaway:** 71, 79, 85, 174, 193; **Dan Hobbs:** 182-183; **Gary Johnson:** 19-21; **Tony Joyce:** 144; **Stanford Kay/Paragraphics:** 14-16; **Kathleen Kinkopf:** 132, 133; **Vesna Krstanovich:** 246-247; **Helen Kunze:** 212, 213; **Chris Lam:** 22, 44, 48, 131, 162, 164, 232; **Tadeusz Majewski:** 62-63, 143; **Claude Martinot:** 80, 81; **Mas Miyamoto:** 114, 184; **Tomio Nitto:** 90-91, 92-93; **Cheryl Kirk Noll:** 155; Julie Pace: 18; **Doug Panton:** 136; **Clarence Porter:** 42, 43, 49, 108, 152, 153, 171, 199, 228, 261; **Teco Rodriques:** 95, 109, 158-159, 166, 169, 170, 176, 187, 192, 197, 206, 234, 241, 244-245; **Robert Roper:** 94, 95, 250; **Marsha Serafin:** 146-148; **Neil Shigley:** 101; **Robert A. Soule:** 41, 119, 120; **Michael Sours:** 126, 127; **Stephen Taylor:** 86-87; **Greg Valley:** 130,131; **K. Watt:** 191; **David Wink:** 100.

PHOTOGRAPHY

Photo Management and Picture Research: **Omni-Photo Communications, Inc.**

Claire Aich: 59, 82, 115, 124, 125, 190, 212, 242, 243, 258, 259; **©Hannah Baker/Bishop Museum:** 205 **©Danilo Baschung/Leo DeWys, Inc.:** 64, 65; **© Allyn Baum/Monkmeyer Press:** 12; **©Hannah Baker/Bishop Museum:** 98; **©Leslie Borden/Photo Edit:** 154,155; **©Robert Brenner:** 252; **©Kathy Bushue/Tony Stone Images:** 175; **©Paul Conklin/Monkmeyer Press:** 96; **Ian Crysler:** 8-9,11, 26, 31, 52-53, 88-89, 104-105, 110-111, 117-118, 134-135, 136, 150-151, 160-161, 162, 172-173, 180-181, 191, 202-203, 224-225, 229, 236-237; **©Grace Davies/Omni-Photo Communications:** 210; **©Everett Studios:** 7, 26, 27, 140, 141, 154, 155, 200, 201, 214-215; **©Kenneth Fink/Photo Researchers:** 46; **©Focus on Sports:** 188; **©Fotopic/Omni-Photo Communications:** 252; **©George F. Godfrey/Animals, Animals:** 64; **©Neal Graham/Omni-Photo Communications:** 134; **©Sylvain Grandadam/Tony Stone Images:** 221; **©The Granger Collection:** 210; **©Joel Greenstein/Omni-Photo Communications:** 95, 102; **Michael Groen:** 178, 179, 194, 195; **©Arron Haupt/Stock Boston:** 114; **Horizon:** 165; **Richard Hutchings:** 74, 149, 255; **©Richard Hutchings/Photo Researchers:** 204, 205; **Ken Karp:** 23, 144, 190, 206, 249, 253, 254, 256; **©Frans Lanting/Minden Pictures:** 121; **John Lei:** i, 17, 66, 68, 70, 132, 188, 190, 211; **©John Lei/Omni-Photo Communications:** 32, 33, 253, 254; **©Alexander Marschak:** 46, 47; **©Megget/Focus on Sports:** 188; **©Ian Murphy/Tony Stone Images:** 220; **Donald Nausbaum/Tony Stone Images:** 221; **©Nurisdany/Prennou/Science Source/Photo Researchers:** 25; **©Raion Oberlander/Stock Boston:** 210 **Steven Oglivy:** 12, 73, 75; **©Laurie Platte/Winfrey, Inc.:** 210; **©M. Richards/Photo Edit:** 154; **©Steve Ross/Leo DeWys, Inc.:** 32, 33; **©Shelly Rotner/Omni-Photo Communications:** 248; **John Running/Tony Stone Images:** 220; **©Nicolas Sapiena/Art Resource:** 204; **©Earl Scott/Charles Eames/Photo Researchers, Inc.:** 204; **©John Shaw/Tom Stack & Assoc.:** 205; **©Hugh Sitton/Tony Stone Images:** 220; **Don Spiro/Tony Stone Images:** 220; **©Dennis Stock/Magnum Photos:** 210; **©Tony Stone Images:** 12, 99, 220; **Super Stock:** 221; **©Joseph Szkodzinski/The Image Bank:** 210; **©Rene Van Dongen/Tony Stone Images:** 221; **©Steve Vidler/Leo DeWys, Inc.:** 204; **©Marvin Wolf/Tony Stone Worldwide:** 206.

CALCULATORS

T-I 108
T-I Math Explorer

MANIPULATIVES

Link-Its ™